Walter F Lonergan

Historic Churches of Paris

Walter F Lonergan

Historic Churches of Paris

ISBN/EAN: 9783337228521

Printed in Europe, USA, Canada, Australia, Japan

Cover: Foto ©ninafisch / pixelio.de

More available books at **www.hansebooks.com**

Historic Churches of Paris

BY

WALTER F. LONERGAN

Illustrated with Drawings
BY
BRINSLEY S. LE FANU
and from Photographs

DOWNEY & CO.
Limited
12, YORK STREET COVENT GARDEN, LONDON
1896

Historic Churches of Paris

*Inde Parisiacas properant cito visere sedes,
  Quo Stephanus martyr culmina summa tenet,
  Quo Germane, tuum colitur, sanctissime corpus,
  Quo Genuveffa micat, Virgo dicata Deo.*

*Nec tua præteriit Dionysi culmina martyr,
  Quin adiens tibimet posceret auxilium.*

ERMOLDUS NIGELLUS, II., 143.

Alluding to the visits of Lewis the Pious, or Louis le Débonnaire, the St. Louis of the 9th Century, son of Charlemagne, to the holy Parisian shrines of St. Stephen, St. Germain, St. Geneviève, and St. Denis.

CONTENTS.

CHAPTER I.
Notre Dame de Paris.
I.

                                                                                                                   PAGE

"A symphony in stone"—Esmeralda and Quasimodo—Historical scenes in Notre Dame de Paris—The cloister and the hospital—The ship-shaped island—Ham Fair—Stacking hay and oats in church—The Feast of Fools—The University in the cloister—Devotion to the Virgin Mary in Paris—The Dominicans and the University—Tests for the Huguenots—Louis XIII. and his vow—Modern veneration of the Blessed Virgin—Her name given to Voltaire and others 1

CHAPTER II.
Notre Dame de Paris.
II.

Historical connections—The third crusade—Philip Augustus and Ingelburgha of Denmark—Formal interdict against a frivolous festival—The Albigenses—Raymond of Toulouse flogged at the doors of Notre Dame—Blanche of Castille and the Chapter of the Cathedral—Philip the Fair and Boniface VIII.—Gallican liberties—On horseback in Notre Dame—Burning of the Templars—A dreadful summons—The big taper of Notre Dame—Cathedral Council *re* the Anti-Popes—Henry VI. of England crowned in Notre Dame—*Te Deums* and thanksgivings from Agnadel to Sebastopol—The League and the Huguenots—Paris an archbishopric—The Goddess of Reason in Notre Dame—Coronation of Napoleon—Marriage of the Third Napoleon—The Communists of 1871 . 13

CHAPTER III.
Notre Dame de Paris.
III.

Gothic architecture—The mediæval architects and sculptors—A lady sculptor . —The monastic and the lay builders—The ravages of revolution . . 29

CONTENTS.

CHAPTER IV.
Notre Dame de Paris.
IV.

The façade—The great portals—The gallery of the kings—The Devil's cauldron—The interior of Notre Dame—The stained glass windows—Great festivals and famous preachers—Lacordaire, Ravignan, Monsabré, Père Hyacinthe, and Monseigneur d'Hulst 41

CHAPTER V.
The Sainte Chapelle.

St. Louis—His piety, and desire to become a Dominican—Fainting from prolonged prayer—The mystic chapel—Joinville's testimony—The Armenians and St. Louis—The Chapel and the Police Court—Boileau's satirical poem—Imperial impecuniosity—Gibbon's version of the cost of the Chapel—The rival architects—Exploiting the young and zealous—Stabbing a rival—Historical events and full description of the monument 59

CHAPTER VI.
The Abbey Church of St. Denis.
I.

Saint Denis town—The Communists and the abbey church—Hatred of kings—Unlovely surroundings—Catulliacum—Dagobert—The supposed damnation of Charles Martel—Pepin and the Pope—The abbey and Charlemagne—The ravages of the Northmen—Descriptions of Sir Francis Palgrave—Abbot Suger—Famous monks—Peter Abelard—His "Book of Calamities"—The Renan of the Middle Ages—The devotion of Héloïse—The lover's tomb 75

CHAPTER VII.
The Abbey Church of St. Denis.
II.

Veneration of monarchs for the Shrine—Fêtes and historical events—Henri Quatre abjuring Protestantism in the abbey—New storms and sieges—The desecration of the tombs in 1792—The coffin of Louis XV.—The head of St. Denis—Speech in the National Assembly—Viollet-le-Duc's restorations—Exterior of the church—The interior and its monuments

CONTENTS.

—The crypt—The dim vault of the Bourbons—Enumeration of the coffins in the royal charnel-house—The pictures in the sacristy—Divine worship restored in the church by the Third Republic 87

CHAPTER VIII.

St. Germain L'Auxerrois.

The Huguenots—Condé and Coligny—The two saints—Etienne Marcel and Charles the Bad—Maurevert, the hired murderer—Coligny and Charles IX.—Catherine de' Medici and Duc Henri de Guise—The Bartholomew massacre—The bell signal—"Down with the Huguenots!"—The window of Charles IX.—Balzac's opinion—Catherine de' Medici praised by the novelist—Her powerful enemies—Maria de' Medici—Concino Concini and Leonora Galigaï—A skilful bird-trainer—Murder of Concini—His body dragged out of the tomb—The service for the murdered Duc de Berri—Description of the church 99

CHAPTER IX.

St. Germain-des-Prés.

A mighty monastery—The remains of the abbey and their modern uses—The Benedictines and the Salvation Army—The rival fairs—Privileges of the monks—The Northern Pirates—Formation of the "Noble Faubourg"—Disappearance of Cow Road and the Froggery—Increasing wealth and worldliness—Reforms effected—Royal and abbatial tombs—Abbot and king—The tombs of the Douglases—The church a powder manufactory during the Revolution—Flandrin's frescoes—Strange career and sad end of the artist—General description of the church—Its connection with the French Academy 109

CHAPTER X.

The Pantheon, formerly St. Geneviève's Church, and St. Étienne du Mont.

"A bad imitation of St. Peter's"—Quinet's view of Soufflot's work—St. Geneviève and Attila—Treatment of the Patroness of Paris by the Republicans—The "Temple of Renown"—Mirabeau's funeral—Voltaire, Rousseau and Marat—Royalist revenge for the desecration of St. Denis—In Napoleon's days—The Restoration and Baron Gros—Changes—In the hands of the Communists—The frescoes of Puvis de Chavannes and others—The tombs in crypt—The church of St. Étienne du Mont—Its splendid rood-loft—Gibbon's account of the finding of St. Stephen's remains—Miracles—The curious architectural features of St. Etienne du Mont—The glasss by Pinagrier—The tomb of St. Geneviève . . . 119

CONTENTS.

CHAPTER XI.

St. Sulpice—St. Julien le Pauvre—St. Séverin.

St. Sulpice and its district—The "Temple of Victory," the banquet to Bonaparte—The "Clarionet" towers—The seminary of St. Sulpice—Ernest Renan's connection with the church and the college—The Sulpicians: Servandoni's façade—The work of Eugène Delacroix—The meridian line—The shells—St. Julien le Pauvre and its pictured screen—A terrible district—St. Séverin—The stained glass—The daughter of Herodias dancing—Historical operation on a criminal 133

CHAPTER XII.

The Sorbonne—The Val de Grace—St. Louis des Invalides—St. Francis Xavier's—The Church of St. Joseph des Carmes—St. Thomas d'Aquin—St. Louis-en-L'Ile—St. Jacques du Haut Pas—St. Médard's—St. Nicolas du Chardonnet.

Richelieu's tomb—Stealing the cardinal's head—Opening of the tomb in 1895—Mignard's frescoes in the Val de Grâce—St. Louis des Invalides. The Hôtel des Invalides—The Sombreuil family—The cup of blood—Napoleon's tomb and funeral—The church of St. Francis Xavier—The church of St. Joseph des Carmes—The massacre of the priests—The spots of blood—The crypt—Joséphine de Beauharnais in the prison of the Carmelites—St. Thomas d'Aquin—St. Médard's 143

CHAPTER XIII.

St. Eustache—St. Gervais, St. Protais—St. Leu, St. Gilles—St. Merri—St. Nicolas des Champs—St. Laurent—Ste. Elizabeth—Notre Dame des Blancs Manteaux—St. Paul, St. Louis—Sainte Marguerite—Notre Dame des Victoires—Notre Dame de Lorette—St. Roch—Notre Dame de l'Assomption.

St. Eustache and its three patrons—Jacob the Hungarian—The butchers—Scarron's wife—A terrified congregation—Mirabeau—Madame Momoro, Goddess of Reason—The Women's Club—The Communists and the market-women—Molière's funeral—St. Gervais—Scarron's tomb—St. Leu—The bleeding statue—St. Merri's—St. Nicholas-in-the-Fields—Mademoiselle de Scudéri's tomb—Other churches—Rabelais and the Man of the Iron Mask—The monuments to the mignons of King Henri III.—Cardinal Richelieu's first mass—The Dutch dauphin—The English converts—Barras, Bonaparte, and the Venus of the Capitol 161

CONTENTS.

CHAPTER XIV.

MODERN CHURCHES.

The Madeleine—St. Philippe du Roule—The Chapelle Expiatoire—St. Augustin - Ste. Clotilde—The Trinité—St. Vincent de Paul—The Basilica of the Sacré-Cœur—The Chapel of the Convent of the Sacré-Cœur, and the smaller Churches.

The fashionable church—The Madeleine and the Commune—A temple of glory—The cemetery of the Madeleine—Louis XVI. and Marie Antoinette—Rossini's funeral—The Sacré-Cœur and the old Church of St. Pierre—A famous hill—The Hallelujah of the Germans—Ignatius Loyola—Henri Quatre and the abbess—The Temple of Reason and the Montmartre Goddess—Montmartre in 1814, 1871, and 1895 181

CHAPTER XV.

The Protestant Church of the Oratory—The Russian Church—The Synagogues.

French Protestants before the Reformers—"Little Geneva"—Calvin and Cop—Abbot Briçonnet and Marguerite de Navarre—Burning heretics—The Protestant tailor—The Huguenot hedge-schools—The first Synod—St. Bartholomew's Day—The League—The Edict of Nantes—George Washington and the French Protestants—The "White Terror"—The Bible Society—Jonathan, the Jew—Early persecutions of the children of Israel—Removal of Jewish disabilities 191

CHAPTER XVI.

Inscriptions and Epitaphs.

A ghastly memorial—The "Sorrows of Death"—Eccentric epitaphs—The Bouvines Memorial—Strange epitaph of Jean de Creil—The glory of Louis XIII.—The tomb of Lulli—The inscription in the Scotch College 199

INDEX . 209

INITIAL LETTERS.

	PAGE
Clovis I.	3
Childebert I.	15
Pepin	31
Louis III.	43
Carloman	61
Robert I.	77
Catherine de' Medici	89
Hugues Capet	101
Philippe III.	111
Jean I.	121
Jean II.	135
Charles V.	145
Charles VII.	163
Louis XII.	183
François I.	193
Henry II.	201

LIST OF ILLUSTRATIONS.

	PAGE
NOTRE DAME	*To face* 1
Monster	12
Ditto.	36
Ditto.	37
Ditto.	50
Ditto.	51
Choir stalls	*To face* 29
West Front	40
THE SAINTE CHAPELLE	*To face* 64
Interior	*To face* 59
The Reliquary	72
Capitals of the Porch of the Upper Chapel	70
Figure at the top of the Chevet	74
ST. DENIS—Tomb of Marie Antoinette	*To face* 75
The Crypt and Tomb of Louis XVI.	*To face* 83
The North Portal	86
Tomb of Henry II.	94
The Crypt	95
ST. GERMAIN L'AUXERROIS	98
Statue of Coligny—Rue de Rivoli	*To face* 104
ST. GERMAIN-DES-PRÉS	*Frontispiece*
Fresco by Flandrin	108
Ditto	*To face* 115
ST. ETIENNE DU MONT—Interior	118
The Rood Loft	126
The Pulpit	129
THE PANTHÉON	123
ST. SULPICE	132
ST. SÉVERIN	140
THE VAL DE GRÂCE	142
THE SORBONNE—The Tomb of Richelieu	146
ST. LOUIS DES INVALIDES—Interior	*To face* 150
Tomb of Napoleon	153
ST. MÉDARD	158
ST. EUSTACHE	160
Parish Arms	168
ST. MERRI	171
ST. NICOLAS-DES-CHAMPS	172
ST. LAURENT	*To face* 173
ST. ROCH—The High Altar	*To face* 177
THE MADELEINE	180
ST. AUGUSTIN	185
THE TRINITÉ	*To face* 187
ST. CLOTILDE	186
THE RUSSIAN CHURCH (Winter)	190
ISRAELITE TEMPLE—Interior	197

ARTIST'S NOTE.

AMONGST the smaller illustrations in this book, the artist desires to acknowledge his indebtedness to the following works :—" Les Églises de Paris," M. l'Abbé Pascal ; " Histoire de la Sainte Chapelle," S. J. Morand ; " Itinéraire Archéologique de Paris," F. de Guilhermy ; and to a work by the same author, " Monographie de l'Église Royale St. Denis," in which copies of the small engravings of the tombs of the Kings of France form part of the letterpieces at the commencement of each chapter.

INTRODUCTION.

In a book of this kind many authorities have to be consulted and a good deal of evidence has to be sifted. Facts and dates are frequently difficult to verify, especially in the case of the old churches and abbeys of Paris which have suffered from the ravages of foreign foes and civil war. The author has done his best to reconcile conflicting testimony, and has gone a little ahead of all writers, either French or English, who have been in the same field before him. He has dealt at greater length than others with the historical events happening in, or in connection with, the older churches. This book is therefore in advance, not only of ordinary handbooks, but of the archæological treatises, like those of Baron F. de Guilhermy, which have chiefly dealt with architectural or other details, and have only touched incidentally on historical events.

Three churches—Notre Dame, the Sainte Chapelle, and St. Denis—stand out in greater prominence than the others. An attempt has been made to describe them as completely as possible, in the first place, because they are often the only edifices of the kind in which average visitors to Paris, and even Parisians themselves, take an interest, and, secondly, because they are the three great legacies of Gothic genius in the possession of the inhabitants of the French mother city. Rouen, Beauvais and Chartres have their

INTRODUCTION.

own monuments to show the skill of the early French architects and sculptors, but in Paris, the cathedral, the chapel of the Law Courts, and, to a large extent, the elegant edifice of St. Denis, are the only structures produced by the genius of the soil, untrammelled by the necessity of imitating Greek temples or Roman basilicas at the bidding or command of Royal or Imperial patrons.

The author must acknowledge his indebtedness to the "Chartularium Ecclesiæ Parisiensis," to the works of Viollet-le-Duc, to Baron F. de Guilhermy, to Gibbon, who has written not a little about Paris churches in his "Decline and Fall," to Sir Francis Palgrave's "History of England and Normandy," to Abbé J. Perdreau, who has issued a little work on St. Etienne du Mont, to Abbé Torré, who has published a useful monograph on the important church of Saint-Eustache, to the compilers of the literary "Paris Guide," which is a valuable compendium of information to those who know how to use whatever is not out of date in the volume, and finally to Dubu, whose treatise on Notre Dame is the nearest approach to an historical, as opposed to an architectural work on the subject.

Notre Dame.   *To face p.* 1.

CHAPTER I.

NOTRE DAME DE PARIS.

I.

"*A symphony in stone*"—*Esmeralda and Quasimodo—Historical scenes in Notre Dame de Paris—The cloister and the hospital —The ship-shaped island—Ham Fair—Stacking hay and oats in church—The Feast of Fools—The University in the cloister —Devotion to the Virgin Mary in Paris—The Dominicans and the University—Tests for the Huguenots—Louis XIII. and his vow—Modern veneration of the Blessed Virgin—Her name given to Voltaire and others.*

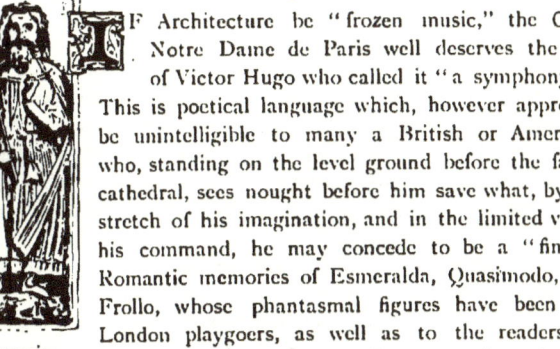

CLOVIS I.

IF Architecture be "frozen music," the Cathedral of Notre Dame de Paris well deserves the description of Victor Hugo who called it "a symphony in stone." This is poetical language which, however appropriate, may be unintelligible to many a British or American tourist who, standing on the level ground before the famous Paris cathedral, sees nought before him save what, by the utmost stretch of his imagination, and in the limited vocabulary at his command, he may concede to be a "fine building." Romantic memories of Esmeralda, Quasimodo, and Claude Frollo, whose phantasmal figures have been familiar to London playgoers, as well as to the readers of Hugo's lurid pages, may, haply, flit across the minds of some visitors from Great Britain and Ireland as they gaze on the fretted *façade*, the pointed archways, the row of kings drawn across the frontage like a belt, the quadrangular towers and all the other noted architectural and sculptural features of the metropolitan church of Paris.

To realize in the proper spirit the grandeur and the associations of the great Gothic pile which, in spite of alterations and defacements, notwithstanding the clumsiness of some of its restorers, like Soufflot, the fury of revolution and the canker of time, still remains a marvellous memorial of mediæval workmanship, one must not depend alone on the literary or stage effects evolved by the novelist and dramatist from the stones of Notre Dame de Paris.[1] History must be laid under contribution in order to enable us to realize the part which this most famous of French monuments has played since it was completed in the thirteenth century.

[1] In the preface to his "Notre Dame de Paris," Victor Hugo states that he conceived the idea of his romance from the inscription 'ΑΝΑΓΚΗ, "fatality," written on the wall of one of the cathedral towers.

HISTORIC CHURCHES OF PARIS.

Notre Dame de Paris is an historical, as well as an ecclesiastical and architectural landmark. It is eclipsed in some points of architectural grandeur by other edifices in France and elsewhere. It disappoints, at first sight, like St. Peter's at Rome. Its low, unfinished towers give it a stunted appearance, and it loses by comparison with the minsters of Cologne and Strassburg,[1] whose springing spires seem to symbolize the heavenward aspirations of those who faithfully follow a religion founded on idealism.

It was one of its ablest restorers, Viollet-le-Duc, who said that, if the pillars of Notre Dame had a voice, they could recount the annals of France from the days of Philip Augustus to our own. This historical connection is, therefore, one of the charms of the chief Paris church for all who have not become too modern and sophisticated to lose veneration for antiquity. Restorations and repatchings have assuredly altered the face of the majestic building. Modern mortar, plaster of Paris, lead, wood, and iron are calculated to spoil one's appreciation of the antique, and to give a prosaic curb to the lively historic imagination which finds its keenest pleasure in re-peopling the present with the phantoms of the past. The intensely new aspect which marks much of the sculptured imagery on the frontage of Notre Dame de Paris, disturbs recollections and jars on the visual nerves of the archæologist, like the propping and cementing of the Coliseum and St. Peter's.

The restorations must perforce be effected, but one cannot help imagining, when they are thrust aggressively in view, that one is being duped by cunning curators and able architects who have been repatching and rebuilding until nothing remains but a mere shell or skeleton of the old structure, buried beneath a mass of nineteenth-century brick, stucco, or concretionary limestone.

Enough, however, remains of Notre Dame de Paris to give a good notion of its antiquity and to satisfy the artist, the antiquarian, and the raiser of historical phantoms. Its lines, as the historian Michelet says, are those of a book. It is an open record in stone, and under its gorgeous rose-windows, whose rays empurple the floor of nave and transept, great historical dramas were enacted, and scenes, solemn and

---

[1] So good an authority as Freeman writes "Köln" and "Strassburg," as well as "Trier" for Treves. "Cologne," the English as well as French form, is here preserved. There will always be this difficulty about the names of foreign places, and if we call the capital of Rhineland, Köln, we must call Vienna, Wien.

pompous, gay and grotesque, were often visible. It is a fane more famous than other European monuments of the kind, with the exception of Saint Sophia's, rebuilt by Justinian in the sixth century, in order to eclipse Solomon's temple. It is, to some persons, more historically interesting than St. Paul's, Westminster Abbey, St. Stephen's of Vienna, or even St. Peter's, for it witnessed more dramatic events than these places. It epitomizes nearly the whole history of the strange and fascinating French nation.

Wandering amid its internal or external recesses one can hardly imagine it to be in busy, brilliant and restless Paris, but rather in some slow, old-world town, where steam, the telegraph, the telephone and all the complicated contrivances of modern civilization are still unknown. It is out of the range of feverish Bourse speculation, of the theatres, music-halls and places where vice flaunts in gaudiest and most fascinating attire. The cries of the backers of favourites do not trouble its tranquillity. The illusion of calmness and antiquity is rather dispelled by the contiguity of the big, modern, barrack-like building of the Prefecture of Police, and by the equally unlovely Hôtel Dieu, whence medicinal odours are wafted on warm days towards the cathedral towers. By confining oneself to the church, however, one can retain the illusion, and, after all, the life that there is now-a-days around the minster is rather slow and stagnant. There is no close on the fine old models of English minsters—like Lichfield or Exeter, for instance—no antique cloister as at Westminster, no God's Acre as at St. Paul's. The houses of the Rue du Cloitre Notre Dame, in spite of a few modern additions, do not, however, give an impression of contemporary bustle and activity. Even the bit of river bounding the church on the south side is sluggish in its course, and the heavy omnibuses from Batignolles to the Jardin des Plantes rumble like old "diligences" around the venerable pile.

For all that, the island of the city on which Notre Dame de Paris stands was once not only the busiest part of Paris, but also the kernel or cradle of the capital of France which, like Rome, has been so important a centre in the world's history. When St. Stephen's and St. Mary's stood where Notre Dame is now, the island formed the chief bulwark against the inroads of the northern pirates.[1] From that small, river-girt strip of land which looks like a leviathan ship, the great mistress and mother city of France sprouted and

[1] Freeman in his "Select Historical Essays" gives a very concise and lucid account of the rise of Paris, comparing it with London, Vienna and other capitals. The accounts of Victor Hugo in his novel, and of Michelet in his history, are picturesque, but facts are sometimes rather evasively treated by these great writers.

grew by degrees until it became the seat of government, after having been an insignificant township under the predecessors of Charles the Bald. The ship-shaped kernel which, according to heraldic writers, gave the form of the arms of Paris, expanded in every direction, bursting its mud or brick barriers and stretching out its hands to grasp the green hills through which the Seine threads its way to the ocean.

In those distant days when men built such majestic edifices as Notre Dame the church was everything to the people, and not a mere meeting-house for prayer and thanksgiving. It was the house both of God and man, an asylum or refuge, the place where the people often assembled to take counsel. The Ham Fair of Eastertide, now held on the Boulevard Richard Lenoir, near the site of the Bastille, on the Tuesday, Wednesday, and Thursday of Holy Week, was of old established on the "Parvis" or "Paradise" of Notre Dame, that is to say, on the ground in front of the church, and from which, as some say, steps led up to the cathedral. Each purchaser had his pig-meat blessed by a priest as he left the Parvis. Hay and oats were also stacked in the church. The sick were tended there, and sometimes there were feasts and dancing. Grave canons joined in sports, and the Feast of Fools, afterwards prohibited by a Papal Legate, was carried out with extraordinary animation. This "Festum Fatuorum" is dealt with in the "Chartularium Ecclesiæ Parisiensis," which contains a chapter descriptive of the "foul language" used and the deeds of blood caused during the junketing.[1] There were likewise feasts in honour of the Ass, an animal identified with the history of the Redeemer of mankind. At these festivals the priest, as we are told by old writers, in finishing the Mass, brayed like a donkey. "In fine missæ sacerdos versus ad populum vice : Ite. missa est, ter hinhannabit," etc. A hymn, half Latin, half French, was sung in which the "fine, strong" donkey was told that he would have abundant fodder. It began,—

> Orientis partibus
> Adventavit Asinus
> Pulcher et fortissimus
> Sarcinis aptissimus
> Hez, Sire Asnes, car chantez
> Belle bouche rechignez,
> Vous aurez du foin assez.

---

[1] Chapter 76. "Contra facientes festum fatuorum in ecclesia." Peter of Capua, Papal Legate, remonstrated with Bishop Eudes de Sully, and the Feast of Misrule was temporarily discontinued. See further references to this subject later on.

NOTRE DAME DE PARIS.

This respect was paid to the ass not only as having been connected with the history of the Saviour, but also because the animal was regarded in the Middle Ages as a model of patience, meekness and resignation.[1] The sacred drama, too, the mystery plays, were represented in the church, and the people joined the priests in celebrating many of the rites. Afterwards came comparative silence and gloom ; only the priests and the choristers were heard, and the voices of the worshipping people were subdued. The mighty edifices raised by the mediæval master-builders at the bidding of princes and prelates, became little more than sacred museums. Divine Service is held in them still, but bereft of many of the popular attractions of old, like the dove-flying at Pentecost, or the fantastic processions around the illuminated galleries and up the towers, which symbolized the life journey of humanity towards the heights of the heavenly Jerusalem.

Learning, as well as religion, had its headquarters at Notre Dame de Paris. The cradle of the university was on the Parvis near the Bishop's Palace, and the Benedictines, in the monumental " Histoire Littéraire de la France,'' call the episcopal school the origin of all the others. The " others " became rather numerous. That of St. Victor[2] was the first and most celebrated of the schools of the canons regular to which William of Champeaux transferred, in 1108, the school of the Cloister of Notre Dame. Next came the school of Sainte Geneviève where Abelard taught, and that of Jocelyn, afterwards Bishop of Soissons. These were attended by many English students. The scholastic institutions near Notre Dame formed what was then called the " Academy," the title University not having been given until the thirteenth century, when Pietro Lombardo was Bishop of Paris.[3]

Turning now to the origin of the cnurcn, we find that Notre Dame replaced in the year 1163, when it was begun by the direction of Maurice de Sully, sixty-second Bishop of Paris, two other sacred buildings. One of

[1] Carlyle refers to "Ass Processions" in his "French Revolution." Animals are still blessed by priests in many parts of provincial France, as is shown by E. H. Barker in his "Wanderings by Southern Waters."

[2] Dante, who studied in Paris, makes several references to the Canons of St. Victor, and the "Vico degli strami," (straw-littered street), or Rue du Fouarre, where scholars met, is also mentioned.

[3] Pietro Lombardo is mentioned in the tenth canto of the Paradiso,—
Quel Pietro fu che con la poverella,
Offerse a Santa Chiesa il suo tesoro,
the " Peter who, like the widow, gave his treasure to the Church." His Liber Sententiarum, containing a system of scholastic theology, is still greatly esteemed. He was Bishop of Paris only one year.

these was dedicated to Mary Mother of God, the other to St. Stephen. The new church perpetuated the memory of the Mother of God alone, that of St. Stephen being preserved elsewhere.

We may take it for granted that those who dedicated the church to the Virgin were not influenced alone by the fact that a previous temple in her honour stood on the banks of the island city, but by the impetus given to what Protestants call her " worship," and Catholics her " cult," or devotion, in the twelfth century. The Virgin had of course been venerated from the early ages of the Church. The history of her " worship," to use the non-Catholic term, has engaged the attention of many an able and distinguished writer, English as well as foreign, and Henry Thomas Buckle has left us a few pages of fragmentary notes on the subject, in the " Miscellaneous and Posthumous Works," published in 1872. In the second century Irenæus attributed extraordinary powers to the Virgin, who, in ancient works, called the " Gospel of the Infancy of Jesus," and the " Gospel of the Birth of Mary," was hailed as " divine." Then there were the Collyridians, so called from the Greek word meaning a kind of cake, who were chiefly women. These offered bread at stated intervals to the Mother of God, whom they treated as a divinity. Their tenets were attacked by St. Epiphanius, A.D. 310 to 403, who also denounced the sect of Antidicomarianites who held views about the Virgin similar to those of non-Catholics of the present day.

Next came the heresy of Nestorius, Patriarch of Constantinople in A.D. 428, who objected to the title of " Mother of God," which had, as Gibbon says in the " Decline and Fall," been insensibly adopted since the origin of the Arian controversy in the preceding century. Controversies of this sort started by Nestorius, continued long afterwards, but there grew with them side by side, increased devotion to Mary, whose festivals were celebrated with great pomp in the churches of the East and West. It was, however, towards the twelfth century, when Notre Dame de Paris was founded, that a real revival of devotion to Mary took place. Hugues, Canon regular of St. Victor, who died in 1142, wrote a treatise maintaining the " Immaculate Conception " theory, long afterwards to be raised to the rank of a dogma by Pius IX. The doctrine was opposed by St. Bernard, in spite of his known veneration for the Mother of God, and he wrote to the Canons of Lyons, blaming them for introducing the new festival of the Conception.[1]

---

[1] The learned Jesuit, P. Colonia, who wrote a literary history of Lyons, gives information on this subject. In the " Vindiciæ Ecclesiæ Anglicanæ," London, 1826, it seems to be supposed, according to Buckle, that the Franciscans originated the Immaculate Conception theory.

NOTRE DAME DE PARIS.

Fleury, in his " Histoire Ecclésiastique," says that both the Greeks and the Armenians celebrated the Conception, but not, however, the " Immaculate Conception," in the twelfth and thirteenth centuries. Thus a vast pile of literature arose at this period of the building or completion of Notre Dame de Paris, around the Virgin. In the century preceding that in which the great Paris church was finished, King Robert of France, who died in 1031, had written hymns and sequences for the Nativity of Our Lady. According to Ceillier, author of the " Histoire Générale des Auteurs Sacrés," it was Robert who ordered that the festival of the Nativity of the Virgin should be celebrated with pomp in France. Other pious writers of the period were St. Bernard, Abbot of Clairvaux, who died in 1153; William of Auvergne, Bishop of Paris, who died in 1248; Yves, Bishop of Chartres, Geoffroi, Abbot of the Trinity of Vendosme; Hildébert, Bishop of Mans; Marbode, Bishop of Rennes; Peter de Celle, Bishop of Chartres, and several others, including even Peter Abelard, the lover of Heloise, who died in 1142. All of these, as well as non-French authors or homilists inspired to write about the Virgin, are mentioned by Ceillier.

Later on, the veneration of Mary attained still more important development, and the Virgin's history furnished a theme for poets and prose-writers of greater celebrity than most of those mentioned. Dante, when in Paris, must have been struck by the devotion paid to Mary, when he wrote those concluding cantos of the " Paradiso," in which he introduces the French Saint, Bernard of Clairvaux, prominently, and after him, Francis, Benedict Augustin, and "all the rest," who joined in the " Ave, Maria, gratia plena!" Bernard is notably described as the Virgin's " fedel Bernardo," her own faithful servant, who, if he objected to the Immaculate Conception theory, was a fervent devotee at her shrine, and composed the fine prayer, " Memorare, O piissima Virgo!" It is he who points out to the poet the " file of Hebrew dames,"—

>Sara, Rebecca, Judit, e Colei
>Che fu bisava al Cantor, che, per doglia.
>Del fallo disse : *Miserere mei*,[1]

---

[1] Cary's translation is—
>" Sarah next,
>Judith, Rebecca, and the gleaner maid
>Meek ancestress of him, who sang the songs
>Of sore repentance in his sorrowful mood."

and is made to conclude the "Paradiso" with the majestic invocation beginning:—

> Vergine Madre, figlia del tuo figlio
> Umile ed alta più che creatura.[1]

Further impetus still was given in Paris to the cult of Mary, after the foundation of Notre Dame, that is to say, in the fourteenth, fifteenth and sixteenth centuries. In 1387, for instance, Jean de Montson, a Dominican, argued that the Virgin was not free from original sin. He was condemned by Peter d'Orgemont, Bishop of Paris, and was excommunicated by Clement VII., the opposition Pope, Robert of Geneva, who was recognized by France, and reigned at Avignon, while the real Pontiff, Urban VI., was at Rome. The University of Paris next issued a decree ordering all its members to take an oath condemning the opinions of Montson, and declared that no one should receive degrees who refused to do this. The Dominicans objected to denounce Montson, and were accordingly shut out from the University until 1401. The same Institution formally decreed in 1496, that all who were admitted into its body should sign an opinion in favour of the Immaculate Conception, as is pointed out by the author of the continuation of Fleury's "Histoire Ecclésiastique." Many instances could be drawn from the same source in order to show to what extent the "Mater Domini," the "Vera Mater magni Dei ac Salvatoris Nostri," as Anastasius of Antioch called her, was venerated in Paris. That veneration continued to increase down to Luther's time, and to the days of the Huguenots, for whom images of the Virgin were purposely placed in the streets of the city. If they passed by without saluting these "tests for heretics," or refused to contribute money for the purchase of tapers for the altar of the Holy Virgin in Notre Dame, they were attacked by the people.

The "Mater Domini" was more glorified still in the time of Louis XIII., son of Henri Quatre and Maria de' Medici. This monarch was noted for

---

[1] "O virgin Mother, daughter of thy Son,
Created beings all in lowliness
Surpassing, as in height, above them all."

Cary, by the way, expresses surprise that Dante should make St. Bernard act so prominent a part, as he opposed the doctrine of the Immaculate Conception. See notes to Canto xxxi. of the "Paradiso," Maclaine's Mosheim being referred to. It is clear, however, that Bernard, if adverse to the doctrine or theory in question, was full of devotion to Mary. The biographical notice of the Saint in the Roman Breviary sets forth that he was buried at Clairvaux before the altar of the Virgin, "quam religione singulari coluerat," whom he specially venerated. The sermons of the holy Abbot, which are quoted for the offices of the Feast of the Assumption, are also full of tender, poetic references to the "Illustrious Virgin."

NOTRE DAME DE PARIS.

his devotion to the Virgin, to whom he consecrated himself, his crown, his kingdom, and his people by a special edict, beginning : " Beatissimam et gloriosissimam Virginem in specialem regni nostri Patronam assumentes, eidem speciali modo nos, nostrum sceptrum nostrum coronam, nostrosque omnes subditos dicamus et consecramus."[1] The solemn procession which he ordered is still organized every year on the Festival of the Assumption, in the Cathedral of Notre Dame de Paris, and the massive silver statue of the Virgin is then exhibited to the faithful. And even in these times, when a "solemn creed" is still undergoing the process of being sapped by many a "solemn sneer," devotion to " Notre Dame " is faithfully kept alive, not only in provincial France, but in the heart of worldly Paris. Multitudes of French mothers still dedicate their children to the Virgin and make them wear garments, blue or white, in her honour. Half the women in France may be said without exaggeration to answer to the name "Marie," and the festivals of " Notre Dame ' are observed by the godly and the ungodly alike. What is more, even male children are baptized at the instance of pious parents as " Marie." Voltaire himself, who terminated his letters to the Encyclopædists by the phrase " Ecrasons l'infâme," which was interpreted as an injunction to wipe out superstition, was christened as François Marie Arouet. The late President of the Republic, who was murdered at Lyons by an Anarchist in June, 1894, was " Marie François Sadi Carnot." The devotion to Mary is, in fact, so universal in France, even in these free-thinking days, that if Notre Dame Cathedral were accidentally burned down, or destroyed by the fury of Revolutionists, funds could be easily collected for the rebuilding of the church on a still larger and more sumptuous scale. There are many thousands of Frenchmen, lay as well as religious, who are as enthusiastic in their devotion as the directors of the old University of Paris, and who, like the young men who give their services to the infirm at Lourdes gratuitously, are completely uninfluenced by the cynicism and the infidelity of the Boulevards.

[1] This is set forth in the " Chartularium Ecclesiæ Parisiensis," and in the " Breviarium Parisiense." In the last-mentioned book it appears in the part prescribing the Divine office for the day of the commemoration of the vow of the "most Christian King," Ludovicus Decimus-tertius, Francorum Rex," which is kept on the Sunday within the Octavé of the Assumption. Viollet-le-Duc calls the edict "letters patent." The most interesting testimony to the revival and development of the veneration for the Virgin, begun in the twelfth century, and carried on later, is to be found in Michelet's " History of France," a much-criticized but fascinating work. He says : " God changed sex, so to speak. The Virgin became the God of the world. She invaded nearly all the churches, and occupied all the altars." From this he deduces the increase of woman's dominion in the world. Goetzius, a Lutheran writer, was so struck by the devotion of Catholics to our Lady, as to call their religion " womanish "—*religio muliebris*.

Demon—Notre Dame.

CHAPTER II.

NOTRE DAME DE PARIS.

II.

Historical connections—The third crusade—Philip Augustus and Ingelburgha of Denmark—Formal interdict against a frivolous festival—The Albigenses—Raymond of Toulouse flogged at the doors of Notre Dame—Blanche of Castille and the Chapter of the Cathedral—Philip the Fair and Boniface VIII.—Gallican liberties—On horseback in Notre Dame—Burning of the Templars—A dreadful summons—The big taper of Notre Dame—Cathedral Council re the Anti-Popes—Henry VI. of England crowned in Notre Dame—Te Deums and thanksgivings from Agnadel to Sebastopol—The League and the Huguenots—Paris an Archbishopric—The Goddess of Reason in Notre Dame—Coronation of Napoleon—Marriage of the third Napoleon—The Communists of 1871.

CHILDEBERT I.

IN dealing with the historical associations of the cathedral of Paris, it is only possible here to touch upon the most striking and important events. The earliest occurrence of note with which Notre Dame was identified was the third Crusade, in 1188, when Philip Augustus of France joined Richard Plantagenet of England and Frederick Barbarossa of Germany in checking the power of the Moslem. There was a council held in Notre Dame de Paris similar to that attended previously by Heraclius, Patriarch of Jerusalem, when an expedition to the Holy Land was discussed. In 1190, Isabella of Hainault, first wife of Philip Augustus, and who died in childbirth at the age of twenty, was buried with great pomp in the choir of the cathedral. Six years later, when the King wanted to divorce his second wife, Ingelburgha of Denmark, in order to marry Agnes, daughter of the Duke of Meranie, a council assembled in Notre Dame for the purpose of condemning the Royal claim. Philip subsequently submitted to the Church, took back Ingelburgha, and had her crowned in the cathedral in 1201.

In 1198 a great blow was struck at the popular and profane ceremony of the "Festum Fatuorum," or "Feast of Fools," which was always carried out with much ribaldry in the diocese of Paris. Notre Dame and its vicinity formed the centre of this festival, which nearly equalled the orgies of the Roman Saturnalia. Peter of Capua, the Pope's legate, being shocked at the sight of one of these spectacles, directed Bishop Eudes de Sully to discontinue the disgraceful foolery. The legate was obeyed, but the "Feast of Fools" was not, for all that, destined to disappear until long afterwards [1]

[1] Dulaure, and also Michelet, were disbelieved when they referred to this fête, but the chapter in the "Chartularium," previously quoted, is explicit on the subject. M. Bourquelet,

HISTORIC CHURCHES OF PARIS.

The next date of any importance in the annals of the church is 1210, when a council condemned the works of Aristotle as dangerous to religion. We afterwards come to the period of the Albigensian Wars.

The Albigenses, so called from the city of Albi, and the district of Albigeois, between the Rhone and the Garonne, have been identified with the Manichæans, the Paulicians, and the Waldenses. Their history is especially interesting to Englishmen, for they were the forerunners of the Reformers. They took their tenets from the Paulicians, a sect started about the year 660 in Armenia and Cappadocia. Its founder rejected the two epistles of St. Peter, agreed with the Gnostics in denying the Old Testament, disclaimed veneration of the Blessed Virgin, and pinned their faith in Christ and the Apostle of the Gentiles. The Paulicians did not want to be classed as Manichæans, although they held some of the doctrines of Manes, but they rallied to their standard all the remnants of that and other Gnostic sects. Like their spiritual descendants, the Albigenses, the Paulicians revolted under persecution. Their city of Tephrice, in Asia Minor, was taken by the Greek Emperor Basil, their lands were laid waste, and many of the Paulicians were eventually transplanted from Armenia to Thrace and Constantinople. In the beginning of the thirteenth century, their Pope or Primate resided on the confines of Bulgaria, Croatia, and Dalmatia, governing through his vicars the congregations of Italy and France, the doctrines of the "New Manichæans," as they have sometimes been called, having reached these countries.[1] The Paulicians were numerous in Languedoc, and as Gibbon says, "the persecutions which had formerly taken place on the banks of the Euphrates were resumed on the banks of the Rhone."

This necessarily succinct summary of the origin of the Albigenses will better enable the intelligent visitor to the Paris Cathedral to realize the historical fact of the presence of Raymond VII., Count of Toulouse, barefooted at the door of Notre Dame in 1229. The father of that nobleman had been called upon by Pope Innocent III., to withdraw his support from the heretics who were turning Languedoc into a battlefield of the creeds, and banding against each other the hot-blooded descendants of Iberians,

---

furthermore, found in a MS. of the thirteenth century, a special " office " for the "Festum Fatuorum," supposed to have been prepared by Peter of Corbeil, Bishop of Sens. This feast was once also observed in England, according to Fosbrooke.—"British Monachism."

[1] See Muratori, Antiquitat. Italiæ, also Mosheim, Institut. Hist. Eccles., Beausobre's Hist. Crit. du Manicheisme, and Gibbon, who has given a summary of the history of the Paulicians in his great work on Rome.

NOTRE DAME DE PARIS.

Gauls, Romans, Saracens and Goths Raymond at first refused, but Innocent III. was not a man to be trifled with. He organized a crusade against the heretics, sent forth Dominic and his preachers, used the terrible engine of the Inquisition, and in a short time brought the bold Count to his knees. Raymond found to his cost that he had provoked the wrath of a man who had anathematized Philip Augustus for his attempt to divorce his wife, and John Lackland because he refused to accept an Archbishop of Canterbury of the Pope's choosing, and who, in the Council of the Lateran, acted as ecclesiastical and almost temporal sovereign of the East and West.

Before so powerful a Pope a Languedoc baron was of small consequence, so Raymond VI. submitted with a bad grace to the inevitable. The war against the Albigenses again broke out, but ended in the submission of his son Raymond VII. to Queen Blanche of Castille, mother of Louis IX., or St. Louis. Raymond VII. underwent the punishment of the "discipline," or lash, before the door of Notre Dame, at the hands of the Pope's legate, gave himself up as a prisoner, and made over large tracts of land to his foes. This was the triumph of Blanche of Castille, the real ruler of the kingdom during the youth of her son. Raymond was compelled to accept the most disadvantageous terms. He had to dismantle the fortifications of his city, receive a royal garrison, allow the Inquisition to be established there, ratify the transfer of Lower Languedoc to the monarchy, and agree that, after his death, Toulouse should serve as a dowry for his daughter, who was to marry one of the brothers of the king. He also made over Upper Provence to the Church, this resulting in the establishment of the Papal authority over the district of Avignon.

Queen Blanche of Castille, backed by the Church, is credited with having begun the reign of woman in France. She had no right or title to the regency, but the daughter of Alphonso the Noble knew how to rule, and asserted herself to some purpose. She not only dominated the clangour of feudal militarism, but set her bar against priestly encroachments. Thus, when the Canons of the Chapter of Notre Dame de Paris, a powerful body then, wanted to impose more taxes on their serfs of Chatenay, the Queen prevented them, and went in person with her followers in order to overcome their refusal to obey her orders.

On his departure for the Crusades, and on his return from the East, King Louis IX. punctually paid homage to the Holy Virgin at Notre Dame. No great ceremonies seem to have marked these visits, but more memorable

HISTORIC CHURCHES OF PARIS.

events with which the cathedral had a connection, happened in the reign of Philip the Fair, the fourth of his name.

This takes us to the period of the Pontificate of Boniface VIII., the celebrated Benedetto Gaetani, a time approaching that when, as Gibbon says, " the apostolic throne was transported as it might seem for ever from the Tiber to the Rhone."[1] The historian refers to the beginning of the fourteenth century, when Clement V. succeeded Benedict XI., who only reigned a short time after Boniface VIII. Benedetto Gaetani had studied in Paris University, and on returning to Rome became Apostolic Notary. After his election to the Papacy, he canonized Louis IX. as being the " model of Christian monarchs." His next act was to consolidate the institution of the Jubilee, which the first French Pope, Sylvester II., who received the tiara in 999, had already partly inaugurated.[2] Boniface, who, as the chroniclers say, " entered like a fox," was elected through the influence of the House of France, and did his best to extend the power of the Capetians. He objected, however, to the imposition of the " maltôte," or some such tax as that which the Third Republic now levies on the property of the religious orders and congregations in France. He published a violent bull anathematizing the cleric who should pay the tax and the laymen who should receive it. Philip the Fair on his side took reprisals by preventing supplies or money gifts intended for the Sovereign Pontiff, from leaving the kingdom of France. This led to the bull " Ausculta Fili," which Philip rejected, and even burned, then convoking the first States-General for the purpose of appealing to his subjects against the Pope.

Clergy, nobility and burgesses were convoked in Notre Dame de Paris, and

---

[1] Avignon. The first Pope who went to Avignon was Clement V., a Frenchman, who, as Bertrand de Got, or Goth, had been Archbishop of Bordeaux. He transferred the Holy See to the banks of the Rhone in 1309, some say 1307, and it remained there until 1377 or 1378. He is the " pastor senza legge" who, with Boniface VIII., is prominently mentioned in the " Inferno," but he is well defended by French Catholic historians against Villani, who said that the Pope's emissary having descended by magic into hell, found a place prepared there for Clement. (See P. Longueval's " Histoire de l'Eglise Gallicane," vol. xiii. ; "Dissertation historique sur le Pape Clement V.," by Abbé Souiry, etc.) The Roman Cardinals who accompanied the Pope to Avignon were the loudest in their lamentations over the " captivity" in the Provençal Babylon, which they called " Avenio ventosa—cum vento fastidiosa—sine vento venenosa." The reference was to the wind called the Mistral: " Windy Avignon, with the mistral blowing is wearisome, without it, poisonous." Yet the Popes, the Cardinals, and Petrarch, who played a prominent part in Avignon, had a tranquil, easy-going time on the banks of the Rhone.

[2] See Chantrel's " Histoire de l'Eglise."

NOTRE DAME DE PARIS.

an initial step was taken not alone towards resenting too much intrusion on the part of the Papacy in the affairs of the Gallican Church,[1] but also towards consultations in which the advice of the people was sought. Pierre Flotte, Vice-Chancellor of the kingdom, opened the proceedings by a powerful speech in favour of the King, who received the full support of the States, which declared that God was the only Master of the sovereign in temporal affairs. In order to make his revenge more complete, Philip sent into Italy William of Nogaret, who, with the help of Sciarra Colonna, attacked the Pontiff in his native town of Anagni. The full and heartrending narrative of this raid may be read in the pages of Dupuis, and in those of the Italian chronicler Villani.

Notre Dame de Paris was again, in 1304, the scene of another half-religious, half-political ceremony, when the French monarch, after having defeated the Flemings at Mons-en-Puelle—uselessly it is true, for he had to give up part of Flanders owing to the stubborn determination of its people to resist him—entered the Cathedral of Paris on horseback surrounded by his warriors, courtiers and people.[2] Another event which happened not in Notre Dame, but in its vicinity, was the burning of Jacques de Molay, Grand Master of the Templars, and others of his order, by Philip the Fair with the consent of Pope Clement V., although this is carefully glozed over by the defenders of that Pontiff's memory. It is recorded that the Grand Master, when dying, summoned the King and the Pope to appear with him before the Tribunal of God inside forty days. The two died in 1314, soon after the burning of the Templars, and truth was thus lent to the terrible summons attributed to the Grand Master. The cause assigned for the persecution of the Templars was

---

[1] The "Libertés Gallicanes," or privileges of the Church of Gaul, had been taught in the Sorbonne from early times. In 1682, Bossuet drew up a declaration of the French clergy which formulates "Gallican" claims as opposed to those of the Ultramontanes.

[2] This is a very debateable point. Viollet-le-Duc says that the equestrian statue in Notre Dame destroyed by the Revolutionists in 1792, was that, not of Philip le Bel, the victor of Mons-en-Puelle, but of his successor (not immediate), Philip of Valois, sixth of the name, who, in 1328, defeated the Flemings at Cassel, and who, on his return to Paris, rode into the cathedral in state, and vowed his harness to the Holy Virgin. On the other hand, the chapter of the church held that the statue was that of Philip IV. (the Fair). Viollet-le Duc is backed by the Benedictines, notably by Père Montfaucon, by the writers who continued the chronicle of William of Nangis, and others. Flanders played a most important part after these reigns, when Edward III. of England was recognized as liege lord of that country. Charles VI. had to return from the Low Countries in order to chastise the Paris " Maillotins," or mallet-men, who wanted to imitate the men of Ghent. As the author of the play " Philip Van Artevelde" says, " Flanders at that time imbued all Europe with ideas of Revolution."

HISTORIC CHURCHES OF PARIS.

the desire of Philip to obtain the money which they were supposed to have brought from the Holy Land. Catholic writers anxious to shield the memory of Clement V., give other reasons, such as the alleged spread of Gnosticism among the Templars, but they wisely throw the whole blame of the burning on the shoulders of Philip the Fair. The Templars, according to some, were burned near the extremity of the Ile de la Cité, facing the great western front of the cathedral. Michelet, however, states in a footnote to the " Eclaircissements " of his history of France, that Jacques Molay, as he calls him, was burned on the Parvis Notre-Dame.

From the death of Philip the Fair until the accession of John the Good, no very remarkable event occurred in Notre Dame de Paris. When John was captured at Poitiers by Edward the Black Prince, and led a prisoner to London, the burgesses of Paris vowed to the Virgin an annual candle as long as the city, if she would deign to bring about the King's liberation. Soon afterwards, a truce having been entered into by France and England, John returned home, but subsequently, owing to the escape of his son, the Duke of Anjou, whom he had left as a hostage with the English, he went back to London, where he died in 1364. During the troubled period before John's death, the Jacquerie, or revolt of the much-oppressed peasants, had broken out, and Etienne Marcel, Provost of the Paris merchants, was temporarily master of the Government and the metropolis. The distracting events of that period had influenced the burgesses in their vow. They wanted their King back, and the big candle was accordingly built and carried to Notre Dame. This votive offering was annually renewed until 1605, when, as the metropolis had become larger, and was manifestly to extend more every year, the worthy burgesses replaced the colossal taper by a handsome lamp, which was suspended in the Virgin's chapel. The "ex-voto" was destroyed by the Revolutionists in 1793, and like many other historical vestiges and memorials collected in Notre Dame de Paris, has disappeared for ever. It must also be recorded that John the Good, when freed by the English, duly repaired to the cathedral in order to render thanks to God and the Holy Virgin for his liberation.

In 1376, Charles V., the Wise, wanted Paris to be made an Archbishopric independent of Sens, the metropolitan see. He accordingly sent the Bishop of Paris to Rome in order to see the Pope on the subject. Gregory XI., a French Pontiff, the same who proscribed Wickliff, and who, by returning from Avignon to the Eternal City, put an end to the so-called " Captivity of Babylon," objected to raise the capital of France to the rank of an Arch-

NOTRE DAME DE PARIS.

bishopric, on the ground that the cathedral church was not sufficiently endowed. He, however, sent the pallium to the Bishop of Paris. Among the chief historic events in Notre Dame soon after this period, was the solemn entry into Paris of Isabeau, or Isabelle de Bavière, in 1389, four years after her marriage with Charles VI. There were, then, great rejoicings throughout Paris, a ceremony at Notre Dame, and mystery-plays were performed—all these solemnities and functions being picturesquely recorded by that king of chroniclers, but bad ecclesiastic, Messire Jehan Froissart:—"Devant la dite église de Notre Dame, en la place, l'Evêque de Paris était revêtu des Armes de Notre Seigneur et tout le Collége (Chanoin) aussi ou moult avait grand clergé, et la descendait la Royne, et la mirent ins hors de sa littière les quatres ducs qui la estoyent—Berry, Bourgogne, Touraine et Bourbon."[1] It was soon after these rejoicings that Charles VI. began to show signs of lunacy, that the famous feuds between the Bourguignons and the Armagnacs broke out under the regency of the Queen, and that the Duke of Orleans, the King's brother, was assassinated at the instigation of the Duke of Burgundy. About this period, too, important Councils were held in Notre Dame de Paris with reference to the claims of the Anti-Popes, and in order to determine the attitude of the Gallican Church towards the conflicting aspirants to the tiara.[2] There were also great thanksgiving services after Charles VI. had been saved from burning. The King, dressed as a satyr at a palace fête with five companions, excited the curiosity of the Duke of Orleans, who put a torch near the masqueraders in order to see who they were. Four of the companions of the monarch were burned to death, but Charles was saved by the Duchess of Berri, who threw a cloak over him. The other person was saved by flinging himself into a tub of water. There was a solemn procession to Notre Dame after these sinister events.

[1] Froissart, tome iv., pp. 4 and 5. For those who do not read French easily, it may be said that the passage refers to the presence of many ecclesiastics at the ceremony, and to the fact that the Queen was helped out of her resting-place, while travelling, by the four dukes of the places mentioned.

[2] The Anti-Popes at the end of the fourteenth century and the beginning of the fifteenth, were:—1378, Robert of Geneva, called Clement VII.; 1394, Peter de Luna, or Benedict XIII.; 1417, Mugnoz, or Clement VIII. The lawful Popes of the period were Urban VI.; Boniface IX.; Innocent VII., etc. The last Anti-Pope was Amédée VIII., Duke of Savoy, who was proclaimed Felix V. by the Council of Basle in 1438. This prince lived in the Augustinian monastery founded by himself at Ripaille lez Thonon. He was supposed to lead there a life devoted to politics, piety and pleasure. Some say that he was rigidly pious, others that he gave himself up freely to pleasures, notably to those of the table, whence originated the oft-quoted French phrase—*faire ripaille*, to gorge, as at a feast.

HISTORIC CHURCHES OF PARIS.

We next come to the time of Henry V. of England, who, profiting by the feuds between the Bourguignons and the Armagnacs, defeated the French at Agincourt, became Regent of France with right of succession to the throne, after his marriage with Catherine, daughter of Charles VI., in 1420, and who, on his entry into Paris, paid a solemn visit to the church of Notre Dame. After his death at Vincennes in 1422, the Duke of Bedford governed France, and, in 1431, had young Henry VI. crowned monarch of the kingdom in the cathedral. The pillars of the great church were more sumptuously ornamented in 1437, when a solemn *Te Deum* was sung in Notre Dame to celebrate the entry of Charles VII., surrounded by both Armagnacs and Bourguignons who had joined in driving the English to Rouen, and in thus paving the way towards freeing France from the invaders.

In the annals of Notre Dame from the days of Louis XI., the rebellious dauphin who succeeded his father, Charles VII., to the reign of the fourteenth Louis, there is chiefly a long record of *Te Deums* after the victories of the French army. Historic Rheims, where Clovis had been baptized by St. Remi in 496, was the favoured city of the French monarchs since the days of the Merovingians, who had accorded it great privileges. It appears to have been a metropolitan see since the third century, the titular of that see being first Duke and Peer of the realm, born legate of the Pope, Primate of Belgic Gaul, and having the exclusive right of crowning and consecrating the kings of France. As, therefore, all the French kings from the days of Philip Augustus were, with the exception of Henri Quatre and Louis XVIII., crowned at Rheims, the Parisians were not able to see coronation ceremonies in their cathedral. After they had been crowned, however, the sovereigns went to Notre Dame de Paris in order to join in the thanksgivings for their advent to the throne. The Parisians had the funeral services of dead kings and queens, who, before being laid to rest in the Abbey of St. Denis, were placed for a while in the cathedral, where a mass was said. This custom, too, was carried out in June, 1894, when President Carnot's remains were taken to Notre Dame before burial in the Panthéon.

A list of the thanksgivings would mean a *résumé* of the whole history of France, from the days of that military monarch, Charles VIII., and of his successor and cousin, Louis XII., to those of the Third Napoleon—the days of the victories of the Crimea and of the campaign in Italy, when the Imperial star shone with its most splendid lustre, long before the disaster of Sedan arrived to pale its light for ever.

There were, for instance, the *Te Deum* for the victory over the Venetians

NOTRE DAME DE PARIS.

defeated at Agnadel, or, as the Italians call it, Vaila, in 1509 by Louis XII., who had with him the famous Chevalier Bayard, the knight "without fear and without reproach;" a thanksgiving for the marriage of Louis XII. with Mary, sister of Henry VIII. of England, which ended a disastrous war. It also brought about the King's death, for being already feeble and worn out, he could not bear the fatigues incidental to the wedding festivities, and died in 1515. Next there were the *Te Deums* for the victories of Francis I.; the visit to Notre Dame of Charles V., Emperor of Germany, when he crossed France on his way to chastise the rebels of Ghent; the thanksgiving of Catherine de' Medici,[1] after the accession of her husband, Henri II., to the throne; the marriage of Mary Stuart with Francis II., then dauphin; the marriage of Henri de Bourbon, King of Navarre, with Marguerite de Valois outside the porch, as the Prince was a Protestant, only a few days before the bell of St. Germain l'Auxerrois rang out for the massacre of St. Bartholomew, and when the cry of "Down with the Huguenots" filled the streets of Paris.

In 1590, all the Catholic lords swore before the altar of Notre Dame to maintain the faith of their fathers in France, and to shed the last drop of their blood rather than obey the Béarnais, Henry of Navarre. About the same time the cathedral was used as a sort of garrison by the troops of the Catholic League under the "Seize," or chiefs of the sixteen divisions of the city. In 1593, there was the great procession to the chief church of the States-General, which had assembled in order to appoint a successor to the Catholic King Charles X. (the Cardinal de Bourbon who of course never reigned). The Leaguers could not agree among themselves. They were perplexed by the prospect of the intrigues sure to arise if on the one hand the Salic law were repealed, and the Infanta Isabella of Spain, daughter of Philip II. and

---

[1] The marriage of Catherine, daughter of Lorenzo II., Duke of Urbino, grandson of the great Lorenzo de' Medici, with the son of Francis I. of France, was accompanied by fêtes which were carried out with great magnificence in Paris during more than a month. Balzac, the novelist, has given a picturesque account of them in his "Études Philosophiques sur Catherine de' Médicis." He introduces the anecdote to the effect that Catherine's father, referring to a certain malformation of Henri, son of the French king, said, "A figlia d'Inganno non manca mai figliuolanza," ("a clever girl will never lack children"), but points out that it was not uttered by Lorenzo, who died before Catherine was born, but by her uncle, Pope Clement VII., Giulio de' Medici, the "offspring of illicit love," to whom historians refer the extinction of the liberties of Florence, the alliance of the Medici family with the Royal House of France, and the expulsion of Henry VIII. of England from the bosom of the Roman Church. See the histories of Machiavelli and Varchi, as well as Roscoe's "Lorenzo de' Medici."

of Elizabeth of France, were chosen to reign, and if, on the other, the young Duke of Guise were selected. The Duke of Mayenne, uncle of young Guise, opposed the abolition of the Salic law in his own interest rather than in that of his nephew. Philip of Spain tried to bring about the repeal of the same law, but he adopted the Machiavellian plan of pretending to favour the cause of the Duke of Guise. The Leaguers were therefore in a quandary, and their doubts, hesitations and difficulties gave rise to that famous "Satyre Ménippée," founded on the Greek and Latin models, and to which "Hudibras" has been compared. The nimble ridicule of the "Satyre Ménippée," directed at the leaders of the League—Mayenne, the Pope's legate, the Archbishop d'Espinac, and others—was as useful to Henri Quatre as was Butler's amusing satire to the cause of Charles II. of England. Henry IV. gave the last blow to the Leaguers in the same year, 1593, by abjuring Protestantism and finding " Paris worth a mass."[1] He *did* go to Mass, and heard a *Te Deum* in Notre Dame on the occasion of his accession to the throne as the first of the Bourbons.

The next date of importance in the annals of the great cathedral is 1622, when Henri de Gondy, Cardinal de Retz, and last Bishop of Paris, died. Pope Gregory XV. then raised the French metropolitan see to the dignity of an Archbishopric. In 1682, under Louis XIV., the big bell or bourdon of the Basilica was christened Emmanuel Louis Thérèse, the Grand Monarque and his wife being the sponsors. Later on, in 1699, the great changes in the church caused in fulfilment of the vow of Louis XIII., who had dedicated himself and his kingdom to the Virgin, were begun. Against this restoration Victor Hugo has raised his voice emphatically in " Notre Dame de Paris." "Who," he asks, "replaced the old Gothic altar by a heavy marble sarcophagus, and stupidly fixed this anachronism in stone in the Carlovingian pavement of Hercandus?[2] Was it not Louis XIV., accomplishing the vow of his predecessor?" The first stone of that altar was laid with great pomp by the Archbishop of Paris, the service used being the same as for the consecration of a church. On the foundation slab was placed the inscription: "Louis the Great—son of Louis the Just—after having subdued heresy, established the true religion in his kingdom, ended gloriously

[1] The expression " Paris vaut bien une messe," is attributed to Henri Quatre, but, like many phrases of the kind, it is rather apocryphal. Another version is that attributed to the Duc de Rosny, who told Henri Quatre that the "crown was well worth a mass." Henry is also reported to have said that "the best of cannons was the mass," for it pu him on the throne.

[2] One of the early bishops of Paris.

NOTRE DAME DE PARIS.

several wars by land and sea, wishing to accomplish the vow of his father, built this altar in the cathedral church of Paris and dedicated it to the God of Arms, Master of Peace and Victory, under the invocation of the Holy Virgin, patroness and protector of his States. The year of our Lord 1699."

The alterations made in the church at this period destroyed for ever many of the old tombs and monuments of the past, as well as the Gothic altar referred to by Victor Hugo. In making a crypt for the burial of prelates, in 1711, the builders found two parts of old walls, on them being bas-reliefs with inscriptions which have led to pages of learned archæological discussion. They were supposed to show that in the reign of Tiberius Cæsar, the Parisian sailors, or rather bargemen, had built on the spot an altar to Jupiter.

There is nothing else to connect Notre Dame with the reigns of Louis XIV. and his successor, except the numerous *Te Deums* and thanksgiving services for the victories of the French army in Flanders and Germany. In 1690, Marshal de Luxembourg sent one hundred flags from Fleurus to the cathedral, and was therefore jocosely called the Tapissier, or upholsterer, of Notre Dame.

With the approach of the Revolution, Notre Dame was destined to undergo a desecration which might have ended in its destruction but for the good sense and art instincts of some of the Terrorists. In November, 1790, the troubles began when the canons were compelled to leave the church after High Mass by order of the National Assembly, which had decreed for the service of religion only "sworn" priests, that is to say, those who had taken the civic oath. In July, 1792, the General Revolutionary Council of the Commune of Paris ordered all the crucifixes and bronzes in Notre Dame and other churches to be melted down for cannon, while the railings and *grilles* or gates were to be used for pikes and gun-barrels. Leaden coffins and some of the church bells were also utilized for military purposes. In 1793, a black flag was placed over the cathedral owing to the defeat of Dumouriez near Liège, a reverse which neutralized the result of the previous successes of that general in the Low Countries. In the same year the Revolutionary General Council ordered the cordon of kings over the façade of Notre Dame to be smashed. The fragments of the statues were thrown into the enclosure behind the apsis of the church, and were afterwards used for building purposes.

The next proceeding of the Terrorists was to make Gobel, the Archbishop of Paris, abjure the faith. " Goose Gobel," Carlyle calls him, and proceeds to

HISTORIC CHURCHES OF PARIS.

describe in his picturesque boil-down of the account of the "Moniteur," and also of the narrative of Mercier, how Gobel acknowledged no religion but liberty, doffed his "priest-gear," and received the fraternal embrace. All this, by the way, did not save the "Constitutional Bishop of Paris" from the guillotine, by which he perished at the same time as the "orator of the human race," Baron Anacharsis Clootz of Prussia, who became a naturalized Frenchman only to lose his head. On the 10th November, 1793, the Cult of Reason was decreed by the Convention; Notre Dame was therefore transformed into the temple of the new rite. A mock mountain was erected in the nave with a Gothic temple on the top, by its sides being busts of famous philosophic writers. On the capital of the temple was inscribed the dedication "À la Philosophie," and on the declivity of the hill there was an altar surmounted by the "torch of truth." Girls in white veils and carrying torches walked up and down the flanks of the mount. Then the Goddess of Reason entered, sat on the top of the hill in state, while hymns were sung and a vow of fidelity to her was made.

The members of the Convention were too busy to assist at the first fête of the Goddess of Reason, but Chaumette, Hébert, Momoro, and other members of the Commune, on leaving Notre Dame, organized a similar ceremony and introduced the Goddess of Reason to their colleagues, who fraternally embraced her. In the evening there was another disgraceful scene in the desecrated cathedral. Historians, by the way, differ as to the identity of the damsel who acted as Goddess of Reason in Notre Dame. Many French writers suppose her to have been Demoiselle Maillard, an opera dancer. Carlyle calls her "Demoiselle Candeille, of the opera," but the actress and authoress, not dancer, of that name, always denied that she had taken a part in the disgraceful procession of blackguards and strumpets organized by the Terrorists. In 1793, the Convention further decreed that the statues of saints ornamenting Notre Dame should be smashed, that a collecting-box for letters, protests, and all documents concerning the public weal, and entitled the "mouth of truth," should be placed in the church or temple, and that a register of Republicans who "had done some service to the State" should be kept in the same edifice. There were also built two galleries, one for elderly and feeble men, the other for "women in an interesting condition."

A stranger use was, however, made of the cathedral in 1794, when it was turned into a sort of "bond store" for the wine stolen from the cellars of the proscribed or guillotined Royalists. Some of the stuff was also "bonded" in

NOTRE DAME DE PARIS.

the Church of Saint Martin-in-the-Fields. In May, 1794, the "Tample of Reason" was made that of the "Supreme Being," by Robespierre, who also induced the Convention to decree "the consoling principle of the Immortality of the Soul." Finally, in 1795, Notre Dame was restored to the professors of the old religion, which had survived the destructive statutes of the Convention, as well as the attacks of the Encyclopædists.

After this, the chief events in the annals of Notre Dame may be more briefly summarized. There were the *Te Deum* for Marengo, the services for Desaix, La Tour d'Auvergne, and others who had fallen for France, and in Easter, 1802, the ceremony for the re-establishment of religion under the Concordat between the First Consul and Pope Pius VII. At this sacred function all the great administrative bodies were present. Cardinal Caprara, the special legate of the Pope, said Mass, and the archbishops and bishops took the prescribed oath. In the following August, the anniversary of Bonaparte's birth was celebrated with great pomp in the church. In 1804, there was the *Te Deum* for the establishment of the Empire, and at the end of the same year Pius VII. came to Paris in order to officiate at the coronation of the new Cæsar. That scene in Notre Dame during which Napoleon took the imperial crown from the Pope's hands and placed it on his own head, as if to show that no one else was fit to invest the master of mighty and successful legions with the symbol of sovereignty, has frequently been described by historians, so that there is no need to dwell on it here.

The next dates of any importance are 1805, when the flags taken at Austerlitz were placed in Notre Dame; May, 1814, when Louis XVIII. and his family attended Mass in the metropolitan church after their entry into Paris backed by the allies; the marriage of the Duc de Berri to Caroline of Naples in 1816; the baptism of the Duc de Bordeaux (Comte de Chambord) in 1820, after the assassination of his father, the Duc de Berri, at the opera by Louvel, in the beginning of that year; the *Te Deum* for the failure of Fieschi's attempt to blow up King Louis Philippe in 1835; the funeral of the Duc d'Orléans in 1842; the restorations effected by Viollet-le-Duc and Lassus in 1844; the service for the First Napoleon in 1840; that for Archbishop Affre, shot at the barricades in 1848; the marriage of the Emperor Napoleon III. with Eugénie de Montijo, Comtesse de Teba, in January, 1853; and the baptism of the Prince Imperial in 1857.

Mention must also be made of the service for Archbishop Sibour, murdered by a priest in January, 1857, in the Church of Saint Etienne du Mont, and of that for Monseigneur Darboy, shot by the Communists in 1871.

HISTORIC CHURCHES OF PARIS.

The Terrorists of 1871, by the way, did not do as much damage to the church as they had intended, owing to the arrival of the Government troops. They managed to rob the Treasury of many valuable relics, and attempted to set fire to the building, but the flames were extinguished in time to prevent the destruction of the great historic and architectural monument which is one of the glories of France. The cathedral founded in the twelfth century has thus survived all shocks, like the remarkable faith which it represents. During the Third Republic, no great ceremonies have taken place at Notre Dame, except the funeral service in June, 1894, for President Carnot, assassinated by an Italian anarchist at Lyons in that year. There was also a service in October, 1895, for Louis Pasteur, who received a State funeral as one deserving to be honoured for his scientific labours.

CHAPTER III.

NOTRE DAME DE PARIS.

III.

Gothic Architecture—The mediæval architects and sculptors—A lady sculptor—The monastic and the lay builders—The ravages of revolution.

PEPIN.

NOTRE DAME DE PARIS is, architecturally, a monument of the transition period from the Romanesque to the early Gothic. With the cathedrals of Chartres, Rheims, Amiens and Bourges, it forms a link in the chain of the great architectural constructions raised by the mediæval builders and decorated by those able sculptors who were called "magistri de vivis lapidibus," masters of the living stones. Who were these marvellous Gothic architects and embroiderers, and whence did they derive their inspiration and their style? History gives various accounts of them, and the records are often conflicting. An author has yet to come forward who shall offer us a clear and trustworthy account of these men, whose lives and labours would undoubtedly be worthy of careful record, and prove highly interesting to readers.

Viollet-le-Duc, Bauchal, De Caumont, De Verneilh and Quicherat, have not seriously attempted to fill up this void in dealing with the origin of French-Gothic architecture and sculpture. M. Courajod, of the Louvre School, in his lectures, Herr Vöge in his work "Die Anfänge des Monumentalen Stiles im Mittelalter,"[1] and to a certain extent, Mr. C. H. Moore in his "Development and Character of Gothic Architecture,"[2] have done something more than the French writers referred to, but they have left a large field open for future research.

The subject is too vast and complicated to be treated at any length here, but interest in such monuments as Notre Dame, the Sainte Chapelle, the Abbey of St. Denis, may be increased by the exposition of a few points connected with the architectural history of cathedrals like that of Paris. In the

[1] Strassburg, 1894.   [2] London 1890. Macmillan.

first place, a summary may be given of the general form and constructive features of a developed Gothic building. Such a summary is provided by Mr. C. H. Moore, and it is worth transcribing here as an accurate description of the manner in which Notre Dame is built :—

1. In Gothic buildings the plan consists of a nave the eastern portion of which forms the choir with side aisles sometimes single, sometimes double, and a transept generally also with aisles, the nave and choir terminating at the east almost invariably in a semi-circle or a polygon, around which the aisles are continued. At the west the termination is square, the aisles at this end finishing in towers. The nave is separated from the aisles, and the aisles when double are separated from each other, by rows of piers, which support the superstructure. The whole is enclosed on the ground story by a thin wall beyond which, opposite the piers, are the far projecting and massive buttresses.

2. The vaults, whose plan and construction determine the number and arrangement of the piers and buttresses, are furnished with a complete set of ribs—transverse ribs, diagonal ribs, and longitudinal ribs. (These are the constructive ribs ; the *tiernes*, *tiercerons*, etc., in the later form of vaulting, especially in England, being mere surface ribs having no real function.) These ribs are independent arches of which the transverse and longitudinal ones are pointed, while the diagonals are usually rounded, and upon them the vault masonry simply rests, the one never being incorporated with the other.

3. The ribs spring from slender shafts compactly grouped and often detached, although having their bases and capitals incorporated with the great piers which arise from the pavement through the successive stories to the nave cornice. Each one of these piers is a compound member consisting of a central body with which are incorporated all the vaulting shafts, besides the columns which carry the pier arches on the ground story, and those above, which support the arches of the triforium and, finally, the buttresses of the clerestory. Upon the piers are concentrated all the side pressure of the vaults, but these side pressures are so neutralized by the buttressing, that the piers require only to be massive enough to bear the weight of the vaults.

4. The clerestory[1] buttresses which receive the thrusts of the nave vaults,

---

[1] Clear-story, an upper story, or row of windows in a Gothic church, rising clear above other parts of the edifice. It is uncertain whether the epithet clear is applied to the story on account of the light admitted through its windows, or from its being clear of the roof of the aisles.

NOTRE DAME DE PARIS.

are reinforced by flying buttresses springing over the aisle roofs and rising from the vast outer buttresses, which are incorporated with the respond piers of the aisles.

5. The walls, required for enclosure only, are reduced to a minimum of thickness and are confined to the ground story and to the spandrels of the arcades. The apertures fill the whole spaces laterally between the piers.

This description of the characteristics of Gothic architecture, as carried out in Notre Dame, is rather technical, but it will be intelligible, in the main, to anyone who takes the trouble to verify it by reference to the actual building.

We now come to the originators of this system, so far as their history can be ascertained. A few names have been preserved here and there. Sabina of Steinbach, for instance, worked as a sculptor in Strassburg Cathedral with her father, one of the architects of the Middle Ages. One Ingelramme was master-builder of Notre Dame de Rouen; Robert de Lusarche built Amiens Cathedral in 1220; Pierre de Montereau built the Abbey of Long Pont in 1227; Hugues Lebergier built Saint Nicaise of Rheims in 1229; and Jehan de Chelles managed to have his name preserved on the southern lateral portal of Notre Dame de Paris, which he constructed, together with the north and south gables and with some of the early choir chapels, about 1257. The inscription found was as follows:—" Anno Domini M.CC.LVII. Mense Februario. Idus Secundo. Hoc Fuit Inceptum. Christi. Genitricis Honore. Kallensi. Lathomo. Vivente. Iohanne. Magistro."—" In the year of our Lord, 1257, the second of the ides of February, this (portal) was commenced in honour of the Mother of Christ during the life of John de Chelles, Mason."

Pierre de Chelles, son or nephew of John or Jehan, has also some posthumous prestige, as well as Jehan Ravy, his nephew, Jehan Le Bouteiller, and Raymond de Temple, whose names have been preserved either by Viollet-le-Duc or by Bauchal in his "Architectes·de Notre Dame de Paris."

These artists—architects and sculptors—have been represented by different authors as working partly for the sake of religion, partly for the glory of their country or their municipality. According to some writers who seem to object to any idea of compulsory service, the churches of the Middle Ages were really built by the people through pure love of God. So says M. Choublier,[1] Professor of History in the Lycée Condorcet and the College Chaptal, in whose excellent summary it is stated that serfs and freedmen,

[1] " Histoire Sommaire de la France."

prelates, lords and ladies manipulated the shovel and trowel. "The Norman pilgrims, headed by banner-bearers, flocked to build the Cathedral of Chartres, the direction being confided to a Master of Works, an unknown architect with some skilled men under him, who were called 'les logeurs du bon Dieu,' or franc-maçons." When the rough work was finished, it was the turn of the "tailleurs imagiers," or sculptors, who created a world of statues, and of the artists in stained glass, whose painted panes flung rainbow-colours on the floors of the churches.

Michelet has a different tale to tell, and talks of the "drudges who were driven to work while the money for the construction of the churches was wrung from a starving people." Referring to the punishment of some citizens of Rheims who refused to pay a tax, and whose figures are sculptured on a part of the cathedral, each bearing a mark of chastisement, the same historian says that "under the stones of the churches there were too many tears," and "that buildings erected by *corvées*, or compulsorily, could hardly please God." These differences of opinion are, however, only recorded here in an impartial spirit. The works of the Middle Ages, whether erected by the people, animated by religious fervour, or driven to the task like galley-slaves, stand for all time as marvels of colossal labour and delicate art-workmanship.

The "franc-maçons," referred to by M. Choublier, were the chief workmen employed on the Gothic edifices. They were established along the Rhine, at Cologne (or Köln), and Strassburg and in the Isle of France, a district so-called because it was comprised within the Seine, the Marne, the Ourcq, the Aisne and the Oise. These masons, as well as the sculptors, or stone-cutters, to use the word in its original meaning, were undoubtedly influenced from Cluny. The monastic or Benedictine architects and sculptors had first shown the way in Burgundy, and many of the lay builders and embroiderers in stone were unmistakably indebted to the Cluniac artists. The monks in the North of France were busy, active, energetic men; they planned and built their own abbeys,[1] although M. Anthyme de St. Paul,

---

[1] The world owes a great tribute to the Benedictines, who, in spite of what Gibbon and Buckle have thought fit to say about them, performed a stupendous work. Gibbon, however, admits that the "monuments of Greek and Latin literature were preserved and multiplied by their independent pens." Montalembert describes in his introduction to the "Life of St. Bernard," how the monks went to work at building, the abbots sometimes acting as labourers. St. Bernard, by the way, like some Protestants of the present day, was no lover of the fantastic sculpturing in the abbeys and churches, as he considered that it took the mind from God.

NOTRE DAME DE PARIS.

contrary to what Viollet-le-Duc has advanced, denies that they created an original architecture.

In any case they had an influence over the laymen employed by the Princes and Bishops in the erection of the churches, and we may take it for granted that some of the architects and sculptors of such cathedrals as Notre Dame de Paris had originally been novices at Cluny, or, perhaps, professed monks who threw off the yoke of conventual discipline. This, however, is one of the points to be cleared up in any elaborate account of the mediæval artists.

The Cluny school must meanwhile be regarded as the art nursery of the period. The monks worked from nature, as is testified by their stone decoration of the church of Vézelay in the Yonne and the cathedral of Autun in the Saône-et-Loire. They were disciplined by the Greek traditions which had arrived through Byzantine channels, and they were also, no doubt, inspired by the illuminated miniatures of the older art craftsmen, like Alcuin, who, with his monks, was invited to Tours by Charlemagne in 796.[1]

All the characteristics of the monastic sculpture appeared in the work of the laymen. There was the same expressive character in the faces of figures. The birds, monsters or devils were accurately carved in beak, talon and claw, as the demons on the parapet of the west front of Notre Dame de Paris, the grotesque creatures gambolling among the foliage of the hood-mould of the archivolt of the Virgin's portal, and the lateral gargoyles of the same church, amply show. The artists copied direct from field, forest and flower, as is demonstrated by the adornment of the capitals and by the crockets of the triforium and the nave of the Paris Cathedral, springtime plants, such as the fern, arum, hepatica and plantain, being mostly chosen. All these were cut out of the "liais cliquart," a finely-grained and strong limestone found in the beds of the Seine and the Oise.[2]

To conclude the question of origin, as far as it has been treated, it may be said that Gothic art grew up out of the commingling of northern and southern blood—that is to say out of Gallo-Roman elements. The north

---

[1] Some foundation for this hypothesis may be seen in the "Fac-Similes of the Miniatures and Ornaments of Anglo-Saxon and Irish MSS.," 1868, published by Westwood. Guizot in his "History of Civilization in France," vol. ii. p. 174, says that, when Alcuin was alive, the "intellectual state of Ireland and England was superior to that of the Continent." He adds that in these island countries there were then no desolating invasions to sweep away monasteries and shelters of learning. Gothic art, after all, may have gone from the British islands to France and the banks of the Rhine, there to find its highest inspiration and development.

[2] Moore's "Gothic Architecture." London, Macmillan

supplied an active imagination and a daring spirit of invention, the south a disciplined feeling for beauty and for the traditions of ancient art. Herr Vöge, previously referred to, inclines to believe that the art really began at Chartres, whose sculptors borrowed from Arles—that is to say, Provence — which was influenced by Greece and Rome. Anyhow, the Gothic school had flourished long before Niccola Pisano and Giotto lived in Italy, and the work produced at so early a period is a wonderful testimony of the skill and originality of the French artists who conceived and executed figures which, according to competent critics, for treatment of form and beauty of modelling, had not been seen since the days of Phidias, the elder Polycletus and Myron.

Viollet-le-Duc describes at great length the changes which have taken place in Notre Dame de Paris since its termination, which may be said to have been effected in 1235. The purely constructive part of the cathedral has undergone comparatively few alterations since that time, although many modifications were made in the clerestory windows. There was a screen

NOTRE DAME DE PARIS.

before the choir, and fragments of it were found by the restorers of 1845. Part of it still exists with the old stone enclosure of the choir. The mutilations undergone by the church, and to which Victor Hugo so scathingly refers in his romance, were begun in 1699, when Louis XIV. was carrying out the vow of his father referred to in a preceding chapter. Splendid tombs in bronze of Isabella of Hainault, first wife of Philip Augustus ; of Geoffrey, Duke of Brittany, son of Henry II. of England, who was killed in a tournament in Paris in 1186, and of several bishops, were destroyed, and the old stalls of the choir were replaced by those now visible, which are of finished workmanship.

The Revolutionists also effected much damage. They smashed many of the exterior statues, notably those of the kings on the façade, and removed the interesting equestrian monument of Philip of Valois, which the Metropolitan Chapter held, contrary to Viollet-le-Duc and others, to be that of Philip the Fair.[1] The

[1] See note on this debatable subject in the second chapter.

HISTORIC CHURCHES OF PARIS.

three rose-windows, one over the western entrance, and those in the transepts, remain the same as of old, but the others were transformed by Levieil in 1741. Most of them are of *grisaille*, a plain sort of glass with fleur-de-lis ornamentation.[1]

The shell of the great building has remained intact. The vast central aisle was so strongly roofed in stone by the Gothic builders that it has stood the test of seven hundred years. The vaults are of the sexpartite form, the filling in consisting of successive courses of arched masonry reaching from rib to rib over each triangular space of the plan. The vaulting shafts are slender, and rise from the great capitals of cylindrical columns which constitute the piers of the ground story. The flying buttresses, consisting of arches which clear both aisles at a single span, are alterations of the thirteenth century. It is thought by competent authorities that quadripartite vaults had been originally intended, and that the sexpartite form was adopted after the building had been carried to the " naissance " or springing of the vaults.

The following are the most important dates in connection with the construction of the cathedral, as given by the various authors who have written on the subject, and notably by M. Queyron, Architect and Inspector of Diocesan buildings in Paris, who has prepared a most careful monograph on Notre Dame.

In 1163, Pope Alexander III. laid the foundation stone. In 1182, the fourth day after Pentecost, the high altar was consecrated by the Papal legate. Towards 1218, the western front was begun, and in 1223, at the time of the death of Philip Augustus, the great portal was finished as far as the bases of the towers. In 1235 was begun the construction of the towers and of the open gallery connecting them. Between 1225 and 1240 a fire damaged the upper parts of the edifice, and the repairs executed were of the less severe Gothic style of the second half of the thirteenth century. Between 1296 and 1300, the lateral chapels of the choir and apse were built. The edifice was

---
[1] The subject of stained glass would merit a whole chapter to itself. Michelet, referring to the introduction of *grisaille*, says, " C'est le protestantisme entrant dans le peinture." In Germany, where there had been great glass-artists like William of Cologne and John of Bruges, the Reformation confined the art to heraldry. The French had acquired so much skill in glass-painting that, in 1506 or thereabouts, Pope Julius II., the fighting Pontiff and patron of Michael Angelo, and who laid the foundation stone of St. Peter's as designed by Bramante, invited William of Marseilles, a Dominican monk, to Rome in order to decorate the windows of the Vatican. The Dominicans had distinguished themselves in this art, and the patron of painters on glass was Giovanni da Fiesole, or Fra Angelico. He had also gone to Rome from the Dominican convent of Fiesole in order to ornament a chapel in the Vatican for Pope Nicholas V. See later on in chapter on the Sainte Chapelle.

thus finished about the beginning of the fourteenth century, the plan of placing stone spires on the towers, after the manner of the old belfry of Chartres, having been abandoned. It is said that these spires would have doubled the elevation if carried out according to the plan of the original architect. The defacements in 1699, and under Soufflot in 1771, as well as the iconoclastic mischief wrought by the Revolutionists, have been already alluded to.

The West Front—
Notre Dame.

CHAPTER IV.

NOTRE DAME DE PARIS.

IV.

The façade—The great portals—The gallery of the kings—The Devil's cauldron—The interior of Notre Dame—The stained glass windows—Great festivals and famous preachers— Lacordaire, Ravignan, Monsabré, Père Hyacinthe, and Monseigneur d'Hulst.

THE great façade or west front of Notre Dame has not been surpassed in beauty and dignity by other constructions of the kind. The Church, which, as has been said, is in the form of a Latin cross, has six entrances, three on the west front, that of the judgment in the centre, of the Virgin on the left, and St. Anne's on the right ; the cloister portal on the north and that of St. Marcel on the south, near the river, while the canons enter by the handsome Porte Rouge on the northern side of the apsis. The ground story has with the three grand portals five niches, of which four appear in front. The four visible from the Parvis are in the buttresses at the springings of the portal *voussures*, or arch curves, and contain statues of Saint Stephen, Saint Denis, the Church and the Synagogue, the latter with head bent, as a sign of humiliation and defeat. Around the southern corner is the niche containing Saint Marcel, a bishop of Paris. Over the portals is the gallery of the kings with twenty-eight arches borne by columns. In the openings are twenty-eight statues of kings. These monarchs have been the subject of a good deal of archæological controversy. In the Cartulary, or ecclesiastical record of Notre Dame, they are set down as the Kings of France. Many foreign and English writers have taken this view, and there are, as the author has found to his astonishment, French clerics as well as laymen familiar with great Paris monuments, who regard the effigies in the " Galerie des Rois " as those of the former rulers of their country. Viollet-le-Duc, on the other hand, energetically maintains that they are the Jewish kings who were ancestors of the Blessed Virgin, and M. Queyron in his " Histoire et Description de l'Eglise de Notre Dame," published under the patronage of the Public Instruction and Fine Arts departments,[1] describes the statues as

LOUIS III.

[1] Paris. E. Plon, Nourrit et Cie. It is based on Viollet-le-Duc's inventory of the Cathedral.

those of Israel and Judah, and gives the names, Joachas, Jehu, Joram, Ochozias, Achab, etc. Above the Royal gallery is that of the Holy Virgin with a pierced balustrade, and inside this five large figures dating from 1854. They are those of Adam and Eve, nude as they were in the garden of Eden, before the temptation and the fall; of the Virgin carrying the infant Jesus on her left arm, and of two angels. Immediately over these statues is seen the great rose-window with its early Gothic tracery. It is forty-two feet in diameter, and is flanked by twin-pointed apertures framed in an arch. These apertures, or windows, have small roses over them. In the fourth section from the ground is a large and bold arcade of twin-pointed arches, about twenty-six feet high, crowned by trefoils and borne by delicate columns. On the top of this arcade is a balustrade on which the famous birds and devils are seen—those monsters that may have served Dante for the description of the tormentors of the damned, like Alichino and Graffiacane. Behind is the statue of an angel blowing a trumpet. This is on the platform called the "Cour des Réservoir," from which rise the two unfinished square towers, each pierced by coupled pointed openings, about fifty-four feet in height, and surmounted by gable-like watch turrets, covering the staircases at the sides.

This sumptuous façade, a good deal of which was altered in detail by Soufflot and later restorers, is perpendicularly divided by four buttresses having an internal structure consisting of a superposed series of inclined masses of hard masonry which conduct a large part of the weight from the inside to the outer face of the great external props. In order to secure the external face against yielding to the outward impetus of these props, the bonding of the masonry is strengthened at the levels, where they find purchase by cramps of iron. The buttress, it must be remembered, is an important part of the structure in all Gothic buildings, as the wall frame is not remarkable for thickness.

The façade is also remarkable for its sculptured work, what remains of this being the finest done by the French stone-embossers and embroiderers of the beginning of the thirteenth century. Some of this fretwork suffered from the ravages of the Revolution, but the main lines of the noble compositions on the portals have been sufficiently preserved to give an idea of early Gothic art. There is first the modern figure of Christ, by Dechaume, on the pier of the middle door or Judgment Portal.

The Redeemer is represented in the act of giving a blessing or benediction. Under His feet are the lion and the dragon. The pedestal of the statue is

NOTRE DAME DE PARIS.

pentagonal in form and in the lower part are seven bas-relief medallions. Those on the left of Christ represent veiled women :—

1. Geometry, a compass in hand, with which she traces lines.
2. Dialectic Philosophy, a serpent entwined around her form.
3. Medicine, with plants, the poppy and the digitalis, at either side of her seat.
4. Theology (on the front of the pedestal), a sceptre in one hand, an open book in the other, and a ladder.
5. Astronomy (on the right-hand side of Christ), holding a disc.
6. Grammar, teaching a child from a book, a bundle of rods in one hand.
7. Music, striking bells with a wand. The whole central pier was destroyed during the alterations in the reign of Louis XIV., and was restored by Viollet-le-Duc.

Above the medallions are bas-reliefs of five prophets, and again on either side of the statue of the Redeemer are the twelve virtues and the twelve vices. Faith is represented holding a standard, under her being Impiety or Idolatry—a kneeling man adoring a demon. The figure of the demon is, however, obliterated. The second virtue, Hope, has also a standard, with Despair, a man piercing himself with a sword, below. Next come Charity, a lamb, and Avarice, a woman, leaning on a coffer; Justice, with Salamander on standard, and Injustice, with unequal scales; Wisdom and Folly, Humility and Pride, Courage and Cowardice, the latter being represented by a soldier running away, letting his sword fall. He is pursued by a hare; and an owl, perched on a tree, adds to his fright. Patience holds a standard, with an ox displayed thereon, while Anger tries to drive from her presence a holy monk. Meekness and Harshness, Peace and Discord, Obedience and its opposite, Perseverance and Inconstancy, are also symbolized. Nearly all these figures bear traces of mutilation. On the right and left, at the same height as the pedestals, are St. Christopher, headless, crossing a torrent; Job on his dunghill, his arms and legs eaten by worms, his wife and three friends standing near; the Sacrifice of Abraham; a warrior or hunter, supposed to be Nimrod making war on heaven. On the jambs are the large figures of the twelve apostles, and also on the side-posts are the five wise and the five foolish virgins. Other figures are those of angels and animals. There is, in fact, a small wilderness of figures, and, without plans, it would be difficult to give an idea of their respective positions.

On the tympanum, or triangular area, at the top of the portal, are, first, the figures of the Dead rising at the angelic trumpet-blasts. These are on the lintel or lower part,[1] and kings, queens, prelates, ladies, knights and serfs, the bond and the free, the noble and the lowly, are seen wearily, yet anxiously, shaking off the sleep of death in order to answer the summons. Above the lintel the souls are weighed in the balance by the Archangel Michael—a noble figure—who holds the balance with a soul on one side of the scales, the devils being occupied with the other. On the right of the Archangel are the Elect, joyfully glancing heavenwards, while on the left, the grinning demons haul a row of chained souls to hell. Crowning all is seen the Redeemer showing the wounds in His hands. Near Him are two angels and behind the Virgin and St. John the Evangelist interceding on their knees for sinful humanity. As a setting to this magnificent composition are six rows of sculptured forms making a *voussure*, or set of curves, with figures of prophets, doctors, martyrs, virgins, devils, toads, damned souls, and a hideous ape with crooked toe and finger nails.

Some of the ornamentation of the six ranges of arch curves is gruesome and terrible. It relates either to the celestial or infernal results of the last judgment. There are among the elect, Abraham, Moses and others— Patriarchs, Prophets, and Doctors of the Church. There is, lower down, a boiler filled with the damned who are pitchforked into the seething cauldron by demons. There is Death on a steed as thin as Rosinante, and represented by a skeletonic woman with dishevelled hair, a sword in each hand. On the crupper, behind her, is Hell, typified by a nude man whose entrails are visible. Also noticeable are a figure of a knight, supposed to be Famine, or some other depopulator of the earth as seen in the vision of St. John, a horrible demon, with gigantic mouth, sitting on and crushing the damned, figures of the lost ones being devoured by toads, and goaded, pricked and hacked about by their satanic tormentors. These uncanny figures form a sort of base to the curves or *voussure*, on the left of the tympanum, or of the statue of Christ on the central pillar, or *trumeau*, of the door. The six ranges or rows of figured curves are all enclosed within a foliated moulding which extends over the whole archway, and is terminated on one side by the form of a happy spirit, admitted to heaven, and on the other by a scowling, ape-like demon who wears drawers.

The portal under the North Tower, called the " Porte de la Sainte Vierge," is near the Rue du Cloître Notre Dame, and is the earliest part of the façade, having been begun about 1205. The figures are noteworthy by reason of the skilful treatment of form, and the harmony of the modelling. They are,

[1] This lintel is modern and is borne up by four angels with thuribles.

therefore, considered equal to any of the plastic specimens of Greek art. Viollet-le-Duc calls the composition the masterpiece of the French school of statuary of the beginning of the thirteenth century. The door is different from the other two, inasmuch as it has a sharp triangular envelopment over the arch. On the pedestal of the central pier are bas reliefs, the first representing the creation of Eve, who seems to emerge from the left rib of Adam. The first man is asleep near a rock, and the Deity is addressing Eve as she comes forth into the light of day. Other bas-reliefs are the "Temptation," with the serpent, having the head and breast of a woman, entwined around a tree and offering the apple to Eve, who bites it and gives it to Adam; and the "Ejection from Paradise" of our first parents by an angel. Above, is the Virgin, crowned, the infant Jesus on her left arm, a bouquet in her right hand. Over Mary is a small gabled and pinnacled construction, supposed by some to represent the Ark of the Covenant.

On the upper part of the arch, or tympanum, are, in the lower division or compartment, three prophets and three kings. In the second the angels hold the winding-sheet in which Mary's body reclines near the tomb, a finely-sculptured coffin-shaped receptacle decorated with quatrefoils. Christ stands over the tomb, His right hand raised to bless His mother and near Him are eight apostles. The composition is bounded at either end by a tree. The third division contains Mary, glorified as Queen of Angels and Men, sitting at the right hand of her son. Her crown has been placed on her head by an angel who is in a cloud, and two other members of the celestial hierarchy are on their knees close by, with tapers in their hands. In the *voussure* are the witnesses of Mary's glorification—angels, patriarchs, kings and prophets, in all sixty figures. Prominent in the stylobate is Saint Denis, carrying his head in his two hands. Constantine, St. John the Baptist, St. Stephen, St. Genevieve, and St. Sylvester also figure here. Under the large statues are medallions. Beneath, two angels, for instance, are represented on bas-reliefs, combats between the good and the fallen inhabitants of heaven. Under St. Denis are his two executioners; under St. John the Baptist, another headsman, and as is supposed, Herod; under Constantine, a kneeling king and a bird on a beast's back; under St. Stephen, a martyr being stoned by the Jews; under St. Genevieve, a woman receiving the Divine blessing, and under St. Sylvester, a Pope and a city.

Thirty-seven other bas-reliefs ornament the sides and pillars. They represent the ocean, a man on a whale's back; Aquarius on a monster's tail; the "ram, the bull, the heavenly twins," and other signs of the Zodiac; the months, with corresponding figures underneath, some of which are amusing. Under April, for instance, is a two-headed person lying down, one part of his body being naked and the other warmly clothed. Below May is a man wearing light drawers, below June a nude figure about to bathe. The summer months are additionally symbolized in the lower bas-reliefs by persons enjoying the *dolce far niente*. The signs of the Zodiac are also accompanied by corresponding sculptures, most of which are damaged. Labour is likewise represented by a mower, a harvester, a grape gatherer, a sower, a pig feeder, and a pork-butcher. The figure of the Earth,[1] facing that of the Ocean, has suffered a good deal from time or man. It represents a big strong woman seated, one hand holding a plant, the other an oak, bending with acorns. A girl kneels before her, holding one side of her breast.

St. Anne's portal, under the South Tower, and near the river, is in a great measure composed of fragments of the old church on the site of which Notre Dame de Paris now stands. The tympanum, the central pier, a sort of square tower with turrets, part of the *voussure*, and the statues of the sides are supposed to be specimens of the best twelfth-century work. The fragments of this work were incorporated in St. Anne's portal by the architects of the thirteenth century, who were manifestly desirous of preserving them for the admiration of future ages. On the central pier stands St. Marcel, a Parisian St. Patrick, who, when bishop of the city, told a serpent, or dragon, which had devoured a wicked woman, to "be off to the deserts or the sea." The bishop had evidently pitied the female although she was sinful. Part of the winding-sheet of the woman is seen on the pier, and from it protrudes the serpent's tail. The statues surrounding the central lower figure are those of St. Peter, St. Paul, David, kings, queens, and angels.

The tympanum, like those of the other doors, is in three compartments, the figures being in the Romanesque and not the Gothic style. In the first zone are the descendants of David; Joseph on horseback with his flowering staff; the marriage of the Virgin Mary; the dream of Joseph, to whom the angel reveals the mystery of the Conception, and the presentation of the Virgin. In the second zone are the Virgin in prayer before an altar, a thirteenth-century figure; St. Joseph and the Angel Gabriel; the Virgin

---

[1] The head of the figure is represented by a spike. It is one of the most damaged bits of sculpture existing on the façade.

NOTRE DAME DE PARIS.

bowing to the will of God; the Visitation; the Nativity; Joseph's sleep; the Infant Jesus in His cradle; the ox and the ass warming Him with their breath; the two shepherds with their barking dogs, and Herod on his throne, giving audience to the Magi. The third zone contains figures larger than those of the lower compartments. They represent the Virgin and child under a round-headed arch, borne by columns and surmounted by a Byzantine cupola with small openings. On either side are angels, a king and a bishop. The monarch is supposed to be Louis VII., father of Philip Augustus. The prelate is either Maurice de Sully or Etienne de Garlande. The *voussure* has four rows and sixty figures of angels, prophets, and elders. The St. Anne's portal, with its Romanesque work, has many points of resemblance with parts of the frontage of the Abbey of St. Denis.[1]

It is supposed that the three great doors on the western front of the cathedral, and their elaborate ornamentation, were finished within the space of five years. The delicate work in wrought-iron of the *pentures* or hinges on St. Anne's door, came from the old church of St. Stephen, and were restored by Boulanger, who made the new hinges on the central portal. The legend runs that the mediæval smith, to whom the iron-work of the three doors was entrusted, being unable to finish them in time, had recourse to the Devil, who agreed to help him, on the usual Satanic conditions—namely, that he should have the soul of the artificer. The demon, however, was unable to do the central door, as the Blessed Sacrament was carried through it when processions took place. Thus the Devil's bargain was not concluded. He could not keep his compact, so the artificer retained his soul, and the middle portal remained without its iron-work until more modern times.

As to the remainder of the exterior of Notre Dame de Paris, the North Transept portal, in the Rue du Cloître, has a fine antique statue of the Virgin. Most of the sculptured work in the tympanum refers to the history of the mythical monk Theophilus, who abjured Christianity for Judaism, signed a contract with the devil, like Faust, in his own blood, but was saved by the Blessed Virgin, whose garments the Devil is seen to pull, as if enraged at her interference. On this side of the church is also the famous Porte Rouge with the "Coronation of the Virgin" in the tympanum, and scenes from the life of St. Marcel around. There are near it, under the

---

[1] The stylobate, or continuous base under the sculptured figures, at both sides of St. Anne's portal, is ornamented by small pointed arches with shafts and a background of lilies. It is thoroughly modern, and looks it. The old stylobate of the thirteenth century was damaged beyond repair.

windows of the choir chapels, towards the garden, seven bas-reliefs of the sixteenth century, representing scenes from the Virgin's life.

The portal of the Southern Transept, on the river side, begun under the direction of Jean de Chelles,[1] as testified by an inscription previously referred to, which runs on one line, is surmounted like the other Transept door by a large rose. The figures are those of Christ, St. Stephen, St. Martin, St. John the Baptist, St. Peter, Moses, Aaron, St. Denis, St. Thomas, St. Bartholomew, David, and angels. In the tympanum is the "Martyrdom of St. Stephen." The saint is seen discussing with the doctors, dragged before the judge, stoned, and finally put in a coffin. All the figures, which include that of God the Father, are good, but the design is unsatisfactory. The doorway belongs to the declining period of Gothic architecture in France.

Notable, too, are the Gothic sacristy on the south side, constructed by Viollet-le-Duc and Lassus; the

---

[1] See Chapter III. The Northern and Southern Transept façades of Notre Dame are under a disadvantage, as, unlike the western frontage, they have no large spaces in front of them to enable their points to be seen properly. The same may be said of the lateral pinnacles and gargoyles. The elevated sides of the church are full of architectural and sculptured marvels which can only be discovered by persistent exploration. The front of the Southern Transept portal is topped by a figure of the Redeemer, that of the other by the form of St. Landry, a bishop of Paris.

NOTRE DAME DE PARIS.

exterior of the chapels with mullioned windows topped by balustrades and gables; the exterior of the choir; the apsis and the flying buttresses; the side pinnacles and grotesque lateral gargoyles, or spouts, with "figureheads," if nautical language may be used, one of which represents the back of a bird which seems to be entering the wall near the tower stairs; the demons and strange nightfowl near and around the towers, and the Fontaine Notre Dame, a tasteful work erected in 1845 on the site of the old archiepiscopal palace, now a public garden. The spire over the middle of the church is made of oak covered by lead, and was erected in 1859.[1] The great bell or "bourdon," weighing sixteen tons, is in the southern tower, the other, brought from Sebastopol, not being used. The "bourdon" breaks the silence of Passion week, and, on the Saturday before Easter Day, gives the signal to the bells of the different churches to ring out for the Resurrection. It was the gift of Jean de Montaign, a Paris magnate and brother of a metropolitan bishop who called it after his wife Jacqueline, but when recast in 1686, it was baptized Emmanuel - Louise - Thérèse,

[1] Oakwood and lead have been largely used in the construction or alterations of the edifice by the builders and restorers. All the high parts of the cathedral, including the tops of the towers, are leaded over. The old spire was destroyed in 1810, but its roots, so to speak, were preserved. The new one is a pyramid ornamented with crockets.

in honour of the Grand Monarque and his consort, Maria Teresa of Austria.

The best view of the exterior of Notre Dame de Paris is obtainable from the Quai de Montebello, on the opposite side of the river. Zola, in one of his novels, " L'Œuvre," describes the cathedral, when seen apsewise, as "colossal, and squatted between its flying buttresses which resemble paws in repose, crowned by the double head of its towers above a long monster-like spine." The prospect from the towers, 223 ft. high, at the present day is fully equal to that described by Victor Hugo in the chapter of his novel "Paris à vol d'oiseau au quinzième siècle." Instead of the antique Paris, however, that of the nineteenth century looms up with its new and intensely modern buildings, relieved here and there by the older edifices which have escaped obliteration.[1] The view may not be so picturesque as in the old times, but it is deeply interesting, and the city, when bathed in spring or autumnal sunshine, fascinates by the brightness and cheerfulness of its general effect, so different to the darker and duller aspects of other northern cities. Notre Dame de Paris should also be seen in the setting sun, when its whole western front is ablaze with light, and each sculptured form seems to stand forth in full relief from the gorgeous fretwork of the façade.

Coming now to the interior, it may be remarked at the outset, that like the external part of the cathedral the internal space if a little heavy in parts is harmoniously designed and constructed. The church, which is in the form of a Latin cross, consists of a nave and double aisles, the latter being continued around the choir. It is 139 yards long and 52 yards broad. The vaulting is 110 feet high in the nave, and is borne by seventy-five pillars, most of which are round. All these, like the choir columns, are finely foliated, the sculptors, as has been shown before, having worked straight from Nature and reproduced the flowers and leaves of the fields around the city. Above the inner aisles runs a triforium, or gallery, with pointed arches, and over all are the high clerestory windows, retouched or altered in the thirteenth century. Near the gallery entrance is the tomb of Etienne Yver,[2] Canon of Paris and Rouen, who died in February, 1467. The monument is in the fifteenth-century style of French sculpture and is nearly free from mutilation. The oak pulpit in the central nave is richly carved with bas-reliefs represent-

[1] Part of the old hospital, Hôtel Dieu, is still seen across the river on the left.

[2] This is a gruesome monument, and repels by its charnel-house aspect. On the base the Canon's body is seen delivered to the worms; above, two saints help him to rise from his coffin.

NOTRE DAME DE PARIS.

ing six apostles and angelic figures from the designs of Viollet-le-Duc, and eight great lustres in gilt bronze hang from the vault. The chapels are those of St. Charles Borromeo, the Holy Childhood, St. Vincent de Paul, St. Francis Xavier, St. Landry, St. Clotilde, St. Genevieve, the Souls in Purgatory, St. Joseph, St. Peter, St. Anne, the Sacré Cœur, the Annunciation, St. Martin, St. Ferdinand, St. Germain, St. Louis, St. Marcel, St. Denis, Mary Magdalen, St. William, St. George, and the Chapel of the Apsis, or that of "Our Lady of the Seven Dolours." There are a few other undedicated chapels, and the baptismal font with fine carvings and *grisaille* windows.

All these chapels contain appropriate statues or frescoes mostly modern; that of Purgatory comprising, for instance, a painting which represents Christ releasing from limbo a soul typified by the jaws of a demon. In St. Martin's chapel is the monument of Jean-Baptiste de Budes, Comte de Guébriant, Marshal of France, who died in 1643, and of his wife, Renée du Bec-Crépin. In St. Ferdinand's Chapel is the monument of Monseigneur de Beaumont, Archbishop of Paris. St. Germain's Chapel has the memorial of another archbishop, Monseigneur de Juigné. The Chapelle St. Louis is full of frescoes and statuettes of the saint to whom it is dedicated, of St. Clotilde, St. Isabella, the Virgin, the Redeemer, and a large marble figure of Cardinal de Noailles, Archbishop of Paris, who died in 1729. The prelate is represented kneeling. The memorial to Cardinal de Belloy, another archbishop, is in the Chapelle St. Marcel, opposite it being that of Monseigneur de Quélen; the tomb of Monseigneur Affré, the archbishop who was shot at the barricades in 1848, is in the St. Denis Chapel. He is represented falling, struck by a bullet. A crucifix is slipping from his left hand as it rests on the ground, while with his right he holds out an olive-branch. A bas-relief on the pedestal refers to the prelate's death in the Faubourg St. Antoine, in June, 1848. Monseigneur Sibour, the archbishop who was murdered by a mad priest, has a memorial in the Magdalen Chapel, where are likewise to be seen, besides mural paintings representing the conversion of the saint to whom the spot is dedicated, the arms of Archbishop Garibaldi, Papal legate, or nuncio, who died in Paris in 1853, and whose body, like those of the Paris prelates above referred to, is in the crypt of the cathedral. A mausoleum to Claude-Henry d'Harcourt, Lieutenant-General of the armies of the king, and who died in 1769, is in the St. William Chapel. Monseigneur Darboy, shot by the Communists in 1871, is commemorated in St. George's Chapel. He is represented giving a blessing, as he dies, to his murderers. In this chapel are mural paintings of scenes from the life of St. George. Decorations with a similar motive are on the stained glass. There are also two other statues, one of St. George overthrowing the dragon, the other of Cardinal Morlot, an Archbishop of Paris.

The chapel of the apsis, dedicated to Notre Dame des Sept-Douleurs, has bas-reliefs on the altar representing the Annunciation, the descent from the Cross, and Christ in the tomb. There is a statue in wood of the Virgin, and mural paintings and windows full of scenes from her life are also to be seen here. The chapel was built by Bishop Matiffas de Buci, who has a memorial in it.[1] Nearly all the monuments visible in the church are of Languedoc marble.

That important part of the church, the choir, is raised above the transepts by three steps, and on the right and left is closed by a low *grille* in wrought-iron, gilt, resting on a stone foundation, and terminated towards the entrance by two stone columns which support the central rails. The wood carvings of the choir, done in the time of Louis XIV., in fulfilment of his father's "vow," are famous, and are treated at great length in a monograph entitled "Album des boiseries sculptées du chœur de Notre Dame de Paris, etc.," published in Paris by Chouvet in 1855. Inside the railings are two episcopal seats, one for the Archbishop, the other for the Dean of the Chapter. The back of the chair on the right is carved with a scene representing Childebert I. being cured by St. Germain, Bishop of Paris; on the other seat being represented, in a similar manner, the martyrdom of St. Denis. The panelling of the choir stalls is ornamented with episodes from the life of the Virgin. There is also a small organ, for accompaniment purposes, in the choir, and near it is the entrance to the burial-places of the archbishops, which are covered over by movable flagstones.[2] Noticeable too, is the fine lectern in green bronze, with its ornamentation, such as the angel, the lion, the eagle and the ox—symbols of the four evangelists.

At the nave entrance to the choir on the right, near the low communion rails, is a large statue of Mary, holding the Infant Jesus, supposed to be the original fourteenth-century statue. On the pillar, under the Virgin, is a bas-relief representing Eve with the serpent's tail. On the opposite side is a

[1] His tomb and recumbent statue are behind the high altar.
[2] The crypt for the archbishops was made in 1711, and the excavations led to the discovery of an altar to Jupiter, which is now in the Cluny Museum. This altar dated from the old Roman days.

NOTRE DAME DE PARIS.

corresponding statue of St. Denis, who, as well as the mother of the Redeemer, is prominently commemorated in the Paris cathedral.

Four steps in Languedoc marble lead to the sanctuary, and the high altar is approached by three additional steps of the same material. The altar itself is of limestone or liais on which the old sculptors worked, and is badly set off by the marble group representing the "Descent from the Cross,"[1] the statues of Louis XIII. and Louis XIV., and the bronze angels carrying the instruments of the Passion. These figures are good, but they do not harmonize with the Gothic character of the edifice. They were placed in the church by those whom Louis XIV. employed to carry out the "vow" of his father.

In the "Pourtour," or ambulatory of the Choir, are the curious scenes from the life of Christ, or "histoires," carved on stone in 1351, by Jean Ravy and Jean Lebouteiller. These are on the wall, outside the choir enclosure, and are in relief supported by clustered columns and Gothic arches. Some of the old reliefs were on the screen destroyed by order of Cardinal de Noailles. The fourteen "histoires" on the north side refer to the Visitation, the Star of Bethlehem seen by the shepherds, the Nativity, the Adoration of the Magi, the Massacre of the Innocents, the Flight into Egypt, the Presentation in the Temple, the Discussion with the Doctors, the Baptism of Christ, the Marriage in Cana, the Entry into Jerusalem, the Last Supper, the Washing of St. Peter's feet by his Master, and the Garden of Olives. On the south side the subjects represent Christ and Magdalen, the Holy Women, or the three Maries kissing the Redeemer's feet, the Apparition of Jesus to the Apostles, who are in a quaint turreted construction, the Disciples of Emmaus with Christ between them, the Breaking of the Bread, the Apparition to the Apostles, a repetition, with some variations, of the other, the Doubt and Conversion of St. Thomas, the Miraculous Draught of Fishes, and the "Mission or Message to the Apostles," who are directed by their Master to evangelize the world. These quaint stone reliefs, of which a cast may be seen in the Crystal Palace, were finished by Jean Lebouteiller in 1351. Underneath them are the names of bishops and archbishops who are buried in the crypt, and the tombs of many of whom were cleared away by restorers. The pavement of the church is in great squares of Grimault stone and black Bourbon marble, alternating in the transepts with liais and Dinan stone. The choir pavement is in multi-

---
[1] This group is also called a Pietà, after the work of Michael Angelo in the Cappella della Pietà, dedicated to the dead, in St. Peter's at Rome.

coloured marble, and that of the sanctuary in mosaic work, part of which represents the arms of France and a fleur-de-lis.

On the stained glass window over the organ are painted the Virgin and Child surrounded by prophets, the signs of the Zodiac, the works of the Months, the Virtues triumphant with lances in hand to attack the Vices. The grand rose-window of the north transept has depicted on it the life and miracles of Mary, with eighteen figures representing kings of France, founders and benefactors of the church. The southern rose has groups of apostles and bishops, to whom angels bring golden crowns. In the angles above this rose are some curious figures :—Antichrist decapitating Enoch and Elias, is in one corner; and God emerging from a cloud in order to put Antichrist to flight, is in the other. Under the rose, in the windows of the arcades of the gallery, are the Jewish kings, ancestors of Mary. The high, mullioned windows of the choir and the apsis have figures of the Virgin, of angels, kings, bishops and fathers of the Church.

The organ does not call for much description. It was rebuilt and enlarged by Thierry Lesclope in 1730, and further developed in 1785 by Cliquot. M. Cavaillé-Coll's improvements have given the instrument 5266 pipes and eighty stops, or five keyboards for the hands, and the " clavier de pédale."

The sacristy is of less historic interest than the other parts of Notre Dame de Paris. It comprises a large hall, the room of the Chapter above which the treasures of the cathedral are placed, and the parish vestry, where one of the ecclesiastics of the church is generally to be found. The great hall has three stained glass windows on which the principal bishops of Paris are depicted. In the central one at the top are St. Denis, St. Rustique, St. Eleuthère; between the mullions and underneath are the less known saints and prelates, among the latter being Peter Lombard, the Italian, who was only bishop of Paris for a year, and Maurice de Sully. Underneath these is seen Monseigneur Affré, shot in 1848, who is represented on his death-bed, near him being the inscription: " The good shepherd gives his life for his flock ; may my blood be the last shed." The right and left windows are less interesting from an historical point of view. Cardinal de Noailles, the vacillating prelate who first backed Fénelon, Quesnel and the Quietists, and afterwards signed the bull " Unigenitus," which Pope

[1] The Quietists only believed in the contemplative life and advocated utter inaction. There were the Hesychastes or Quiescentes of Mount Athos, who lived idly, watching, as has been said, "their noses and their navels," and the sect founded by the Spanish theo-

NOTRE DAME DE PARIS.

Clement XI. directed against the revival of Jansenism, is on the right window.

The hall of the Chapter, or Salle Capitulaire, "Capitulum Ecclesiæ Parisiensis," is noteworthy by reason of the archbishop's choir, the canons' stalls, and the carven work on the great oak press on which are also painted scenes from the life of St. Louis. The glass arcades of the cloister are composed of nine mullioned windows with roses. On these arcades are scenes from the life of St. Genevieve, patroness of Paris, who, according to the legend, saved the city from Attila, king of the Huns, in 451. In the cloister and sacristies are likewise to be seen various pictures, some of which were given to the Church from time to time as "Maïs," or offerings from trade guilds. Most of the "Maïs," however, are now in the Louvre. Notable, too, is the cloister fountain, with its stone cross, and, above on the buttresses, the seated figures of eight bishops of Paris.

Most of the reliquaries and relics shown in the "Treasury" are imitations of the old ones, which were formerly in the Sainte Chapelle. The crown of thorns was removed to Notre Dame by order of the First Napoleon, and among other sacred or merely historic souvenirs shown, are the holy nail given to Charlemagne by Constantine V.; fragments of the True Cross; steel coffret and gold cross of St. Thomas à Becket, in English work of the thirteenth century; a slipper and gloves of Pope Benedict XIV.; the Palatine Cross in gold of the Emperor Manuel Comnenus, which survived the Revolution;[1] a cross worn by St. Vincent de Paul, the crozier of Eudes de Sully, and the "discipline" supposed to have been used by St. Louis. Among the other souvenirs or gifts are the vestments sent by the First Napoleon to the church for his coronation; the Mitre and Missal given by the Third Napoleon to Archbishop Sibour; the ornamental taper for the baptism of the Prince Imperial; Russian banners from Eupatoria: sontanes worn by Archbishops Affre, Sibour and Darboy; the ring and cross of Vicar-General Surat, who was also shot in 1871 by the Communists.

Little more remains to be said about Notre Dame de Paris, except that the festival services, notably that of the Assumption, which has already been alluded to, are conducted on a sumptuous scale. The myriads of lights, the

loginn Molinos in 1675. The doctrines of this sect found their way to France, and were supported by Fénelon, at least for a time, by Madame Guyon, and others.

[1] It was given to a king of Poland by Manuel in the twelfth century, and passed into the hands of Anne of Cleves, who left it in 1684 to the church of St. Germain-des-Prés. It is idle to enter into the question of the authenticity of relics.

HISTORIC CHURCHES OF PARIS.

gorgeous vestments of prelates and priests, the high overarching pillars, the organ music, the voices of choristers, and the deep, rich colours flung over all by the great rose-windows, combine to bring home to the worshipper or spectator the Gothic conception of heaven. Even the unbeliever is often impressed by such scenes, and has to concede that there must be some foundation for the mystical theory as to the existence of a world beyond the stars.

The Lenten sermons or conferences at Notre Dame are historical in interest, inasmuch as they were begun by Lacordaire, the Dominican, who was called " le Romantique de la Chaire." [1] It was the period of Romanticism in France, and the eloquent Friar, who had thrown off the lawyer's robes for the black and white habit of the sons of St. Dominic, was supposed, rather irreverently, to represent in the pulpit, what Hugo, Gautier and De Banville represented in literature, and Delacroix, Scheffer, Horace Vernet, Ingrès, and Paul Delaroche in painting. Another historical preacher of Notre Dame was Père Ravignan, a Jesuit, of noble family, and in later years, the famous pulpit has been occupied by Père Hyacinthe, now M. Hyacinthe Loyson, Père Monsabré and Monseigneur d'Hulst, Rector of the Paris Catholic University.

[1] Lacordaire began his conferences in 1835.

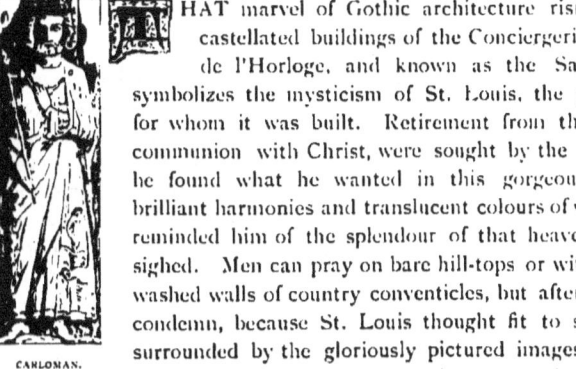
CARLOMAN.

HAT marvel of Gothic architecture rising above the castellated buildings of the Conciergerie on the Quai de l'Horloge, and known as the Sainte Chapelle, symbolizes the mysticism of St. Louis, the pious monarch for whom it was built. Retirement from the world, close communion with Christ, were sought by the holy king, and he found what he wanted in this gorgeous chapel, the brilliant harmonies and translucent colours of whose windows reminded him of the splendour of that heaven for which he sighed. Men can pray on bare hill-tops or within the white-washed walls of country conventicles, but after all who shall condemn, because St. Louis thought fit to say his orisons surrounded by the gloriously pictured images of saints and angels, in an edifice raised to the Creator by architects and artists whose skill and services were nobly employed?

We have only to glance through the chronicles of old Matthew Paris, the English Benedictine of St. Alban's, or the memoirs of the Sire de Joinville, the faithful follower of the Ninth Louis, and the recorder of the saint's actions, in order to realize how far this devout monarch carried his zeal and piety. He did not want the crown, and would have gladly given it up in order to bury himself in a monastery, like the Emperor Charles V., who retired to San Yuste, and, like his son Philip II., who prepared for death inside the walls of the gloomy Escurial.[1] It was, in fact, a marvel to

[1] The difference between the Escorial or Escurial, and the Sainte Chapelle, is that between the gloomiest night and the loveliest morn. The Escorial, in the graphic words of Ford (Handbook for Spain), is "an ashy pile looming like the Palace of Death, who hence sends forth his blasts of consumption which descend from the peeled Sierras to sweep human and vegetable life from the desert of Madrid." The Sainte Chapelle is a place of cheerful colour, but both edifices were used for the same purposes by their royal founders. St. Louis also sought seclusion in the forest of Fontainebleau, where he built a hermitage.

find a monarch so imbued with religious sentiment as was Louis IX., remaining on the throne, but there is the testimony of the chaplain of Queen Margaret (Margaret of Provence), who said that the king was eagerly desirous of becoming a Dominican, but his wife, with great trouble, dissuaded him from abandoning the palace for the cloister and the royal robes for the cowl of the Preaching Friars. Louis compensated himself for his enforced retention in the world by fasting, praying, alms-giving and scourging his body with the "discipline." He surrounded himself with Dominicans and Franciscans, whom he consulted in every doubt and difficulty. The Secular Church of the Popes and prelates was not enough for him. He even favoured the league formed against the secular clergy by Pierre Mauclerc, the Duke of Burgundy, and the Counts of Angoulême and Saint Pol in 1246, and whose claims against the "arrogant clerics"—"sons of serfs who judge, according to their own law, the free and the sons of freemen "—are formulated in a curious legal document in the "Trésor des Chartes," and the "Preuves des libertés de l'Eglise Gallicane." Rarely have the laymen of a Catholic country dared to attack the privileges of the clergy in so outspoken a manner as that adopted by the lords and lawyers who were headed by Mauclerc.

An old writer tells us that even prayer and meditation were not sufficient for St. Louis. He found himself unable to weep while engaged in his devotions, and was afraid that his fervour had waned, even after he had fainted away in his chapel owing to the prolongation of his prayers. Here is what the ancient chronicler says in his delightfully quaint French, which it would be a pity to translate word for word : "Li beneoiz rois désirroit merveilleusement grâce de lermes, et se compleignoit à son confesseur de ce que lermes li défailloient, et li disoit débonnèrement humblement et privéement, que quant l'en disoit en la létanie ces moz : Biau Sire Diex, nous te prions que tu nous doignes fontaine de lermes, li sainz rois disoit dévotement : O Sire Diex, je n'ose requerre fontaines de lermes ainçois me souffisissent petites goustes de lermes à arouser la secherèce de mon cuer." The king only wanted one small tear to water the aridity of his heart.

"These pious tears, these mystic ecstasies, these mysteries of divine love are all to be found," says Michelet, "in that marvellous little church of St. Louis, the Sainte Chapelle. Church all-mystical, Arabesque in its architecture, which he caused to be built on returning from the Crusade, by Eudes de Montreuil, whom he had taken with him to the Holy Land. A world of religion and poetry, a whole Christian East are in these windows and in these fragile and precious paintings." Michelet must not be taken as having meant that the church is Arabesque except so far as some of the decorative motives resemble that style, and it is to be remarked that Viollet-le-Duc and nearly everybody else mentioned Pierre de Montereau, and not Eudes de Montreuil, as the builder of the Sainte Chapelle.

Joinville's testimony as to the extraordinary piety of the king is also quaint and interesting. The chronicler relates that a crowd of Armenians wanted to see the "saint roy "—" Je alai au roy là ou il se séoit en un paveillon, apuié à l'estache (colonne) du paveillon, et séoit on sablon sanz tapiz et sanz nulle autre chose dezouz li. Je li dis: 'Sire, il à la hors un grant peuple de la grante Herménie qui vont en Jérusalem, et me proient Sire, que je leur face monstrer le saint roy; mès je ne bée ja à baisier vos os (cependant je ne désire pas encore avoir à baiser vos reliques).' Et il rist moult clèrement et me dit que je les alasse querre; et si fis-je. Et quant ils orent veu le roy, ils le commanderent à Dieu et le roy eulz." From this it will be seen that Joinville was not a bad courtier, and that Louis was not insensible to a joke about his own sanctity.

The Sainte Chapelle nowadays has strange surroundings. When it was built for St. Louis, the present Palais de Justice was a royal residence, and the king went from his chambers to his chapel. The gem of Gothic architecture, with its magnificent jewelled windows, was at that time in its proper place. The Salle des Pas Perdus, where lawyers and litigants now congregate, was then the festival-hall of the monarchs. The Parliament also shared the palace with the king, but in the reign of Henri II., husband of Catherine de' Medici, the royal residence was transferred to the Tournelles, and the palace of the city was left to the full possession of the Parliament, and subsequently passed into the hands of the lawyers. Boileau, who was the son of a Parliament Registrar, and who studied both law and theology could not find anything better to do when he became a versifier, than to satirize the canons of the Sainte Chapelle in the "Lutrin." This satire the author of "The French Humorists" ascribes to the non-poetic temperament of a man who saw nothing else in the gorgeous Sainte Chapelle save the squabbling of the rotund ecclesiastics. These church dignitaries do not seem, however, to have been much annoyed by the amusing pile of verse built around their lectern. Boileau's brother, by the way, was a canon of the Sainte Chapelle, and when the author of the "Lutrin" died, he was buried in the lower oratory of the edifice, his body being afterwards removed to Saint Germain-des-Prés. There are no rubicund canons nowadays in the Sainte Chapelle to call forth the jibes and jokes of another Boileau, no fat sinecures, no paid deputy-clerics like those who chanted themselves hoarse and officiated while the others sat or slumbered in "cushioned ease,"[1] and only thought of comfortably killing the time between meals. The Sainte Chapelle is now devoid of seats and stalls, and is only used for the annual " Messe Rouge," or " Red Mass," with which the Law Courts open in the autumn. This ceremony is still carried out, contrary to what has been stated in some books on Paris. There was a rumour of its approaching abolition in newspapers of anti-clerical tendencies, but it is duly celebrated every year. The judges and lawyers with their families punctually attend it, and the Archbishop of Paris lends to the ceremony the dignity of his presence. It is to the law-people that the once royal chapel now practically belongs. Its frontage faces the tribunal of Correctional Police, and almost touching the monument of mediæval architecture is the depôt, or Bow Street of Paris, where all the drunkards, demireps, thieves, murderers, tramps, swindlers, pickpockets and garrotters arrested overnight by the police are interned, while awaiting examination before a magistrate, or trial and imprisonment. Close by, in the Rue de la Sainte Chapelle, may be seen every day rows of black prison-vans disgorging candidates for jail, or receiving those who have been condemned. The noise of the cursing, swearing and coarse jokes of hardened criminals frequently reaches the sanctuary where St. Louis sought seclusion and prayed.

The Sainte Chapelle was begun about 1242, and finished in 1248, in order to receive the Crown of Thorns which St. Louis purchased from the needy Emperor Baldwin II. The whole history of the affair may be read in Gibbon, as well as in the work of Canon Morand, who has written about the Sainte Chapelle in a voluminous manner. Baldwin, the adopted son of that John of Brienne who was named by Philip Augustus the most worthy champion of the Holy Land, "in armis probum, in bellis securum, in agendis providum,"[2] having become impoverished, sought the pecuniary aid of the Western monarchs. Although Emperor of Constantinople and King of Jerusalem, he had to beg at Courts, and was snubbed in England, where with much difficulty he raised seven hundred marks. He was reduced to

---

[1] " The cushioned ease of immemorial deans." See J. A. Symonds' "Sketches in Italy and Greece." In the essay on Perugia he talks of Salisbury Close and its clergy.

[2] See Marinus Sanutus, " Secreta Fidelium Crucis," and also the English Benedictine Matthew Paris. John of Brienne is described as " tried in arms, sure in wars, and far-seeing in actions." Paris is also full of details about Baldwin's impecuniosity.

THE SAINTE CHAPELLE.

seemed to shun mankind and to nurse some secret woe in mystery and silence. When the chapel was finished the architect disappeared. He had buried himself in a monastery, there to do repentance for his enormous crime. The young architect, on recovering his health after the attack made upon him in the dead of night, went mad. Five years after, he left the inn where he had been carefully nursed, wandered somehow to Paris, and seeing the realization of his plan in stone, suddenly recovered his reason, but it was too late. The work was attributed to the other, and the young artist remained in obscurity. This legend is related at great length in the encyclopædia of Larousse, and the question is asked, Could the robber have been Pierre de Montereau ?

This is not likely, for Pierre de Montereau did not enter a monastery. He and his wife Agnes were buried in the Abbey of St. Germain-des-Prés, and his monument recorded that he was "vivens Doctor Lato Morum," that is to say, the doctor or teacher of architects or masons. It is also suggested that Pierre de Montereau might have been the young artist, whose claim to the plan of the holy chapel was successfully advanced by the priest to whom the would-be murderer had confessed before entering the cloister. The whole legend may, however, have its basis in the fact that somebody had used a plan, or passed it off as his own, when it was in reality the work of some young, poor and retiring craftsman. This often happened in the Middle Ages, among the painters and architects, nor is it uncommon in our own days, when even Eiffel's Tower, although by no means an artistic monument, is said to have been designed by a young and obscure man. His identity is, however, lost in that of the able organizer and constructor whose name stands for ever associated with the modern Babel. In the Middle Ages many leading "magistri de vivis lapidibus" had pupils as skilful as themselves. In the church of St. Ouen at Rouen there is to be seen, on the same stone, the figures of Alexandre de Berneval and the disciple or pupil whom he stabbed to death. Berneval made the southern rose-window of that church in 1439. His pupil made the northern rose, and was murdered by his master for having surpassed him. For this crime Berneval was duly and justly hanged.[1] Dædalus did the same by his nephew, Talus, in Athens, of old, because the youth promised to eclipse him in statuary, and the story is told in stone in the churches of Caen and Rouen.

In 1248, the Sainte Chapelle was consecrated, the ceremony taking

[1] Michelet, "Histoire de France." The youth is represented with the rose on his breast.

place on Quasimodo Sunday. The upper chapel with the high stained-glass windows was dedicated to the Holy Crown and Cross, for Louis IX. had also obtained part of the instrument of Christ's crucifixion. Eudes or Odo of Châteauroux, Bishop of Tusculum, and legate of the Pope, officiated at the ceremony. The lower and crypt-like chapel was dedicated to the Holy Virgin by Philip Berruyer, Archbishop of Bourges.

The object of the foundation of the chapel is clearly set forth in a document given by Canon Morand among his " Pièces justificatives," and entitled " Prima fundatio Sanctae Capellae, An. 1245." King Louis states for the benefit of all whom it may concern that the chapel " was founded for the salvation of his soul, for commemorating his father, Louis, and his mother, Blanche of Castille, and his ancestors, in honour of God and of the holy Crown of Thorns of Jesus Christ." The document begins :—" In nomine Sanctae et individuae Trinitatis, amen. Ludovicus Dei Gratia Francorum rex. Notum facimus universis tam praesentibus quam futuris praesentam paginam inspecturis, quod nos pro salute animae nostrae, et pro remedio animarum inclytae recordationis regis Ludovici, genitoris nostri, charissimae Dominae et genitricis nostrae Blanchae reginae, et omnium antecessorum nostrorum, in honorem Dei Omnipotentis, et sacrosanctae Coronae spineae Domini nostri Jesu-Christi, fundavimus et aedificavimus infra septa domus nostrae Parisiensis, Domino concidente, Capellam, etc."

Among the historical events with which the holy chapel was connected soon after its foundation, was the coronation of Queen Mary of Brabant, who had married, at Vincennes, Philip III. (le Hardi), son of St. Louis. This was the queen who was accused by Pierre La Brosse, the barber-surgeon of St. Louis and Lord Chamberlain under that king's successor, of having poisoned her stepson in 1276. The youth in question was Prince Louis, son of Philip III. and of Isabella of Aragon, his first wife, who died at Cosenza in Italy in 1271. La Brosse was subsequently hanged for his slanderous charges and insinuations. The second wife of Charles le Bel, Marie de Luxembourg, daughter of Henry VII., Emperor of Germany, was also crowned there, as well as Jeanne d'Evreux, her successor. In 1292, the Emperor, Henry VII., was married there to Margaret of Brabant, niece of the widow of Philip III. The Bishop of Paris, Simon de Buez, officiated at the ceremony. Isabeau or Isabelle of Bavaria, wife of Charles VI., was crowned in the chapel, and her daughter, Isabelle, was there betrothed to Richard II. of England. In 1378, there were great ceremonies in the chapel on the occasion of the visit of the Emperor Charles IV., and his son Wenceslaus.

THE SAINTE CHAPELLE.

Reference must also be made to the ceremonies in connection with the canonization of Louis IX. by Pope Boniface VIII., which led to much division of the relics of the holy monarch, part of his body remaining at St. Denis, while his skull was enclosed in a magnificent reliquary and placed in the Sainte Chapelle. Pope Boniface had expressly written to the Abbot of Saint Denis on the subject of the king's remains telling him to accede to the request of the reigning monarch in every ..icular. The skull of St. Louis was therefore attributed to the cha   and a rib was given to the Cathedral of Notre Dame. The Ab'   nd monks of St. Denis, however, put a stop to all this division of re'   in the reign of Charles VI. That monarch was giving fragment·   h is sainted ancestor to his dukes and others, so the monks justly re   u to close the reliquary altogether.

There were solemn requ   . services in the Sainte Chapelle for all the kings, queens, princes an(princesses of France, from the death of Louis XI. in 1483 to that of L u: XIV. in 1715. The service which was to have taken place for Louis XV. was countermanded, owing to disputes between the legal authorities and the canons relative to the choice of a preacher and to the distributio n f seats.

Councils, royal, parliamentary, and ecclesiastical, which assembled in the 'alace were usually preceded by a mass—that of the Saint Esprit— in t   Sainte Chapelle, just as the same mass, also called " Messe Rouge," is   ./ said every year before the opening of the Law Courts. The Council called on the death of the French opposition Pope Clement VII., was preceded by this mass in 1395, the Cathedral of Notre Dame having also a close connection with the same event. Of minor importance was the ceremony of the angel and the "biberon," or feeding-bottle. In this function, an angelic figure descended from the roof and projected water on the hands of the Mass celebrant. It was repeated twice for the delectation of Charles VIII., at Pentecost. The Sainte Chapelle was desecrated in a terrible manner in the year 1503. · Edmond de la Fosse, a scholar, entered the chapel one morning, and snatching the Sacred Host from the hands of the priest who was saying Mass, carried it out into the courtyard, and there broke it into fragments. The youth was arrested, his mother died with grief, especially as he had manifested no anxiety to make reparation for his act, and he was ultimately burned at the stake, the hand with which he had seized the Host having been previously cut off. The doctors regarded the youth as a lunatic, but that did not prevent his execution or burning. The "Feast of Fools," "Fools' Festival," or "Festum Fatuorum," was

HISTORIC CHURCHES OF PARIS.

observed in the chapel in a peculiar manner. Choir-boys sat in the canons' stalls on St. Innocents' Day, and aped the venerable ecclesiastics. As has already been shown in the chapters on Notre Dame, this festival was strongly denounced by a Papal legate, Peter of Capua, but, if it disappeared from the cathedral, it seems to have lingered on for several centuries in the Sainte Chapelle.

Reference has already been made to the modern surroundings of the Sainte Chapelle. These environments prevent the whole of the splendid edifice from standing forth prominently, and its architectural details are

CAPITALS OF THE PORCH OF THE UPPER CHAPEL (SAINTE CHAPELLE).

accordingly seen only in part. The building was thus enclosed, or rather hemmed in, after the fire which damaged the Palace of Justice in 1776. The builders of the new edifices around the chapel even went so far as to destroy part of it, consisting of a three-storey [1] construction added by Peter of Montereau to the north side of the apsis. The upper storey of this building contained the "trésor des chartes" of the Crown, and underneath

---

[1] The spelling of this word is enigmatical. Fergusson, "History of Modern Architecture," and others, write "storey." Most of the dictionaries have "story." The French word "gargouille" is also rendered in English by "gargoyle," or "gurgoyle." So, too, we have in English "apsis" and "apse."

CHAPTER V

THE SAINTE CHAPELLE.

St. Louis—His piety, and desire to become a Dominican—Fainting from prolonged prayer—The mystic chapel—Joinville's testimony—The Armenians and St. Louis—The Chapel and the Police Court—Boileau's satirical poem—Imperial impecuniosity—Gibbon's version of the cost of the Chapel—The rival architects—Exploiting the young and zealous—Stabbing a rival Historical events and full description of the monument.

The Sainte-Chapelle—
Interior.

THE SAINTE CHAPELLE.

was a double sacristy. The old staircase of forty-four steps connecting the lower and upper chapel also disappeared. The two stories of the chapel, the upper and lower, are borne on pointed arches resting on isolated columns. On the pier of the lower porch is a statue of the Virgin, and in the tympanum is sculptured her coronation. A legend exists, according to which the former or original statue of the Virgin placed on the lower porch bowed its head to John Duns Scotus, the celebrated British theologian, as a token of recognition for his defence of the doctrine of the Immaculate Conception. The upper portal is more richly sculptured, in the tympan being a reproduction of the "Last Judgment," imitated from that on the central door of the Cathedral of Notre Dame. Over all is the grand rose-window with flamboyant mullions, made in the fifteenth century.

It is the interior, however, of the Sainte Chapelle which offers the most attraction, as it deserves the most attention, by reason of its wealth of brilliant colour. The lower chapel, with its arches and decorative work, would stand as a marvel by itself, but it is eclipsed by the splendour of the once royal oratory overhead. The "vitraux" here seen show the art of painting on glass, so minutely described by the monk Theophilus in his "Diversorum artium Schedula,"[1] carried to perfection. There are fifteen windows, on the walls of the chapel, so high that they seem to form the sides of the edifice. They are forty-nine feet by thirteen, those on the right, or south side, giving most light and colour, as the opposite windows are rather dimmed by the contiguous Palace of Justice. Some of the glass dates from the days of St. Louis, but, in general, the windows are restored work due to M. Gerent, M. Steinheil, and others, who deserve all praise for their skill and taste. On fourteen of the panes are storied the

[1] Theophilus, who lived in the middle of the twelfth century wrote chiefly about colouring for walls, wood, windows, parchment and mosaics. He also treated niello work, and left a receipt for mixing colours with linseed oil. The process of glass-painting described by him is primitive. The artists worked on sheets of glass coloured, while in a molten state, by metallic oxide. The drawing was done by means of a pencil dipped in a neutral pigment. The colours used were blues, yellows, reds, greens, purples, etc., of various *nuances*. The designer aimed at subduing the light and producing harmonies of colour, then adding as much pictorial work as he could accomplish within necessarily limited conditions. In cold, northern climes, where Gothic stained-glass painting was practised, the artist had also to produce a sense of warmth and comfort by his combinations of tints and tones. The English styles of glass-work are divided into—Early English, from oldest specimens to 1280; the Decorated, 1280-1380; Perpendicular, 1380-1530; and Cinquecento, 1500-1550. The Italian styles are best known by the names, Pisan, Florentine, Sienese, Umbrian, Lucchese, Bolognese, Lombard and Venetian. William of Marseilles, the French glass-painter, called also Marsillat, has been referred to already in this volume.

different episodes narrated in the Old and the New Testament. The remaining window of the fifteen, not counting the great rose, is pictured with the finding of the true Cross, the despatch of royal envoys for the Crown of Thorns, their arrival in Constantinople, the return to Paris, and other scenes connected with the origin of the chapel. On the rose is represented the weird vision of the Apocalypse of St. John. The interior is also richly ornamented with designs on grounds of glass enamelled in blue and gold, representing martyrs such as St. Stephen, St. Catherine and St. Denis. On either side of the nave, near the third bay, are niches over which are figures of Christ. These recesses were used of old by the kings and their court, while attending devotions in the chapel. On the southern wall is an oblique recess, supposed to have been an oratory used by Louis XI., that strange king who wore medals and crosses in his headgear, was superstitious, dissembling and autocratic, and who, when dying, directed that some of the relics from the Holy Chapel, as well as from other places, should be brought to him at Tours. The altar has disappeared long since. Behind where it stood is a large archway, or rather, open arcade, borne by slender shafts decorated with mosaic work. Above this is a platform crowned by a pointed canopy in sculptured wood under which the holy reliquary once stood. On great festivals the relics were shown to the faithful, and St. Louis sometimes exhibited the Crown of Thorns to his subjects. Two wooden staircases lead to this platform, that now existing on the northern side, where the entrance to the Palace of Justice lies, dating from the time of Saint Louis.

THE RELIQUARY (SAINTE CHAPELLE).

The figures of the Twelve Apostles, painted and gilt, stand against the main pillars of the chapel on pedestals, and a few of them are antique,

THE SAINTE CHAPELLE.

having survived Vandalism. The floor of the chapel is ornamented with foliage, animals, and geometrical figures on stone. Formerly a rood screen separated the nave from the chancel, but this, like the altars, the carved stalls, and the pulpit, has disappeared. The interior of the oratory, or rather the straight nave, without aisles or transept, looks bare now, and the whole place is like a museum. The relics on which so much value was once set,[1] or what remains of them, are in Notre Dame. The "Chasse," or reliquary, was melted down during the great Revolution.

In 1791 the Sainte Chapelle was converted into a clubhouse by the Revolutionists. It afterwards became a flour store, and until the First Empire the sides were lined with shelves, which seriously damaged the gilding, the figures, and the windows. Louis XVIII. and Charles X. intended to have the chapel thoroughly cleaned and restored, but the work was not begun seriously until 1837, when Duban, Lassus and Viollet-le-Duc took up the difficult and delicate undertaking. Lassus, after a time, remained the only architect in charge, and he carried the restoration to a successful completion. He had the new spire in gilt lead placed on the centre. It is the third "fleche" since the foundation. The first gave way in the reign of Charles VI., the next was burned in 1630, and the third, erected in the reign of Louis XIII., was half-destroyed by the Revolutionists, and had to be almost entirely replaced by the present spire, with its royal lilies as crockets. Noticeable on the summit of the church is also the great angel in lead bearing up a cross. It is over the polygon-shaped apsis, and on its pedestal are crowned masks, like the heads of French kings, but supposed to represent the artists and artificers employed in restoring the building.

In 1871, when the Communists were in temporary possession of Paris, the chapel narrowly escaped destruction. The Palace of Justice was fired by the insurgents, but luckily the flames did not touch the superb monu-

---

[1] Not only St. Louis, but other kings also showed the relics periodically to the people, the English Duke of Bedford performing the ceremony for young Henry VI. of England, who had been crowned King of France. With reference to the Crown of Thorns, bought by King Louis IX. from Baldwin II., a transaction already alluded to, it would appear from Racine's "History of Port Royal," that the crown was not complete, for the poet, dramatist and historian describes in a naturalistic manner, eclipsing the ulcerous horrors depicted in M. Zola's "Lourdes," how a Mademoiselle Perrier, niece of Pascal, was cured of an ocular malady by the application of a thorn from the holy crown. Now this thorn was not from the Sainte Chapelle as Gibbon seems to suppose, or at least leads to suppose, in his note on the transaction between Louis IX. and the Eastern Emperor, but was in the possession of a priest, the Abbé de la Poterie.

ment which commemorates the piety and the munificence of St. Louis, and the skill of the great artists whom he employed. The Sainte Chapelle may be flamboyant, and lack the simple dignity of edifices built on the severer lines of the early French-Gothic architects, but it none the less remains a marvellous and magnificent landmark of the past—fully worthy of the admiration of all who love antique art.

FIGURE AT THE TOP OF THE CHEVET
(SAINTE CHAPELLE).

Tomb of Marie Antoinette—
St. Denis.

CHAPTER VI.

THE ABBEY CHURCH OF ST. DENIS.

I.

Saint Denis town—The Communists and the abbey church Hatred of kings—Unlovely surroundings—Catulliacum - - Dagobert—The supposed Damnation of Charles Martel— Pepin and the Pope—The abbey and Charlemagne—The ravages of the Northmen—Descriptions of Sir Francis Palgrave —Abbot Suger—Famous monks—Peter Abelard—His "Book of Calamities"—The Renan of the Middle Ages—The devotion of Heloise—The lovers' tomb.

ROBERT I.

THE old abbey church, or basilica of Saint Denis lifts its light and graceful pinnacles and battlements amid the dingy streets and dreary houses of the great manufacturing suburb of Paris. The square in front of the abbey, and of the Hôtel de Ville (which bears over its doors the city arms and the words, " Montjoie et Saint Denys," the rallying cry of the French knights), is fairly quiet, except on market days. Not far away, there is the ever-whirring noise of forge and furnace, of saw-mills and steam-engines, to interfere with the repose which ought to reign around the monumental tomb of the kings, queens, and princes of the royal families of France. The intensely modern and rather grimy town of St. Denis, with its docks, wharves, factories and yellow canals, seems to trouble itself little about the royal basilica and its tombs. Red Communism stalks near the antique abbey, and execrates those who were once carefully interred in a costly monument, instead of in the " fosse commune," the common ditch, where the paupers are thrown when they have come to the end of their cheerless term in a world which has no regard for those vanquished in the struggle for existence. There are terrible Revolutionists in the town who would burn the basilica to-morrow if they dared. These people are imbued with as much hatred of kings, aristocrats and priests as their predecessors of the " Terror," who desecrated the royal tombs at St. Denis, scattered the bones contained therein to the four winds of heaven, or buried them in a promiscuous heap in the general ditch.

The journey from Paris to the manufacturing suburb is not long, but it is uninteresting while it lasts. St. Ouen, another very Revolutionist borough, lies straight on the road thither, for those who drive out by the Avenue de

HISTORIC CHURCHES OF PARIS.

Clichy, and it has nothing to recommend it. The place is more unlovely than St. Denis. Its streets, and the plain around then, are monotonous in the extreme. All this, however, is forgotten or overlooked when one approaches the cathedral. The reality of the monotonous environment of the splendid monument is temporarily effaced as one enters and sees the colours from the windows making radiant altar, walls, pillars, arches and marble tombs.

On the spot where the old abbey church now stands was the villa of a pious lady named Catulla, by some called a Roman matron, who lived so far back as the year 272.[1] It was on her threshold that St. Denis, or Dionysius, sought security, carrying his head in his hands, according to the legend, and followed by the guards who had decapitated him, and the other holy missionaries from Rome, St. Rusticus and St. Eleutherius, on the hill of Montmartre. Catulla received the saint, made the guards intoxicated, and then buried the holy bishop, who was by that time lifeless, in her grounds. A chapel was afterwards built over the grave, and long enjoyed the reputation of being the scene of miraculous cures.[2] Dagobert ran into the holy place one day in order to avoid the anger of his father, who wanted to chastise him for misconduct, and while there the prince was gratified by the vision of St. Denis, who appeared to him and promised him a place in heaven if he would build a church in lieu of the chapel. When he became king, Dagobert fulfilled the promise made to the saint, by building a church and founding an abbey which he handed over to the Benedictines. According to old chroniclers, Dagobert's church was only the size of the transept of the existing edifice, but it was a marvel of splendour, being enriched from floor to vault by gold, silver, and jewelled ornamentation, much of this

[1] St. Denis town was once called Catulliacum.
[2] There is another version to the effect that St. Denis was none other than Dionysos, or Dionysus, the Greek name for Bacchus, who was fervently worshipped of old by the vine-cultivators around Paris. These people had their Dionysiac festival, as well as the Athenians, and a semblance of one of these fêtes is kept up every year at Argenteuil, near St. Denis. As to the legend about the head of St. Denis, good Catholics do not see any harm in believing in it. On the other hand, Voltaire's fair friend, Madame du Châtelet, wittily said of the saint's expedition from Montmartre, with his head in his hands :—" Mon Dieu, vous avez tort de plaisanter et de vous récrier sur l'invraisemblance de cette aventure ; moi, je ne vois là rien de suprenant ; en pareille circonstance, *il n'y a que le premier pas qui coûte.*" Madame du Châtelet, who uttered this in general conversation, does not get the credit of the phrase, for her friend Voltaire is supposed to have supplied her with it. St. Denis is also sometimes confounded with Dionysius the Areopagite. A plaster of Paris head of the holy bishop is shown in the sacristy of the church. It is said to have been blown off the exterior by a Prussian shell in 1871.

THE ABBEY CHURCH OF ST. DENIS.

work having been executed by the famous metal artificer, St. Eloi. Two years later Dagobert I. was interred in the church. His successor, Dagobert II., and the Merovingian monarchs who came after him, were equally generous towards the church and abbey. In 741, Charles Martel, mayor of the palace, was buried there, although according to the Bishop of Orleans, St. Euchère, who had a vision, he was condemned to eternal damnation, for having wrung money from the prelates in order to carry on his campaigns. Pepin the Short, son of the mayor of the palace, supposed to be in hell, had his father's tomb opened, and was terrified to see a " horrible and hideous serpent issue from the sepulchre, which was blackened as if by smoke." So writes old Jacques Doublet, author of a history of the abbey. Pepin's experiences on this occasion were used with remarkable ability for political purposes. He added more adornment to the church of St. Denis, and then, through his envoys, induced Pope Zachary to connive at the dethronement of the Merovingian, Childeric III. That monarch, accordingly, had his head shaved, and was then sent to a monastery. Pepin le Bref, or Pippin, as he is called after the Latin form of his name, exchanged his post as mayor of the palace for the sovereignty of the whole Frankish realm. He was crowned at Soissons by Archbishop Boniface, and later on, having received a visit from Pope Stephen III., who came to implore his help, he induced that Pontiff to re-consecrate him in the Basilica.[1] According to Professor Freeman, whatever importance Paris possessed at this period, seems to have been derived from " its neighbourhood to the revered sanctuary of St. Denis." Pepin, when he was " sick unto death," was carried from Saintes to Tours to ask the aid of St. Martin, and thence to Paris to seek the assistance of St. Denis. When he died he was buried in the Basilica, as Eginhard, Charlemagne's chronicler, tells us

---

[1] Pippin the Short is supposed to have laid the foundation of the temporal power of the Popes. Freeman says ("Select Historical Essays"), "Constantine, or Pippin, or Charles, or Matilda, or Rudolf, gave Romagna to the Holy See ; but the sovereignty of the Holy See was of the most unpractical kind till its rights were at last enforced by the sword of Cæsar Borgia." With reference to Pope Stephen, it must be remembered that there were three of the name in succession, the first, who succeeded Pope Zachary, having reigned only a few days. French writers nearly always say that it was Pope Stephen II. who consecrated Pippin, or Pepin. Gibbon, on the other hand, distinctly says that Pepin's coronation was twice performed—" by St. Boniface, apostle of Germany, and by the grateful hands of Pope Stephen the Third, who, in the monastery of St. Denys, placed the diadem on the head of his benefactor." Michelet merely says " Pope Stephen." Gibbon seems to be right, according to the "Annuario Pontifici," which gives Stephen II. as reigning only three days, his successor being Stephen III., who sat in St. Peter's chair from 752 to 757.

in his annals of the French kings :—" Inde quum ad Parisios venisset, VIII. Kal. Octobris diem obiit, cujus corpus in basilicâ beati Dionysii martyris humatum est."

In 769, or thereabouts, the abbey church was rebuilt, and was completed in the time of Charlemagne, or Karlmann, one of the two sons of Pepin the Short. About 834, the Emperor Lewis, third son of Karlmann, having been freed by his rebellious son Lothair, who had been king of the Franks, was led to the Basilica of St. Denis, and there, as Bertiniani describes in his annals, he was restored once more to his Imperial rank.[1] The Northmen, the " Piratæ Danorum " of the old chroniclers, played havoc with Carolingian or Carlovingian Paris, its churches and monasteries. Prudentius of Troyes thus includes St. Denis in the number of the churches :—" Præterque ecclesiam Sancti Dionysii, pro quibus tantummodo, ne incenderentur, multa solidorum summa soluta est." This part of the sentence is of course incomplete, the *quibus* referring to other churches which, like St. Denis, bought their deliverance by " big sums of money," or Danegelt. Sir Francis Palgrave, in " England and Normandy," says, however, that the pirates did not keep to their contract, for the " monastery was burnt to a shell, and a most heavy ransom paid for the liberation of Abbot Louis, Charlemagne's grandson." St. Denis fell into bad hands also, even when rebuilt, for the fighting abbots neglected it.[2] Hugh Capet introduced reforms into the monasteries, but the Basilica of St. Denis remained, nevertheless, in a very neglected and dilapidated condition until the time of Abbot Suger, Minister of France, and at one period Regent of the kingdom.

This remarkable man was, in common with many a powerful ecclesiastic of ancient and modern times, both popes and prelates, of lowly origin. Like numerous French archbishops and bishops from Maurice de Sully, founder

[1] This historical event is worthy of a quotation here from Professor Freeman, whose objections to the titles " Emperor of Austria " and " Emperor of the French " are well known. He says : " Once then in the course of its long history did Paris behold the inauguration of a lawful Emperor. But it was the re-inauguration of an Emperor whom one Parisian revolution had overthrown, and whom another Parisian revolution had set up again ; and in the moment alike of his fall and of his restoration the force of loyal Germany forms at one time a threatening, at another time an approving, background."—Select Historical Essays.

[2] An abbey in the old days was, according to Chateaubriand, the dwelling of a rich patrician, the abbot being master and the monks his freedmen, who cultivated science, letters and arts. He also says, in the "Génie du Christianisme," that the monks were originally like the Greek philosophers. St. Basil was the first to introduce vows.

THE ABBEY CHURCH OF ST. DENIS.

of the cathedral of Notre Dame de Paris, to Monseigneur Dupanloup,[1] the famous Bishop of Orléans during the Second Empire, he sprang from the humblest ranks of the people. He is still to be seen, in effigy, on the stained glass in the Lady Chapel of Notre Dame, and several portraits of the celebrated abbot were once visible in the Basilica of St. Denis. This is testified by the Benedictine of St. Maur, Dom Millet, who refers notably to one in which Suger was portrayed "in his habit as he lived," a mere monk, with nothing to distinguish him from the simplest novice of his monastery, save the abbatial cross which he carried, as the chronicler says, "pour marque de sa dignité, et pour monstrer que c'est luy qui est là représenté." Suger was received by the Benedictines, who educated him, and in their monastery he was in the same class as Louis, son of Philip I., afterwards Louis VI.[2] (le Gros), the first to use the "oriflamme," or old banner of the Abbey of St. Denis, when he marched against the Emperor Henry V. in 1124. When Louis became king, he selected his old school-fellow as his guide and counsellor. Under Louis VII., son of Louis le Gros, Suge retained his authority at Court. He protested against that monarch's departure for the Crusades, and also against his divorce with Eleanor of Guyenne. The abbot, in spite of his opposition to the monarch's departure for the Holy Land, subsequently organized a Crusade himself, and was preparing to set out for Palestine with ten thousand men, when he died in 1152.

It was Suger who restored and embellished the abbey where he had received his education. He adopted for his plan of restoration the pointed arches and the ribs of the Gothic style which vies with the Romanesque in the façade of the Basilica, but is pre-eminent inside the church. He built the frontage between 1137 and 1140, and ornamented the windows with splendid glass of which, unluckily, very little remains. The abbot was not destined to see terminated the transept and nave. He left detailed instructions, however, to his successor, but it was not until 1231, in the reign of King Louis IX., that the works were actively taken up. Abbots Eudes de Clement, and subsequently Matthieu de Vendôme, carried on the

---

[1] It is recorded that Dupanloup, when at the zenith of his power as a politician and a prelate, while once visiting his native place, repeated the words from the Psalms, "Suscitans a terra inopem, et de stercore erigens pauperem, etc." In the Protestant version of the Bible, this is in the 113th Psalm, "He raiseth up the poor out of the dust, and lifteth the needy out of the dunghill." The Roman Catholic version runs, "Raising up the needy from the earth, and lifting up the poor out of the dunghill," and it appears in the 112th Psalm

[2] In his youth, he was called Louis l'Éveillé, the wide-awake. Suger acted as his tutor also, having been so appointed by the abbot.

construction energetically, and the main part of the solid building which we now see was completed, the choir and apsis not being fully finished until 1281.

Before proceeding to the description of the tombs, or what remains of them, more may be said about the abbey or monastery of St. Denis, which played so prominent a part in the past. The second abbey, which was built for the monks, is nowadays used as the "Maison de la Légion d'Honneur," founded by Napoleon the First in 1811, for the education of young ladies, daughters of poor nobles, officers and civil servants, on the model of the famous institution of St. Cyr, over which Madame de Maintenon ruled on the death of Louis XIV., in 1715, and where she herself passed away, after much prayer and penance, in 1719.[1] Of old, the monks of this celebrated abbey distinguished themselves as historians and chroniclers. Among these were Odon de Deuil, author of a "History of the Crusade of Louis VII.," Guillaume de Nangis, writer of the "Chronique," Rigord, who wrote the life of Philip Augustus, Jean Chartier, chronicler in the reign of Charles VII., Jean Doe, Jacques Doublet, Jacques le Bossu, and half a dozen others.

The most celebrated man, not an abbot, who was connected with the monastery of St. Denis, was Peter Abelard, the lover of Heloise, immortalized in verse by old François Vilion:—

> "Ou est la très sage Heloïs?
> Pour qui fut chastré et puis moyne,
> Pierre Esbaillart à Saint Denys,"[2]

and by Pope, who refers to the story as "afflicting." Abelard had succeeded Bérenger of Tours, who doubted the Eucharist, Canon Roscelin of Compiègne, who had dared to disseminate strange ideas about the Trinity, and the others who were so hotly opposed by Lanfranc and St. Anselm. The daring lover of Heloise was of noble birth, and as he relates in his "Liber Calamitatum Mearum," and as is shown in the epistles of Heloise, he was handsome, amiable, and could compose, recite and sing amatory verses.

[1] The Institution of the Legion of Honour at St. Denis is usually governed by the widow of some distinguished general. The rules are very strict, and the pupils are taught according to the usual modern methods in young ladies' colleges.

[2] Thus rendered by Dante Gabriel Rossetti in the "Ballad of Dead Ladies," from Villon:—

> "Where's Heloise, the learned nun,
> For whose sake, Abeillard I ween,
> Lost manhood and put priesthood on?
> (From Love he won such dule and teen!)"

The Crypt and Tomb of Louis XVI.—St. Denis.

THE ABBEY CHURCH OF ST. DENIS.

Pope calls him "learned according to the kind of learning then in vogue," in the notes to the poem "Eloisa to Abelard," but Michelet, who classes him with evident satisfaction among the free-thinkers of the period, is loud in his praises, and says that he knew Greek and Hebrew. The same historian, however, adds a trait of Abelard's character which does not show him to be a model student, for he delighted in embarrassing and mocking at William of Champeaux, whose lectures he attended, on the hill of Saint Genevieve. "He would have done the same," adds Michelet, "to Anselm of Laon,[1] but the professor, who was a bishop, expelled him from his diocese."

One cannot help calling Abelard the Renan of the Middle Ages. The two men attacked old, long-cherished dogmas, and both had a lingering respect for the religion which they assailed. Abelard, in particular, wanted to defend Christianity, when attacking it, but his arguments were feeble and made matters worse. He maintained that original sin was chiefly an imposed penalty or burthen, "Moins un péché qu'une peine," and if so then the Redemption was futile. Abelard did not publicly proclaim that conclusion. He even denied it, but the harm was done, and he was not able to undo it. He also condemned the terrible and gloomy asceticism of the age, the mortification of the flesh practised by self-made martyrs and mystics, proclaiming that God was amiable and easy-going, and did not want such an annihilation of the body. There is no need to dwell at length on the story of Abelard and Eloisa here. It is as old as the hills and has been often narrated in prose and verse. Let it be sufficient to state, for the benefit of those who are unversed in the history of the Middle Ages, that Abelard was at the zenith of his power and prestige when he taught Heloise, the niece of Canon Fulbert of the chapter of Notre Dame de Paris. Like every other woman of the time who heard the young scholar speak, and beheld his handsome face, she fell deeply in love with her tutor. Her passionate declaration of love has been recorded in Latin by Abelard. She preferred him "to the Emperor himself." The words are strong in the so-called dead language[2] :—"Tua dici meretrix, quam illius imperatrix," which Pope thus renders :—

[1] A disciple of St. Anselm, Archbishop of Canterbury.

[2] The term "dead languages," seems rather a misnomer, considering that they live in the English tongue, which is so largely based on the Latin, to say nothing of French, Italian, etc. It would be more correct to say, the "transmigrated languages," since they have undergone metempsychosis. The "strength" of Latin, alluded to above, is amusingly referred to in Boileau's well-known line, "Le latin, dans les mots, brave l'honnêteté," alluding to Juvenal's Satires.

HISTORIC CHURCHES OF PARIS.

> " Not Cæsar's empress would I deign to prove ;
> No ; make me mistress to the man I love ;
> If there be yet another name more free,
> More fond than mistress, make me that to thee."

Some of the other phrases written by the young lady show that she was undoubtedly the " New Woman " of her time. Her theory of concubinage is clearly and eloquently expressed, and her reasoning is almost word for word like that of those young Frenchwomen of the present day who object to the fetters of matrimony while remaining passionate partisans of Free Love.

In 1119, or thereabouts, Abelard, after the punishment inflicted upon him by Canon Fulbert, for having taken Heloise away into Brittany, where she bore him a son called Astrolabius, became a Benedictine monk in the Abbey of St. Denis. He did not remain long here, as the temptations of the world were too strong. He was also pressed by his former disciples to resume teaching, so he left the cloister, but did not prosper. His powerful antagonists, St. Bernard of Clairvaux and the Archbishop of Rheims, condemned him at the Council of Soissons, and he was nearly stoned by the people. He again took refuge in St. Denis, but fell into greater trouble than ever, by refusing to believe in the story of the beheaded saint. The Court now rose against him and he had to fly. Condemned by the council, summoned by Pope Innocent II., who hated Abelard because the latter's disciple, Arnold of Brescia, was giving trouble in Italy, the lover of Heloise took refuge in the monastery of Cluny, where he became reconciled to the Church, and died in 1142. Heloise was in the meantime Abbess of the Paraclete,[1] where she taught theology, Greek, and Hebrew. She had not gone to the nunnery in the true spirit of a religious. Her whole life was devoted to the memory of her earthly lover, and she cared little for the unseen, the mystical spouse whom she was supposed to wed when she took the veil. It is said that, when she went to the altar to repeat the vows, she used the words: "Tua me ad religionis habitum jussio, non divina traxit dilectio," " Your will and not divine love has led me to assume the religious habit." She died in 1164, and her body was buried by the side of that of her lover in the Church of the Paraclete. The tomb was removed to Paris in or about 1790, by the painter Alexandre Lenoir, who was empowered by

---

[1] It was so called by Abelard, who founded it, because he was soothed or consoled there, by the presence of his followers. It was in the department of the Aube, near Nogent-sur-Seine.

THE ABBEY CHURCH OF ST. DENIS.

the National Assembly to found a museum of old monuments. The sarcophagus with the recumbent statues of Abelard and Heloise, under a Gothic canopy, now in the cemetery of Père Lachaise, was rebuilt from miscellaneous fragments preserved by Lenoir.

Michelet calls it a "graceful monument," and alludes to its attractions for lovers and sentimental people generally. Viollet-le-Duc, however, takes us into Lenoir's manufactory of restoration, and shows us how work was done there. The tomb of Abelard and Heloise was made out of bits of an arch from the church of St. Denis, of bas-reliefs from the monuments in the same abbey to the brother and son of St. Louis, of window fragments from the demolished chapel of St. Germain-des-Prés, and of two fourteenth-century statues of persons unknown. Lenoir, who had collected all the fragments of church monuments saved from the Revolutionists in the Museum of the Petits Augustins, was imitated by the restorers of St. Denis in the time of Louis XVIII. These people behaved in the most shame-faced manner to the old statues, some of which they re-baptized. As the real restorer of Gothic monuments, Viollet-le-Duc, wrote: "They had duplicates of Charles V. and of Jeanne de Bourbon, so they turned one set into a St. Louis, and a Marguerite de Provence, a matter which caused our historical painters to make singular mistakes." This is always bound to occur in Paris, where so many perplexing changes have been brought about by the whirlwind of Revolution.

The North Portal—
St. Denis.

CHAPTER VII.

THE ABBEY CHURCH OF ST. DENIS.

II.

Veneration of monarchs for the Shrine—Fêtes and historical events—Henri Quatre abjuring Protestantism in the abbey—New storms and sieges—The desecration of the tombs in 1792—The coffin of Louis XV.—The head of St. Denis—Speech in the National Assembly—Viollet-le-Duc's restorations—Exterior of the church—The interior and its monuments—The crypt—The dim vault of the Bourbons—Enumeration of the coffins in the royal charnel-house—The pictures in the sacristy—Divine worship restored in the church by the third Republic.

CATHERINE DE' MEDICI.

ALL the French monarchs venerated the famous Basilica of St. Denis. From the days of Dagobert to those of Louis Philippe and Napoleon III., the abbey church was regarded as a holy and precious place, the monumental tomb of royalty, the last and sumptuous resting-place of the rulers of France. St. Louis caused to be erected a number of mausoleums to the memory of his predecessors. First came Dagobert who had a mausoleum on the epistle side of the chancel, and it still stands much restored, near the high altar. Under the memorial were placed the remains of this prince with those of Nanthilde, his wife, and of his son Sigebert. Then on either side of the choir of the monks, that is to say in the transept, were effigies of kings and queens, princes and princesses of the earlier dynasties. A bronze tomb of Charles the Bold stood in the centre of the monks' choir. From that time until the reign of Henri II., husband of Catherine de' Medici, the erection of monuments went on, but afterwards, the dead sovereigns were placed in a large crypt. Their coffins, which rested on iron trestles, were broken by the revolutionists, but all this must be dealt with later on.

In 1389, Charles VI. organized splendid fêtes at St. Denis. They were at first of a religious character, but degenerated into licentious diversions which had to be stopped. Joan of Acre, whose memory, despite the sneers of Voltaire, has recently been revived even by French Republicans, hung up her arms in the abbey in 1429, before she was burned by the English.[1]

[1] All French patriots h nour Joan. So do all French poets and prose-writers from Villon to Verlaine, Voltaire being about the only exception; Villon wrote, in his famous ballad before quoted,—
"Et Jehanne, la bonne Lorraine
Qu'Anglois bruslèrent à Rouen,"
but not a few Frenchmen hold that she escaped the pyre, and that somebody else was burned in her place—perhaps her understudy or deputy.

HISTORIC CHURCHES OF PARIS.

When the tombs were restored in St. Denis, a tablet was placed with some old armour, near where her saddle and accoutrements had once been seen. In 1436, the English sacked the abbey, before they were defeated and thrown back on the Bastille, where they took refuge in their retreat towards Rouen. In the year before, Isabeau or Isabelle of Bavaria, wife of Charles VI., died, and as she was unpopular owing to her negotiations with the English, her body was carried to St. Denis by boat, and she was buried unmourned. In 1589, the town surrendered to Henri Quatre, and a few years afterwards, that monarch abjured Protestantism in the Basilica. The ceremony is thus described by an old chronicler:—"On Sunday, between eight and nine o'clock in the morning, when the king left for the old abbey, the princes, officers of the crown, and other persons of the nobility formed more than a thousand in number, and marched before him. He was also preceded by the Swiss of the guard, with drum beating, at the head of whom, according to an old custom, was the provost, with a lieutenant and more than fifty archers. The streets through which his Majesty had to pass were decorated and carpeted, and the road was covered with plants and flowers. His Majesty wore a white satin robe, hose and doublet of white silk, white shoes, black cloak and hat of the same colour. Having arrived at the great portal of the church, his Majesty was accosted by the Archbishop of Bourges, who sat there on a chair in his robes. The archbishop said to the king, 'Who are you?' The monarch replied, 'I am the king.' 'What do you want?' 'I want to be received into the Catholic and Roman Church.' The Archbishop of Bourges then said, 'Do you really desire it?' and the king answered, 'Yes, I do so desire.' Then the archbishop gave him a book, and his Majesty, bare-headed, and on his knees, made his profession of faith. After this, he was admitted into the Church amid the acclamations of the people."

Many French queens, notably Mary de' Medici, wife of Henri Quatre and mother of Louis XIII., were crowned at St. Denis. From that time and after having passed through the stormy period of the wars between the Armagnacs and the Bourguignons, the English Invasion, the religious strifes between Catholics and Huguenots, and the Fronde, the Abbey was undisturbed save by some of the Abbots themselves who are reproached with having caused many precious relics of the past to dissappear, notably the bronze doors given by Dagobert, the mosaics of Suger, some of the stalls, and the altar of relics, on the pretence of restoring the church. It was not, however, until the Revolution, that the Basilica of St. Denis was

THE ABBEY CHURCH OF ST. DENIS.

most desecrated and damaged. The Abbey was suppressed in 1792, and in the following year the Convention decreed, on the motion of Barrère, that "the powerful hand of the Republic should pitilessly efface those proud epitaphs and destroy those mausoleums which recall the dreadful remembrance of the kings." According to some, the first coffin opened was that of Turenne, for many of the great warriors of France had also been buried at St. Denis by order of their sovereigns. Marshal Turenne's body was consigned to the care of "nos chers et amez les abbé, prieur et religieux de l'Abbaye Royale, de Saint-Denys, en France," by Louis XIV., who wrote a long epistle on the subject. The remains, after many vicissitudes, are now in the Hotel des Invalides. Others state that the Revolutionists first found the body of Henri Quatre, which was in such a good state of preservation that the workmen hesitated before throwing it into the "common ditch," to which it eventually came. In most of the coffins, dry bones, fleshless, crumbling, were seen by the side of crowns, sceptres and other royal ornaments. The coffin of Louis XV., who died of "confluent smallpox,"[1] only contained a black, oozing liquid, diffusing an unbearable odour. So at least we are told by M. Alexis Martin, author of an interesting work entitled "Tout autour de Paris."

After the desecration of the funeral monuments, and the burial of the bodies, or what remained of them, in two common graves, or pits, statues, tombs and fragments of sculptured work from the church were removed to Paris. St. Denis town was named Franciade, and a deputation went thence to offer the National Assembly busts of saints, objects from the treasury of the Basilica, and the supposed head of Saint-Denis. The language used on the occasion of the presentation, by the orator of the delegates, was disgusting in the extreme:—" Citizens," he said, "a miracle conveyed this head which we bring you from Montmartre to St. Denis. Another miracle, greater and more authentic, the miracle of the regeneration of opinions, brings back this head to Paris. There is but one difference between the return of the skull now, and its journey from Montmartre of old. The saint, according to the legend, embraced his head respectfully at every step,[2] but we, Citizens, have by no means been tempted to embrace this offensively smelling relic! The return journey will not be marked in the martyrology,

---
[1] Carlyle's expression. See first volume of the "French Revolution."
[2] This seems to be an expression of the "bull" order, but Frenchmen, as well as Englishmen occasionally, are guilty of the verbal ambiguities and contradictions said to be peculiar to Hibernians.

but registered in the annals of reason, will be doubly useful to the human race. This skull and these consecrated rags around it, will cease at last to be the ridiculous objects of the veneration of the people, and will no longer feed superstition, fanaticism and falsehood. The gold and silver surrounding them will contribute to consolidate the empire of reason and liberty. The treasures amassed during many centuries by the pride of kings, the stupid credulity of deceived devotees, and the Charlatanism of cajoling priests, have been reserved by Providence for this glorious epoch. It will soon be said of kings, priests and saints, that they have been, and are no more. Thus, Citizens, reason is the order of the day at last, and you, ye saints, male and female, formerly instruments of fanaticism, show yourselves to be patriots! Rise *en masse*, for the sake of the country, and start for the Mint and may we by your assistance obtain in this life the felicity you promised us in the next!" This closing sentence was addressed to the enamelled bronze, gold, and silver busts taken from the Basilica to be melted down. The profanation of the tombs, and of the church in general, is fully set forth by the Benedictine, Dom Poirier, once Archive-keeper of the abbey, and has been incorporated by Baron de Guilhermy in his monograph on St. Denis. The destruction of the tombs and the extraction of the bodies were two distinct operations. It is said by Poirier that some of the men employed in the work fell ill owing to the horrible stenches which assailed their nostrils. The account of the soldier cutting off Henri Quatre's beard and sticking it on his own face is considered apocryphal by some. Poirier makes no allusion to it, but he mentions the opening of the coffins of Henrietta Maria, daughter of Henri Quatre and wife of Charles I. of England, and of Anne Stuart, her daughter, the wife of the only brother of Louis XIV. Guilhermy's work should be consulted, however, for the full history of the desecrated tombs and the restorations which, as he said, were effected in a most immoral manner, archæologically speaking. It was the patchwork of Lenoir, already alluded to, which replaced the old monuments when Louis XVIII. ordered the restoration of the church and of its tombs. This monarch had the remains, or supposed remains, of his ancestors, including Louis XVI. and Marie Antoinette, who had been buried near the Madeleine, put back in the crypt, which the Revolutionists had found literally choked with coffins, some of which were on the steps leading to the Royal charnel-house. Louis XVIII., his son, the Duc de Berri, assassinated in 1820, and others of his family, were the last of the Bourbons buried in St. Denis. The First Napoleon also decreed that he should be interred there,

THE ABBEY CHURCH OF ST. DENIS.

but he is at the Invalides. The Third Napoleon issued a similar decree, but his body rests in English soil.

Viollet-le-Duc has obtained the credit, and no doubt deserved it, of having put the monuments from Lenoir's museum back again in as careful a manner as was possible after the complications caused by the Revolutionists. Before alluding, however, to the monuments arranged by this able architect, it will be necessary to give some description of the church itself The western exterior, with the enclosure before it, is highly interesting, and equally so is the north side, the whole of which may be seen, that of the south being obscured by the old abbey building, now the Institution or House of the Legion of Honour. The three western portals which first strike the visitor, contain some sculptured work dating from Suger's time. These recessed doorways are round-headed in the Romanesque style, but the pointed Gothic arch appears in some of the smaller openings overhead. On the tympan of the central bay is depicted the Last Judgment. Christ holds a scroll in each hand, and on the right side of the Saviour are the words, " Venite, Benedicti Patris Mei," and on the left, " Discedite a Me, Maledicti !" an invitation to heaven for the good, and consignment to hell for the others. The story of the wise and foolish virgins is on the stylobate, around being apostles and elders holding musical instruments and vases, and watching the damned being taken to hell. Other Latin inscriptions, indifferently seen, are on the bronze door and on the marble slabs overhead, supposed to have been brought from Italy by Abbot Suger. The rose-window over the same portal has a clock face. On the northern door is seen St. Denis. He is supposed to be on his way to Montmartre and martyrdom, chained with his two companions. The signs of the Zodiac are around. On the southern portal are visible St. Denis and his colleagues in prison before martyrdom, the Virgin appearing to them. The whole frontage bears the marks of time and weather. On the northern transept door, which can only be well seen, like that of the south, by special permission, are depicted the martyrdom of St. Denis, and the statues of the ancestors of Christ, not, as has been supposed, of the Capetian monarchs. The battlements over the western front were erected during the fourteenth century. Behind them is a statue of St. Denis perched on the top of the nave. The old north tower was placed on a level with the frontage by restorers, so that only one turreted construction now crowns the Basilica. The interior of the church consists of a vestibule, a nave and two aisles crossed by a transept, with seven chapels. The vestibule, which dates from Suger's time, betrays its

HISTORIC CHURCHES OF PARIS

antiquity, and forms a strong contrast to the newer nave with thirty-seven large windows, on some of which episodes of Louis Philippe's reign have been incongruously depicted. All the glass in fact in the triforium or gallery, and in the clerestory, is modern, but in the apsis there are a few windows dating from the twelfth century, and on one of which in the Lady chapel, the figure of Abbot Suger is visible. The clerestory contains four great windows between each main archway. These are subdivided into twin partitions with two small and one large rose over them. The high altar, approached by steps, is a fine imitation of thirteenth century work.

TOMB OF HENRY II.

The wood carving of the stalls is of the fifteenth century, and came from the Abbey of St. Lucien les Beauvais, the marquetry decoration on the back of the seats having been originally in the Chateau de Gaillon, built by Cardinal d'Amboise, Minister of Louis XII. The entrance to the choir was formerly enclosed by a rood-screen, on which episodes from the life of St. Denis and his martyrdom were carved in stone. The nave was also shut off from the choir by a great gold cross, said to have been made by St. Eloi. All these valuable and artistic memorials of an early period were destroyed by the Huguenot soldiers, whose chief, the Prince de Condé, justly hanged some of the authors of the sacrilege. The abbots also, as has been said, removed many old monuments and art treasures during their injudicious restorations.

The following are the chief monuments replaced in their proper order, after restoration, inside the church by Viollet-le-Duc. The first recumbent figure seen on the left, on entering by the central porch, is that of Catherine de Courtenay, a princess of the Royal house of France.[1] This is in the

---

[1] Helena de Courtenay, married to Louis de Beaufremont, was the last of the race who bore the title of Princess of the Blood Royal of France, which was suppressed in 1737. See Gibbon's digression on the family of Courtenay, one of the most noble in Europe. The historian of the Roman Empire, in introducing the subject into his great work, begins:— " Before the introduction of trade which scatters riches, and of knowledge which dispels prejudices, the prerogative of birth is most strongly felt and most humbly acknowledged."

THE ABBEY CHURCH OF ST. DENIS.

St. Hippolyte Chapel on the north side, beyond being the tomb of Louis XII. and his wife, Anne de Bretagne. The king is represented on the top in the attitude of prayer. The monument is in the Renaissance style, and is surrounded by twelve arches under which are the Apostles. Reliefs on the pedestals represent scenes from the Italian campaigns of Louis XII., in 1499, 1507 and 1509. To the right of this is a truncated column commemorating Henry III. From this point is shown the tomb of Dagobert I., to the right of the chancel. It has figures representing the soul of the king leaving earth and its entrance into heaven. Beyond the monument of Louis XII., and also on the north side, is the splendid marble tomb of Henry II. and Catherine de' Medici.

Another monument beyond also commemorates this monarch and his famous Florentine wife. Towards the southern side, in the apsis, is the tomb of Frédégonde, that "terrible queen of the sixth century, of lowly birth," who is said to have caused Galswinthe, sister of Brunehaut, to be strangled on her way to be married to King Chilperic I. That monarch then married Frédégonde. Her tomb in St. Denis is very antique in appearance, and her weird figure, curiously represented in mosaic work, with inlaid circular ornaments of brass, is on the top.[1]

The crypt, gloomy and sepulchral, cold as death, and containing the dust of the "rois anéantis," the "annihilated kings," referred to by Bossuet in his funeral oration over the wife of Charles I. of England, strikes the most hardened with awe. The light of day struggles through the windows where the statues, busts and medallions are arranged, but the charnel-house of the Bourbons is only dimly illuminated by the feeble flickerings of lamps placed in the apertures of the vault by the caretakers of the church for the benefit of visitors. Looking through the openings, one of which is protected by curved bars or rails of iron, like the gate of a prison, one can see inside the rows of coffins with the dust thickly piled

[1] The work is said by some to date from the sixth century; others say the eleventh.

on their lids. Here, surely, is a place infinitely smaller than the grand and gloomy Escurial of the Spanish kings, but equally calculated to remind prince and plebeian alike, of the awful and stupendous reality of Death.[1] . . .

The coffins are those of Louis XVI.; Marie Antoinette; Louis XVIII.; Adelaide and Victoire de France: the Duc de Berri, father of the Comte de Chambord, who was to be Henry Cinq, assassinated by Louvel in Paris, February, 1820. and two of his children; two princes of the Condé family; Louis VII., formerly in the Abbey of Barbeau; Louise of Lorraine, wife of Henri III., from the vanished Capuchin Church of the Place Vendôme. In another vault are the remains recovered from the "fosse commune," in 1817, by order of Louis XVIII. Close at hand is the burial place which Napoleon III. had intended for himself and his descendants, according to an imperial decree of the 18th November, 1858. Opposite the vaults, in the small chapels or recesses of the crypt, are several stone statues, notably of Louis XVI., Marie Antoinette kneeling, robed in a ball dress, Charlemagne, Diana of France, and four gigantic figures intended to ornament a monument to the memory of the murdered Duc de Berri. There is also on the wall of one of the recesses a curious puckered faced portrait of old Louis XI. Few of these subterranean memorials are of great artistic value. Many bear pompous epitaphs which remind one forcibly of Gray's lines in the oft-quoted "Elegy."

On the south side of the church proper, over the crypt, is the monument of Du Guesclin, the champion of France in the wars with England, who died in the year 1380, being soon followed to the tomb by his master, Charles V. The tombs of Louis de Sancerre, a friend of the warrior Du Guesclin, of Renée de Longueville, daughter of the Duke of Longueville, aged seven, of two children of St. Louis, Blanche and Jean, of Francis I., his wife Claude, and three children, are also here. This large memorial is attributed to Philibert Delorme, the architect, Pierre Bontemps, master sculptor, Germain Pilon, and half a dozen other artists of the time —1552. Other memorials are those of Louis d'Orléans and Valentine

[1] " Il n'y a donc plus ici," says Baron de Guilhermy, in his monograph on the abbey and its tombs, " dans cette demeure dernière de rois, que des souvenirs de bannissement, de meurtre, et d'échafaud "—only reminiscences of exile, murder and the scaffold. The -Baron was not able to see clearly the paintings, sculptures and inscriptions on the gloomy vault, as the coffin bars or trestles intervened. He says that the subjects treated there represent Cain and Abel, the Ark of the Covenant, the Passage of the Red Sea, Christ in the Temple, the Magi, Lazarus rising from his charnel-house, and the Last Judgment.

THE ABBEY CHURCH OF ST. DENIS.

de Milan, erected by Louis XII., and a fourteenth-century tomb of Charles d'Etampes, who died in the reign of Philip VI.

The sacristy contains modern paintings—the Coronation of Maria de' Medici; the Emperor Charles V. and Francis I. in the abbey; the death of Louis VI.; Philip III. presenting the relics of St. Denis; St. Louis receiving the Oriflamme, of which an imitation is in the chancel; St. Louis restoring the vaults; Charlemagne at the consecration of the Basilica; the Funeral of Dagobert I.; St. Denis evangelizing, and the discovery of the bodies in 1817. In the treasury are seen many crosses, crucifixes, altar vessels, mostly given by King Charles X. Some of the old treasures are now in the National Library.

The famous Basilica has long been only a museum, with occasional services. It is now open as a parish church, and it is to be hoped that steps will be taken to protect the place from the iconoclasm of future Revolutionists, as well as from any damage during the Lenten services. The other churches in the town of the "Apostle of the Gauls" are the scenes of free fights between the "Libre Penseurs" and the Catholics, on Lenten evenings; and every lover of the antique and the artistic must desire that such quarrels shall be excluded from the historic fane of St. Denis.

St. Germain L'Auxerrois.

CHAPTER VIII.

ST. GERMAIN L'AUXERROIS.[1]

The Huguenots—Condé and Coligny—The two saints—Etienne Marcel and Charles the Bad—Maurevert, the hired murderer—Coligny and Charles IX.—Catherine de' Medici and Duc Henri de Guise—The Bartholomew massacre—The bell signal—"Down with the Huguenots!"—The window of Charles IX.—Balzac's opinion—Catherine de' Medici praised by the novelist—Her powerful enemies—Maria de' Medici—Concino Concini and Leonora Galigaï—A skilful bird-trainer—Murder of Concini—His body dragged out of the tomb—The service for the murdered Duc de Berri—Description of the church.

[1] St. Germain l'Auxerrois, a right bank church, is placed here after St. Denis owing to its historical importance.

HUGUES CAPET.

ATHOLICISM and Protestantism, the two great offshoots and developments of the Hebraic system of theocracy, confront each other on that historic bit of ground between the Rue du Louvre and the Rue de Rivoli. In one street stands the plain Oratory church with the statue of Admiral Coligny, an open Bible at his feet, outside it ; and on the other, St. Germain l'Auxerrois, with its symbolic pinnacles, pointed windows and canopies of stone. The contrast is striking for those who have time or inclination in these busy days to meditate for a while on the bitter religious wars of the sixteenth century, when the followers of the Duc de Guise fought against those of Condé and Coligny. For the present, however, the Church of St. Germain l'Auxerrois must be dealt with. This edifice, standing opposite the eastern entrance of the Louvre Palace, replaced an older one built by Chilperic I., and sacked by the Normans. Archæologists are not agreed as to whether the older church was dedicated to St. Germain, Bishop of Paris, or to his namesake, the Bishop of Auxerre, who died at Ravenna in 430, and who had done some apostolic work in England before retiring to Italy. The newer church was built by King Robert after the Norman invasions, and in order to distinguish it from St. Germain-in-the-Fields, it was dedicated to the holy Bishop of Auxerre, whose rather legendary life is recounted by the Bollandists.[1] Nowadays nothing remains of King Robert's church, owing to the numerous reconstructions undertaken since his time. The spire belongs to the twelfth century ; the principal entrance, the choir and apsis, to the first part of the thirteenth century ; while the porch, the greater part of the façade, the nave and the chapels, date from the fifteenth and the sixteenth centuries.

[1] The Latin name of the church, as set forth in the "Chartularium," is Sanctus Germanus Autissiodorensis Parisiensis.

101

HISTORIC CHURCHES OF PARIS.

The church is rich in historical associations. It was in the cloister around it that Etienne Marcel, the Provost of the Merchants, called a meeting and protested loudly against the spurious money circulated by order of the Dauphin, son of Jean le Bon, in 1356. From this arose the troubles between the nobles and the bourgeoisie. The former, supporting the Dauphin, whose father was a captive in London, attacked the Parisians, who were led by Marcel. This agitator offered the crown to Charles the Bad of Navarre, grandson of Louis X., or Le Hutin, so called from his quarrelsome disposition. Marcel was murdered before Paris could be given up to Charles. It is, however, with the religious wars of the sixteenth century that the church is chiefly identified. It was near the cloister that Maurevel, or Maurevert, hid while waiting to murder Admiral Coligny. The admiral, it will be remembered, was charged by the Catholic party with having instigated the assassination of their great leader, François, Duc de Guise. In August, 1572, Coligny seemed to be gaining a great ascendency over the young king, Charles IX., whose mother, Catherine de' Medici, concerted with Duc Henri de Guise on the matter. The duke, who wanted revenge on the Huguenot admiral, was only too eager to act upon the hints of the queen. Accordingly, the hired assassin fired a shot from an arquebuse at Coligny as the admiral was leaving the Louvre. The great Huguenot chief was wounded only, and his would-be murderer escaped. The Huguenots now became exasperated and asked for justice. The queen accordingly pressed her son to take extreme measures in order to chastise the insolence of the Calvinists, and the memorable massacre on St. Bartholomew's Day, 24th August, 1572, was decided upon. The king is reported to have said to his mother, " God's death, Madam! as you want to kill the admiral, why not murder all the Huguenots in France ? I do not care! Let none of them remain alive, so that I be not reproached by some survivor hereafter."

The signal for the massacre was given by the bell of the Church of St. Germain L'Auxerrois, in the small hours of Sunday morning, 24th of August, 1572. Coligny was the first to be murdered. The deed was done in the Hôtel de Ponthieu, Rue des Fossés St. Germain L'Auxerrois, near where his statue now stands. The assassins, who came out of the Louvre Palace, wore white crosses in their hats and had white cloths tied around their arms. According to Davila, an officer of the guards stood in the courtyard of the Louvre and read out from a list the names of the Huguenot lords and gentlemen who were the king's guests in the Palace.

ST. GERMAIN L'AUXERROIS.

These to the number of two hundred were slain, the king looking on from a window. In the meantime, the massacres were being carried on throughout the city. The blood of the Catholics was up, and the cry, " Kill, kill—Down with the Huguenots ! " resounded through Paris. The king's brother, afterwards Henri III., who was slain by the knife of Jacques Clément, stood in the middle of the bridge of Notre Dame superintending the useless butcheries which were carried on in the name of religion. Protestant pastors, shopkeepers, clerks, went down before the butchers as well as the noble Du Resnels, D'Astaracs, Montauberts, La Roches, La Forces and De La Rochefoucaulds. Even Catholics who were the marks of private vengeance were slain, among them being some celebrated men. Towards seven o'clock in the morning, as is related by some writers, King Charles IX. resolved to have a few shots at the Huguenots, but his arquebuse did not carry far enough. The king is erroneously said to have stood at a large window on the quay, at the end of the Apollo gallery of the Louvre. Balzac the novelist, in his elaborate whitewashing of Catherine de' Medici (Études Philosophiques), points out that this part of the Louvre did not exist in the time of Charles IX. Balzac also denies that the monarch fired at fugitive Huguenots as they were crossing the river in boats. Brantôme, D'Aubigné, Goulard and others maintain the contrary, and Voltaire was told all about it by Marshal de Tessé, who knew the page, then a centenarian, by whom the royal arquebuse was loaded. A few Huguenots were saved from the massacre, notably the king's surgeon, Ambroise Paré, the royal nurse, Philippe Richard, and Renée de France, daughter of Louis XII., a zealous Calvinist who gave shelter to some of her co-religionists in her palace on the left bank of the river. It is estimated that about one hundred thousand Huguenots were put to death at this period in Paris and other parts of France.[1]

Such was the massacre of St. Bartholomew's Day, 1572, instigated by the Italian woman who was the wife of Henri II. Catherine's memory has been loaded with reproach, and it is perhaps just to point out, as Balzac does, that being a woman she could only maintain her influence by the exercise of those arts in which her fellow-countrymen are past masters, and

---

[1] Carlyle compares the massacre of St. Bartholomew and that of September, 1792, in the third volume of the " French Revolution." " Kings themselves, not in desperation, but only in difficulty, have sat hatching, for year and day, their Bartholomew business; and then, at the right moment, also on an autumn Sunday, this very bell (they say it is the identical metal) of St. Germain L'Auxerrois was set a-pealing with effect."

of which Nicholas Machiavelli is the chartered exponent. Catherine had to face the factions of the Guises and the Bourbons, of the two Cardinals de Lorraine, the two Princes of Condé, Queen Jeanne d'Albret, Henri Quatre, the Constable de Montmorency, Calvin, Coligny, and Theodore de Bèze. She had thus opposed to her powerful Catholic as well as Protestant princes and commoners. She held her place proudly among all these, or, as Balzac says, "like a great monarch." She had none of the weakness of her sex, and "lived chaste amid the amorous intrigues of the most gallant court in Europe, and, despite the want of money, built admirable monuments as if to repair the losses caused by the demolitions of the Calvinists." These are the words of Balzac, who also attempts to defend the horrible massacre of St. Bartholomew by political exigencies. The question, however, has nothing to do with the present purpose, the object of the author being merely to revive historical interest in a notable church.

On the 25th of April, 1617, the Church of St. Germain L'Auxerrois was the scene of a popular tumult. Mary of Medicis, or de' Medici, according to the Italian form, the daughter of Francis II., Grand Duke of Florence, she who had married Henri Quatre after his divorce from Margaret de Valois, sister of Charles IX., was now Regent of France, during the minority of her son, Louis XIII. One of her first acts was to depose Sully, the Minister of Henri Quatre, a Protestant who when a youth escaped the massacre of St. Bartholomew by going through the streets reading a Catholic prayer-book. Sully was replaced by the Florentine, Concino Concini, husband of Leonora Galigaï, who was made Marquis of Ancre, a town in the Somme, nowadays called Albert, and a Marshal of France. This Italian soon gained an ascendency over Louis XIII., but he was ousted by Albert de Luynes, a young Court gentleman from Avignon, who was as poor as a church mouse. De Luynes captivated the young monarch by his skill as a bird-fancier. He was especially adroit in training birds of prey, and had charge of the Royal falcons. When the troubles began, owing to the discontent of the people with the Government, and to the revolt of the nobles under the Prince de Condé, De Luynes secretly joined the malcontents and persuaded his master to blot out the Marshal D'Ancre, who was really ruling the kingdom and usurping the place of Louis himself. Accordingly, Concini was attacked one day as he was leaving his house for the Louvre palace, by the Baron de Vitry, Captain of the Guards, and his men. The Florentine had scarcely time to utter an exclamation of surprise, when he was laid low by a volley of pistol shots. He was despatched by sword thrusts, and the Baron de Vitry

Statue of Admiral Coligny—
Rue de Rivoli.

To face p. 104.

ST. GERMAIN L'AUXERROIS.

kicked the body to make sure that the Marshal was dead. Then the house of D'Ancre was pillaged. His wife was despoiled of all the money and jewels which she had hidden under the mattress of her bed; his son, aged eleven, was stripped stark naked and left without food for a whole day. Finally, brutal vengeance was carried so far that Leonora Galigaï was condemned and burned as a witch, and the people broke into the Church of St. Germain L'Auxerrois in order to drag the body of Marshal D'Ancre out of the grave into which it had been hastily thrown, enveloped in a tattered winding-sheet. The corpse was suspended by the feet to a gibbet on the Pont Neuf, was afterwards cut up, and some of the pieces were sold, others burned, others flung into the Seine. These horrible incidents were really brought about by lackeys, who led the rabble on and incited them to dig out the body of the Marshal from the place inside the church where it had been interred.

In 1831, a little more than two hundred years later, the church was the scene of another tumult, after the funeral service in commemoration of the Duc de Berri, son of Charles X., who had been assassinated by Louvel, when leaving the opera, on the 13th of February, 1820, while his uncle, Louis XVIII., was reigning. The clergy of St. Germain L'Auxerrois were noted for their attachment to the Legitimist or Bourbon cause, so the royal Church which had been patronized by French monarchs since the days of Philip Augustus, was terribly damaged both interiorly and outside. It thus required another restoration.

The church is in the form of a cross, and looks a rather light construction when compared with the Renaissance building of the Louvre opposite. The portico is interesting, although the frescoes are in a lamentable state of decay, and give an idea of what may be expected to happen, through the influence of time and a cold climate, to the mural paintings under the arcades of the Hofgarten in Munich. The frescoes of St. Germain L'Auxerrois are indeed pitiful to contemplate. The porch has five arcades surmounted by a balustrade. Above is a flamboyant rose-window, flanked by two turrets. On the gable is an angel sculptured by Marochetti. The whole of the exterior is richly and capriciously carved by the stone-workers of the fifteenth century; and near the pierced terraces, or galleries, are gables, gargoyles, crockets, cornices, brackets, corbels, mullioned windows, and pinnacled flying buttresses. The sculptors seem to have given full rein to their fancies, and on the corbels and gargoyles have chiselled griffins, monkeys, wolves, dogs, bears, showmen with their animals, a savage with a club in hand issuing from the mouth of a river-horse, a man carrying a lion

HISTORIC CHURCHES OF PARIS.

on his shoulders, another with a hooded ape, a sow on its litter, the terrestrial globe gnawed by rats, to symbolize the wicked who devastate the earth, while the devils are represented by watching cats. Two of the statues on the exterior are said to be old. One represents St. Francis of Assisi, the other St. Mary of Egypt, with the three loaves on which she fed when in the desert. Other statues of saints adorn the three doors of the main entrance. By the side of the church is the Mayor's Hall of the first arrondissement, which is connected with the church by a species of cloister and a flamboyant campanile or bell-tower. This construction was supposed to have been necessitated in order to give symmetry to the church and its environments, but it is universally condemned as useless and unlovely, or at least out of keeping with the older building at its side.

The interior of St. Germain l'Auxerrois has suffered from so-called "Classic" restoration, but some of the Gothic has been preserved. The pillars have no capitals and are devoid of decoration in the nave, but in the choir they are fluted and otherwise ornamented. The long choir was formerly separated from the nave by a magnificent screen of the Renaissance period, the work of Pierre Lescot and Jean Goujon. In 1744 this was removed on the ground that it prevented the congregation from seeing the officiating priest. The old tombs were also taken away. Among these were the tombs of Malherbe the poet, who has been so terribly satirized by Regnier, as the founder of a pedantic milk-and-water school of versifiers, of Guy Patin the physician, Sanson the geographer, and predecessor in that line of M. Elisée Reclus, of the painter Coypel, the sculptor Coysevox, and the engraver Israel Sylvestre. These burying-places are now represented by a few statues and inscribed flagstones.[1] The great peculiarity of the interior is the existence of a large chapel on the southern side. This is literally a church within a church. It is called the Chapelle de Notre Dame and also the Chapelle des Catéchismes, and has its own altar, organ, jubé or screen, pulpit, lateral oratories, stained glass windows and a reredos forming the tree of Jesse in stone which envelops with its branches a statue of the Virgin of antique origin, but the date is uncertain.

The windows of St. Germain L'Auxerrois give the interior of the church the appearance of an immense illuminated missal. The eye meets deep, rich, and mellow colours at every corner, and the place is well worthy of a

[1] There was formerly in this church a splendid mausoleum erected by order of Charles V., the Wise, to his Court buffoon. Another jester had a similar monument in St. Martin's, Senlis.

ST. GERMAIN L'AUXERROIS.

visit if only for its pictured panes. It is very difficult, however, to see the figures on the upper windows, but most of those in the chapels and around the aisles are visible enough. The two windows at the entrance of the church are by Maréchal, and of the splendid fifteenth and sixteenth century glass there remain but the north transept rose, on which appears God the Father, with angels, martyrs and confessors; the opposite window, south side, on which the Holy Ghost, or Spirit, in the form of a dove, is visible, and six other windows—four on the north with scenes from the Passion and the life of Christ, and two on the south depicting the Ascension, the Assumption, the Coronation of the Virgin, and a few other scenes. Of the modern frescoes may be noticed Quichard's "Descent from the Cross," in the southern transept. Notable, too, are the smaller chapels, one of which, the fourth of the choir beyond the sacristy, contains monuments of Etienne d'Aligre and his son, who were Chancellors of France in the middle of the seventeenth century, the woodwork of the Compassion Chapel, near the north transept, that of the covered "banc d'œuvre," or churchwarden's seats, and the holy water font, with its three shells surmounted by angels, designed by Madame de Lamartine.

The vaulting of St. Germain L'Auxerrois is low, and gives the interior a correspondingly depressed appearance at first sight, especially after one has seen the high-pitched Gothic roofs. This is atoned for, however, by the harmonious blending of light and colour in the holy place. You feel that the church is admirably fitted for the development of the devotional faculties, and that here, if anywhere, it would be possible to prepare for the next world. Even the materialist must feel impressed when inside St. Germain L'Auxerrois. Exteriorly, the church is less impressive, but few can fail to take an interest in the handsome and historical edifice.

Fresco by Flandrin—
St. Germain-des-Prés.

CHAPTER IX.

ST. GERMAIN-DES-PRÉS.

A mighty monastery—The remains of the abbey and their modern uses—The Benedictines and the Salvation Army—The rival fairs—Privileges of the monks—The Northern Pirates—Formation of the " Noble Faubourg"—Disappearance of Cow Road and the Froggery—Increasing wealth and worldliness—Reforms effected—Royal and Abbatial tombs—Abbot and king—The tombs of the Douglases—The church a powder manufactory during the Revolution—Flandrin's frescoes—Strange career and sad end of the artist—General description of the church—Its connection with the French Academy.

PHILIPPE III.

LOOKING at the massive church of St. Germain-des-Prés, one can easily realize that it was the centre of a mighty monastic stronghold in the days of widespread ecclesiastical domination. The long, high-pitched roofs of the edifice and of the existing part of the Palace of the Abbots at the back are imposing, and give an idea of strength, power and durability. The church vies in antiquity with Notre Dame de Paris, and was the burial place of the Merovingian monarchs before the shrine of St. Denis became a Basilica and the charnel-house of royalty. In the days of its power the great abbey stood towering aloft by itself, strongly fortified in the midst of the meadows bordering the river, whence it derived its name—Sanctus Germanus de Pratis.[1] Nowadays the church is the most striking building on the Boulevard St. Germain, that broad, monotonous thoroughfare, with its lofty houses all alike and all of the same height, which pierces part of the old Latin country wherein many generations of poor scholars have struggled and starved. The mighty monastery, however, is gone, and will no longer tempt the cupidity of revolutionists as it tempted that of the Northmen, whose ravages are described in the annals of Fulda and of Prudentius of Troyes, and in Sir Francis Palgrave's "History of England and Normandy." The part of the abbatial palace, with its red brick frontage facing the modern Rue de Furstemberg, so called after a cardinal who ruled the monastery in the seventeenth century, is now converted into a surgical and dentistry institute, and also contains an antique furniture store. Near the old home of the Benedictines stands a place sometimes used by the very modern Salvation Army. General Booth's followers have intoned their hymns over ground where the matins, lauds, and vespers of the monks once resounded. Of the meadows no trace exists, and of the abbatial

[1] See the "Chartularium Ecclesiæ Parisiensis."

III

gardens there are three strips, one in the interior of the palace, another near the main entrance to the church, and a third on the Boulevard St. Germain side, wherein stands the statue of Bernard Palissy, the famous art potter, who died in 1589.

Near the monastery was formerly held one of the oldest and most celebrated fairs in Paris, which opened before Easter. The monks reaped substantial profit from this institution, and in the twelfth and thirteenth centuries their privileges were interfered with by the kings.[1] The fair was then transferred to the Markets, but Louis XI. re-established the right of the monks to control a "foire franche." This was opposed by the monks of St. Denis, who had a fair called the "Landit," but an arrangement was eventually made by which the religious of St. Germain-des-Prés shortened the duration of their annual bazaar. The arrangement only continued for a brief space of time, as the fair of St. Germain soon passed the limits assigned to it, and lasted much longer than the stipulated week. The fair extended from the market, near the church, to the proximity of Saint Sulpice and the Luxembourg Gardens. The booths were sheltered from the rain by an immense wooden construction which was burned in March, 1762, and from that date the open-air bazaar continued to decline until it disappeared altogether.

Some say that the abbey was founded in the year 543 : others, like the Benedictine Félibien, who was one of its monks, in 567. The church was built on a site once consecrated to Isis, its founder being Childebert I., who dedicated it to St. Vincent. The outside was gorgeously decorated, probably with the spoils brought by Childebert from Spain. It was thence called by the people St. Germain-le-Doré, and traces of the influence of this lavish ornamentation are still to be seen inside the church. The king also endowed the abbey with the domain of Issy, and St. Germain, Bishop of Paris, gave the monks the right to elect their abbot and free ownership of all their conventual property. The monks originally came from the monastery of St. Symphorien of Autun, or Augustodunum, the old Roman town in the department of Saône-et-Loire, whose modern bishop, Monseigneur Perraud, is a member of the French Academy. These brethren followed the rules of St. Antony, "the godly eremite," and of St.

---

[1] The charter of the abbey of St. Germain, defining the jurisdiction of the monastery, is in the Paris Cartulary. One clause, dated July, 1211, has the ring of a modern document. It refers to a dispute between John the Humble, Abbot of St. Germain, "ex una parte," and the bishop and others, "ex altera parte," about parish bounds.

ST. GERMAIN DES PRÉS.

Basil, but soon afterwards they adopted the rule of St. Benoit, or Benedict. In 754 the abbey of St. Vincent took the name of St. Germain when that venerated bishop's body was removed from the chapel of St. Symphorien and placed in the choir of the church. This removal was effected with great ceremony, King Pepin, his sons and vassals leading the procession. During the Norman invasions, the monastery was destroyed, but in the year 1000 it was rebuilt by the Abbot Morard, who was assisted in the undertaking by the pious King Robert, son of Hugh Capet, a monarch who frequently joined the monks in singing psalms. This period was distinguished by a revival of activity and religious zeal in Italy and Gaul, and many of the basilicas were restored or rebuilt. It is supposed that, of all the monastery of St. Germain-des-Prés, only the great tower, still partially existing, most resisted the fire of the pirates. The new constructions were finished in 1163, and the abbey and church were in that year consecrated by Pope Alexander III. On its restoration the abbey became more powerful than ever, and around it was formed the borough, or bourg, which is to-day the most fashionable district in Paris, namely, the Faubourg Saint Germain. The Champs-Elysées vies with this district by the wealth of its residents and the magnificence of its buildings. The Champs-Elysées district is, however, modern, and to a certain extent the locality of the mushroom nobility and of the parvenus who sprang up under the two empires. Many of its best houses are also tenanted by the magnificent plutocrats of the New World, Americans of the north, who have made their money in mines and stores, and who come to spend it in the European paradise ; and Brazilians, Peruvians and Cubans, who imitate their neighbours of the States in their love for Paris. In the Faubourg St. Germain live the old nobility, or those of that class who were enabled to survive the wreckage caused by the great upheaval at the end of the eighteenth century. Here dwell the descendants of many of those Crusaders who, as Montalembert said on a famous occasion, would not recoil before the sons of Voltaire. Around the old Church of the Benedictines, now only part of the parish of St. Sulpice, live the bearers of the greatest names in French history. The "noble Faubourg," as it is called, stands on the once marshy ground environing the old monastery, and some of its finest streets are built on places which were known formerly as the Chemin-aux-Vaches, or Cow Road, the Froggery, and other unpicturesque names. It was only in 1688 that the district was chosen by the nobles as their dwelling-place, and the "quartier monastique," as it has been called, was soon invaded by the

HISTORIC CHURCHES OF PARIS.

Montmorencys, the De Luynes, the De Chevreuses, the Des Broglies, the Des La Rochefoucaulds, the Des Chabrillans, the Byrons and the Maillys. The descendants of these families, or some of them, still inhabit the " noble Faubourg," but the glory of the old salons has departed, and the traditions of the fashionable district are regarded as too antiquated for modern tastes.

To return, however, to the abbey and its church. St. Germain-des-Prés was further enlarged in 1237, and in the reign of Charles V., the monastery was so strongly fortified that it looked like a military construction planned by the Vauban of the epoch. Shortly after this period the monks seem to have fallen away from their practices of piety, either on account of increasing wealth, or through lack of fervour. A reform was instituted by the Abbot Briçonnet, who called in some other monks. Another reform was effected in 1631, when the religious of St. Maur introduced there the strict rule of St. Benedict. This, however, did not have an effect in diminishing the power of the abbots, or the influence of the monastery. The monks had full jurisdiction, temporal and spiritual, over the district. They were more than the vice-Chancellors, the Proctors and pro-Proctors of Oxford and Cambridge nowadays. They virtually ruled the district, and were the " Hauts justiciers et censiers " of the south bank of the river, until they were interfered with in 1668 by an Archbishop of Paris, and in 1674 by a Royal edict. They still, however, had judicial power within their own property limits. Before the cessation of their jurisdiction they had a pillory for offenders, and the prison of St. Margaret, afterwards known as the abbey prison,[1] was in their keeping, and under their control.

Among the famous persons buried in the church after the Merovingian monarchs were Marie de Clèves, Princess of Condé, with whom Henri III. was violently in love, 1574 ; Catherine de Bourbon, daughter of Henri de Bourbon, Prince of Condé, who died in 1595 ; William Douglas, Earl of Angus, who died in 1611 ; his grandson, James Douglas, killed before Douay, in the beginning of the reign of Louis XIV.; other members of the same Scotch stock; François de Bourbon, brother of the Cardinal ; Casimir V., King of Poland, who died Abbot of St. Germain-des-Prés in 1672 ; and of many other princes and abbots. The only tombs left intact by the Revolution are those of King Casimir V., of the Douglases, and of the Castellans. In 1821, the remains of Descartes, the famous philosopher, of the great

---

[1] For a striking description of the horrors perpetrated in the Abbaye Prison in 1792 English readers must be referred to Carlyle's third volume of the " French Revolution." Nothing can equal the Scotchman's lucid picture

Fresco by Flandrin—
St. Germain=des=Prés.

ST. GERMAIN DES PRÉS.

Benedictines Mabillon and Montfaucon, and of Boileau, the poet, were placed in the choir chapels. According to some, only Boileau's heart was removed from the Sainte Chapelle. It is generally admitted, however, that all his body is in St. Germain-des-Prés, as well as that of the philosopher Descartes, which was removed from the church of St. Geneviève. The inscription over the tomb of Descartes sets forth that " he whose intelligence pierced the secrets of earth and sky had to yield to fate, like any ordinary person, but he would have lived for ever, like the divine works which he described, if his wisdom had enabled him to emancipate himself from the bondage of death."

Having suffered from the Revolution in 1793, when it was turned into a powder manufactory, and from an explosion in 1794, when many of the valuable books of the abbey were destroyed, although, luckily, the bulk of them is now in the National Library, the church was restored in the year 1845. Partial restoration had been effected between 1834 and 1836. In 1852 and the following years the interior was redecorated with much gilded ornament and polychromatic paintings. Hippolyte Flandrin also painted frescoes, but the artist unluckily died before he was able to complete his important work from which St. Germain-des-Prés derives a good deal of the interest attaching to it nowadays.

The principal entrance to St. Germain-des-Prés is in the Rue Bonaparte and dates from the seventeenth century. Over the door are bas-reliefs, representing the last supper, and the Romanesque tower with its round-headed bays and slate-covered spire rises over the porch. The other towers over the choir and the transept were destroyed in 1822, and only their bases remain. Still, the single tower, the high-pitched roof and massive flying buttresses, combine to make St. Germain-des-Prés one of the most striking and interesting of the old, historic churches of Paris. The interior of the edifice is remarkable, as it shows the early Gothic style struggling with the Romanesque which it supplanted. The nave, with its heavy and restored capitals, has round-headed Romanesque arcades, but the Gothic style appears in the choir and in the arches of the roof. The upper windows of the apsis are also pointed. Some of the columns of the triforium, or gallery, are said to date from the time of the old church constructed by Childebert I., but this is open to doubt. Their bases and capitals are admitted, however, to be twelfth-century work. The polychromatic decoration of the church, undertaken by Baltard, is interesting, but the green columns, red, arabesqued pilasters and gilded capitals are open to the objections of the admirers of simpler Gothic.

HISTORIC CHURCHES OF PARIS.

Flandrin's much-appreciated frescoes include, in the nave, the Preliminaries of the Last Judgment, and the Ascension, done by his brother Paul from his designs, the Dispersion of the Apostles, the Scattering of Men after Babel, the Resurrection of Christ, Jonas emerging from the belly of the whale, the Death of Christ, Abraham's Sacrifice, the Betrayal by Judas, the Sale of Joseph. These are on the right of the nave, and on the left are the Annunciation, the Burning Bush, the Nativity, the Promise of a Redeemer, in which is seen a beautiful female figure, that of Eve, the Adoration of the Magi, Balaam's Prophecy, the Baptism of Christ, the Passage of the Red Sea, a fine composition, the Institution of the Eucharist and Melchisedech. Above these on the wall spaces, between the windows, are figures of the Prophets and Judges of Israel. In the choir are depicted the Carrying of the Cross, and the Entry of Christ into Jerusalem.

Flandrin's compositions, however, must be seen in order to be appreciated in a proper manner. No amount of bald cataloguing or verbal description, like that indulged in by salon critics, can convey an idea of this painter's religious compositions, and several visits must necessarily be made to the church in order to take in every detail of the art legacy left by this nineteenth-century imitator of Blessed Fra Angelico of Florence. Like the great Dominican artist, Flandrin, too, was pious. His was no skin-deep Christianity flavoured with the æstheticism so much in favour with the cultured admirers of the traditions of Papal Rome. If any man, artist, or prosaic workaday being deserved Heaven, Flandrin assuredly ought to merit a place in the angelic choir, and this on two grounds. In the first place he led a life of bitter struggle on earth, and secondly, in spite of his trials and afflictions, he was a firm and fervent follower of the religion whose traditions he endeavoured to depict on the walls of St. Germain-des-Prés. Hippolyte Flandrin was a pupil of Ingres, and won the grand prize of Rome. He died of small-pox in the Eternal City in 1864, and is buried in Père Lachaise cemetery. His monument stands in the north aisle of the church which contains his frescoes. It " implores the passing tribute of a sigh " from all who can sympathize with struggling poverty and regret the stern decrees of a fate which unmercifully cuts down genius before it gives the full measure of its worth.[1] Of his work in St. Germain-des-Prés the finest specimen is, undoubtedly, the Entry of Christ into Jerusalem, which is on a gold ground, after the Byzantine School, in the choir. The

[1] Hippolyte Flandrin also left a good many portraits, and was called ".le peintre des honnêtes femmes."

ST. GERMAIN DES PRÉS.

figure of the Redeemer is particularly imposing, and the composition of the picture shows the artist at his best. The Crucifixion, or Death of Christ, in the nave, on the right, is also noteworthy.

Other paintings in the Church are St. Germain distributing alms, by Steuben, Baptism of a Eunuch, by Bertin, Resurrection of Lazarus, by Verdier, the Death of Sapphira, by Le Clerc, and Scenes from the Life of St. Peter, by Le Masurier and Jeaurat. In addition to the monuments or memorials already mentioned there are several statues, notably one of Notre Dame la Blanche, or Notre Dame de Consolation, which had been given to the abbey of St. Denis in 1340 by Queen Jeanne d'Evreux, in a niche designed by Lassus, a statue of St. Francis Xavier, the Apostle of the Indies, by the younger Couston, and one of St. Margaret, by Dourlat. The high altar is not a remarkable construction. It replaced one made in 1408, which was destroyed by the Revolutionists in 1792. Some of the windows are composed of fragments of stained glass of the thirteenth century, representing the Annunciation, the Marriage of the Virgin, St. Anne and St. Joachim, and Works of Mercy.

The church of St. Germain-des-Prés has some connection with the French Academy, or "Institut de France." On Wednesday, 21st October, 1895, the fête of the centenary of the five academies forming the institute, namely, the Académie Française, the Académie des Inscriptions et Belles-Lettres, the Académie des Sciences, the Académie des Beaux-Arts, and the Académie des Sciences Morales et Politiques, was begun by a mass in the old abbey church, and Bishop Perraud of Autun, one of the academicians, officiated thereat.

Interior—
St. Étienne du Mont.

CHAPTER X.

THE PANTHÉON, FORMERLY ST. GENEVIÈVE'S CHURCH, AND ST. ÉTIENNE DU MONT.

A " bad imitation of St. Peter's"—Quinet's view of Soufflot's work—St. Geneviève and Attila—Treatment of the Patroness of Paris by the Republicans—The " Temple of Renown"—Mirabeau's funeral—Voltaire, Rousseau and Marat—Royalist revenge for the desecration of St. Denis—In Napoleon's days—The Restoration and Baron Gros—Changes—In the hands of the Communists—The frescoes of Puvis de Chavannes and others—The tombs in crypt—The church of St. Étienne du Mont—Its splendid rood-loft—Gibbon's account of the finding of St. Stephen's remains—Miracles—The curious architectural features of St. Étienne du Mont—The glass by Pinaigrier—The tomb of St. Geneviève.

JEAN I.

THE Panthéon is not an antique building, nor is it now a church. As it, however, occupies the site of the very old edifice dedicated to St. Geneviève,[1] the celestial Patroness of Paris, and as it formerly bore the name of that holy shepherdess, it may be treated after the historic churches already described, and before some of the smaller, but more antique places of worship. Much criticism has been levelled at the Panthéon and at Soufflot, its architect. Victor Hugo described the church as the " finest Savoy cake ever made in stone," and called it a bad imitation of St. Peter's, unwieldy and out of line. Soufflot in reality did not care a jot about St. Geneviève or the legends attached to her name when he began the work. Accordingly, there is nothing idyllic about the Panthéon, which is merely a colossal, cold and formal temple, fit resting-place for the men who tried to pull down the old faiths and to sneer away everything which humanity was taught to hold sacred. The architect only wanted to do something big, to imitate the dome of Michael Angelo, and perhaps, as Quinet imagines, to shelter under his cupola the thought of the eighteenth century. And so it comes to pass that St. Geneviève, once so fervently venerated, has now no church or shrine of her own in the city for which she so often prayed, and from whose gates, as Gibbon says, " she diverted the march of Attila." Revolutionists and republicans have despoiled her of her rights; her " chasse," or reliquary, is no longer carried about in processions, her bones were burned on the Place de Grève, and the recovered stones from her tomb had to be placed in the church of St. Étienne Du Mont, at the back of the Panthéon, where, with her relics, they are now daily displayed for the veneration of the faithful.[2]

The foundation stone of the Panthéon was laid by Louis XV., in 1764, shortly after the death of the butcher's daughter, Madame de Pompadour

[1] The French form is Sainte Geneviève.
[2] This is fully dealt with further on, in the chapter on St. Étienne du Mont.

HISTORIC CHURCHES OF PARIS.

who had during her lifetime been ruling France and its king. The edifice was completed in 1790 and elicited much admiration. Fears were, however, entertained that the whole construction would give way. Soufflot, in his desire to eclipse Brunelleschi, Michael Angelo, and Sir Christopher Wren, tried to keep up his cupola by four columns only. These, it was said, were dangerously insufficient, so another architect, Rondelet, was called in, and erected pillars with arches to support the dome. Hardly had the first mass been said in the church when the Constituent Assembly decreed that it should be secularized and re-named. Count Gabriel Honoré Riquetti de Mirabeau, the man who had opened a cloth shop at Marseilles in order to ingratiate himself with the Third Estate, had just died. His body was borne, with great pomp, to the church of St. Geneviève, which had been turned into a Temple of Renown, the Panthéon for the great men of the country. "Aux grands hommes la Patrie reconnaissante," according to the inscription over its colossal portals. This was to be the crypt of great citizens, as St. Denis had been the burial place of the kings and princes.

Voltaire was the next to be placed in the Temple of Renown on the top of the hill of St. Geneviève. On the 10th July, 1791, the remains of the great cynic were taken from a country grave, in the Abbey of Scellières, and conveyed to the Panthéon with a solemnity greater than that marking the funeral of Mirabeau. The procession first stopped on the ruins of the Bastille, speeches were made there, and then the antique funeral car was drawn, accompanied by mourners in Roman garb, to the dome built by Soufflot. Three years later "Evangelist Jean-Jacques, too, as is most proper, must be dug up from Ermenonville, and processioned, with pomp, with sensibility, to the Panthéon of the Fatherland," as Carlyle tells us. Rousseau ousted Mirabeau, whose body was disinterred, and placed in the cemetery of St. Catherine, for the Revolutionists had begun to suspect that the dead man had been a fraud during his lifetime, and that his democratic principles were only skin-deep. Marat was likewise buried here after his murder by Charlotte Corday, but his remains were also removed by order of the Convention. Later on Voltaire and Rousseau were treated in a similar manner. During the restoration the Royalists rather uselessly and inadequately revenged the desecration of the tombs of the kings at St. Denis.

In the time of the first Napoleon, the Panthéon again became the church of the Patroness of Paris. Marshal Lannes was buried there as well as some of the Imperial Senators and State dignitaries. Then came the Restoration, when Baron Gros was commissioned to emblazon the ceilings with episodes

THE PANTHÉON.

from the life of St. Geneviève. That was after the tombs of the philosophers and revolutionists had been broken by order of the government. After the Revolution of July, 1830, the church again became the Panthéon and an attempt was made to obliterate the memory of the sainted shepherdess. The government of Louis Philippe, however, in putting back in their places the groups and bas-reliefs of the first Revolution, added the marble monument by Maindron, of St. Geneviève and Attila. The Republic of 1848 left the edifice as it was, but in 1851 it again became a church. Another change was effected in 1885, when the building was once more secularized in order to receive the remains of Victor Hugo.

THE PANTHÉON.

Thus the Panthéon has changed with the different political transformation scenes of modern French history. St. Paul's, Westminster Abbey, Santa Croce in Florence, retain the impress of consecration from age to age, but the Panthéon is alternately laicized or restored to its original uses as the French weathercock veers from Royalty to Republicanism. In June, 1848, the Revolutionists temporarily held the building, and in 1871 it fell into the hands of the Communists, who were ousted before they could blow it up.

The Panthéon is built in the form of a Greek cross. The length of the edifice is 370 feet, and the breadth 276 feet. The dome is 272 feet in height, and more than 75 feet in diameter. The great frontage is composed of a portico with twenty-two fluted Corinthian columns supporting an entablature. The tympan was ornamented by David d'Angers and represents France distributing garlands or laurel wreaths to her sons. The figure of the Patrie is flanked by Liberty and History, and around are Malesherbes, Mirabeau, Carnot, the "Organizer of Victory," Voltaire, Rousseau, Napoleon Bonaparte and other famous men whose writings or deeds deserved record in the Paris Temple of Fame. Behind Bonaparte are an old grenadier of the guard and the drummer boy of Arcola. The words "Aux Grands Hommes La Patrie Reconnaissante," are on the architrave below the pediment. Under the portico are Maindron's marble groups, " St. Geneviève beseeching Attila to spare Paris," and the " Baptism of Louis by St. Remigius." The dome of the Panthéon is topped by a big lantern, and there is a fine view from the summit.

The interior of the Panthéon is imposing, but cold and gloomy in its vastness. The pictures in oils and on canvas, though usually called frescoes, are fastened to, not painted on the walls. The dome is decorated with the frescoes by Gros, representing the Apotheosis of St. Geneviève; around her being Louis XVI., Louis XVIII., and other French kings. The spandrels are painted by Carvallo with allegorical subjects relating to the First Empire. The most interesting feature in the interior is the work of Puvis de Chavannes depicting the life-history of St. Geneviève. According to the admirers of that painter of the vague, the ethereal and the delicate, in landscape, and of the attenuated and even ugly, in figure work, the mural decorations of Puvis de Chavannes are the only paintings which are in their proper place in that framing of stone. One of the ugliest figures on these canvases is that of St. Germain, Bishop of Auxerre, who is giving his blessing to the shepherdess. The scenery is that of Nanterre, outside Paris, and in it the river is visible threading its silvery way towards the sea. Other paintings are the " Death of St. Geneviève," by J. P. Laurens; the scenes from the life of St. Louis, by Alexander Cabanel; the Coronation of Charlemagne, by Lévy; the procession of Geneviève's relics, by Maillot: a picture of the shepherdess saving Paris from famine by Meissonier: scenes from the life of Joan of Arc, by Lenepveu; the great women of France, frescoes by Humbert; Bonnat's " Martyrdom of St. Denis;" the mosaics of Hébert in the apsis, and the " Battle of Tolbiac," by Blanc. In this work the artist has drawn Gambetta, Lockroy, Arago and one of the Coquelins. A considerable number, in fact, of the portraits seen on the walls of the Panthéon are those of modern Parisian celebrities in art politics and literature. The statues in the edifice are those of St. Geneviève, St. Gregory of Tours, St. Bernard, St. Jean de Matha, St. Vincent de Paul, St. Martin; and in time Victor Hugo, Renan and others who, if not saints, were celebrated Frenchmen, will be added to the others.

In the vaults or crypt of the Panthéon are the tombs of Victor Hugo, opposite which is an indifferent statue of Jean-Jacques Rousseau, and another of Voltaire; of Soufflot, architect of the building; of Marshal Lannes; of Lagrange, the scientist; of Bougainville, the navigator; and of functionaries

ST. ÉTIENNE DU MONT.

of the First Empire. Since 1889 there have also been placed in the crypt the remains of Lazare Carnot, the "Organizer of Victory;" of General Marceau; of La Tour d'Auvergne, the "First Grenadier of France;" and of Baudin, the deputy, who was killed at the barricades in December, 1851. The remains of Carnot, Marceau and La Tour d'Auvergne were conveyed to the Panthéon from Germany. Marceau is immortalized in the lines of "Childe Harold,"

> "By Coblentz on a rise of gentle ground
> There is a small and simple pyramid," etc.;

but the stanza is bereft of some of its meaning. The young soldier, whose career was "brief, brave and glorious," and who was killed at Altenkirchen, in 1796, now lies, it is to be hoped, in permanent rest. The body had already been moved in 1819 from its first grave.

The last great interment in the crypt of the Panthéon was that of President Sadi Carnot, who was murdered at Lyons by an Italian anarchist, in June, 1894. The burial was preceded by a solemn service in the Cathedral of Notre Dame.

ST. ÉTIENNE DU MONT, at the back of the Panthéon, is one of the most interesting churches of Paris, from the architectural point of view.[1] Its most important feature is the rood-loft, next to which comes the peculiar triforium or gallery around the nave, supposed to have been constructed after the model of a similar building in the Cathedral of Rouen. It also possesses the tomb, or part of the tomb, of St. Geneviève. King Clovis first founded a church on this site, dedicated to St. Peter and St. Paul. It afterwards became the Church of St. Geneviève, and nothing remains of it, and the abbey attached thereto, but the tower rising from the quadrangle of the Lycée Henri Quatre, close to Saint Étienne du Mont. The devotion to the holy shepherdess increased so much that a large parish grew up around her shrine. The monks of the Abbey, therefore, obtained leave to build a church, or chapel, in addition to their basilica, and the new structure was dedicated to the great martyr, St. Stephen. This was in the beginning of the twelfth century, soon after Notre Dame had replaced the old Church of the same martyr in the Island of the City. As the population on the "mountain," or hill, of St. Geneviève still increased, the church of St. Stephen was found to be as insufficient as the basilica had been before, and

[1] Fergusson, "Hist. Mod. Architecture," describes St. Étienne du Mont as a "Gothic church disguised in the trappings of classical details."

in 1517 the foundations of the existing edifice were laid. Ninety-three years after, Marguerite de Valois, first wife of Henri Quatre, and the chief benefactress of the church which is worthy of her artistic attentions, laid the foundation stone of the principal portal, and the works were only finished in 1624. St. Étienne du Mont was consecrated by Jean-François de Gondy, Archbishop of Paris, in February, 1626. The event is commemorated on a black marble slab in the church, and so, too, is the accident which occurred during the ceremony, two girls of the parish having fallen from the choir galleries without injury to themselves or to any of the congregation.

THE ROOD-LOFT, ST. ÉTIENNE DU MONT

During the course of the eighteenth century the church was subjected, like many other monuments, to restorations which were not always effected with care and taste. An architect of this period, named Hivert, proposed to remove the splendid rood-loft, as had been done at St. Germain l'Auxerrois, but his suggestion was fortunately negatived.

There are few historic associations connected with this church since its foundation. It is the shrine of St. Geneviève, whose old church has long since disappeared, and who has been deprived of the Panthéon by the Republicans. Thither flock thousands of the faithful every January for the

ST. ÉTIENNE DU MONT.

Novena or nine days' devotion, following the fête of the canonized shepherdess of Nanterre. It was in this church that Archbishop Silour was murdered by a mad priest on the 3rd of January 1857, during the progress of the Novena of St. Geneviève. The procession had taken place around the church and was entering the nave, when the Archbishop, who was moving slowly towards the rood-loft, was struck down by his assassin. The prelate died a few minutes after in the drawing-room of the presbytery, having shown only a feeble glimmer of consciousness before he expired.

The exterior of the church is rather heavily ornamented in Renaissance style. Over the chief portal is a bas-relief of the martyrdom of St. Stephen, with the inscription " Lapis templum Domini destruit lapis astruit," alluding to the stoning of St. Stephen, who was a " temple of the Lord," and to the construction with stone of the real edifice. On the right and left are statues of St. Stephen and St. Geneviève. The Resurrection is on the pediment, and on the lintel is another Latin inscription recording the dedication of the church to St. Stephen, the head or chief of the martyrs. This saint is also called the Proto-martyr, or first of those who suffered for the Christian faith, and whose remains were removed, in the reign of the younger Theodosius in the fifth century, from Caphargamala, near Jerusalem; to a church on Mount Sion.[1] Gibbon thus relates the miracle of the discovery of St. Stephen's body: " In the reign of the younger Theodosius Lucian, a presbyter of Jerusalem, and the ecclesiastical minister of the village of Caphargamala, about twenty miles from the city, related a very singular dream which, to remove his doubt, had been repeated on three successive Saturdays. A venerable figure stood before him, in the silence of the night, with a long beard, a white robe, and a gold rod ; announced himself by the name of Gamaliel, and revealed to the astonished presbyter, that his own corpse, with the bodies of his son Abibas, his friend Nicodemus, and the illustrious Stephen, the first martyr of the Christian faith, were secretly buried in the adjacent field. . . . The ground was opened by the bishop, in the presence of an innumerable multitude. The coffins of Gamaliel, of his son, and of his friend, were found in regular order, but when the fourth coffin, which contained the remains of Stephen, was shown to the light the earth trembled, and an odour, such as that of paradise, was smelt, which instantly cured the various diseases of seventy-three of the assistants. The companions of Stephen were left in their peaceful residence of Caphargamala : but the relics of the first martyr were transported, in solemn

[1] Gibbon, " Decline and Fall," Chapter XXVIII.

procession, to a church constructed in their honour on Mount Sion; and the minute particles of those relics, a drop of blood, or the scrapings of a bone, were acknowledged, in almost every province of the Roman world, to possess a divine and miraculous virtue." This quotation would, of course, be a comfort to the pious Catholics who believe firmly in miracles and the efficacy of saintly relics, if the historian had not, in the succeeding sentences, cast slurs on the statements in St. Augustine's great work "De Civitate Dei," and sneered away miracles with Hume. In spite of the historians and philosophers, however, saints continue to be venerated, and miracles believed in. St. Stephen, in particular, has been fortunate in the perpetuation of his memory. Two gorgeous churches, one in Vienna,[1] the other in Paris, record the triumph of his faith over the pains of violent death.

In the interesting interior of St. Étienne du Mont, with its nave, two aisles, triforium, pendant keystones, high vaulting, organ loft, round arches, old stained glass, and rood-loft, the lover of the antique finds much to admire. There is, in fact, no church in Paris which arrests the attention so much or fascinates to so great an extent by the artistic originality of its interior. It is one of the curiosities, and one of the best monumental or old-time treasures of Paris, and all who love the antique must hope that the church will always escape the ravages of war, time, and revolution. The architectural curiosity of the church is the triforium, or gallery, supported by round pillars with round arches between them. Over this elevated platform or aerial passage, called also *tournée* as well as triforium, in this case, there is another row of round pillars and arches. On the sides of the passage facing the altar and nave, *tourelles* or round projections like bay windows, facilitate circulation. The clerestory windows are very high and contain some of the old glass. The jubé or rood-loft attracts as much attention as the peculiar passage over the aisles. It is the work of the elder Biart, a seventeenth-century sculptor (1600), and is splendidly carved and embossed with foliage, palms, garlands, corbels, modillons, or brackets, buds, thuribles or incense-censers and figures. The word jubé, used in French for roodloft or screen, is from the Latin "jubere," to order. At high mass the deacon, after the gradual, asks the blessing of the celebrant according to the formula, "Jube Domine benedicere," and then reads the gospel. The "jubé" was therefore used to designate the elevated place where the gospel was sung. The ascent to the loft is by two handsome spiral staircases, and

[1] In the Vienna Cathedral there is a high altar of black marble, on which is a representation of the stoning of St. Stephen the proto-martyr.

two large doors at either side of the towering crucifix placed in the centre of the screen, make the latter extend across the whole width of the church. These doors, or the spaces near them, are inscribed with the words " Ascende qui evangelizas Sion," " Audiam quid loquatur Dominus meus," " Ascend thou who evangelizest Sion," " I shall hear what my Lord God says." These words are on the right side, and on the other are. " Quam dulcia faucibus meis eloquia tua," and " Levavi manus meas ad mandata tua." " How sweet are thy words to my taste,"[1] and " I have uplifted my hands towards thy commandments." These words are supposed to be uttered by the youths whose figures are sculptured on the doors. The pulpit is another curiosity, and the sculpture shows Samson on a lion, the strong man of the Jews supporting the construction. Other figures are those of the Evangelists, the Doctors of the church, St. Stephen, the theological and cardinal virtues, Jesus, and on the summit an angel, a trumpet in one hand, and a gospel in the other. The angel is supposed to repeat the words " In omnem terram exivit sonus eorum," " Their voice went forth to every land."

In one of the lateral chapels, that of Purgatory, or the Virgin's Death, as represented by a picture, there are lists of the names of persons buried in the church, such as Pascal, the famous author of the " Pensées," Racine, poet, dramatist, and historian of the Abbey of Port Royal, famous for its Jansenism, Jean Benigne Winslow, an anatomist, converted by Bossuet, Antoine Lemaistre and Lemaistre de Lacy, who had been buried at Port Royal, Rollin, Rector of the Paris University, and half a dozen other men of minor celebrity. In another chapel, that of the Crucifix, is seen a fine glass painting by Pinaigrier (1568). It represents the wedding feast, with the unready guests. Above is the Deity and underneath the inscription, " Many are called, but few are chosen," " Multi vocati, pauci electi," with the coat of arms of Madame de Viole, a benefactress of the church. Next to this is a holy sepulchre, with quaint figures, and farther up, the oratory of St. Bernard, where there is a portrait of the saint by Latil, as well as a notable picture

---

[1] The Hebrew and Catholic version is " palate." The phrases are translated without reference to either Catholic or Protestant versions of the scriptures.

HISTORIC CHURCHES OF PARIS.

of the Last Judgment, dating from 1605. Close to the screen is the chapel of St. Charles Borromeo, the Archbishop of Milan, with a painting by Varin, whose disciple, Poussin, is better known. Racine and Pascal, whose names are recorded in another place, have their epitaphs in the chapel of the Sacré Cœur, their remains being buried behind the choir. In this chapel there is also a good picture by an artist of Le Brun's school. The chapel of the Virgin is flanked by two columns from the old Basilica, but otherwise it is uninteresting.

The finest stained glass is in or near the apsis, notably the St. Stephen's window with scenes from the martyr's life; the Virgin's window, over St. Vincent de Paul's chapel; the St. Claude's window and the Pentecost window near the screen. The latter is attributed to Henriet, and most of the others to Enguerrand le Prince, whose work has been supplemented in the church by M. Filon, a modern painter. Magnificent, too, is the Apocalypse window, which was unluckily damaged by the shells of the Communists in 1871. Above is the Lamb before the throne, with angels, elders, and kings, and, beneath, the donor's family. The window was the gift of Le Juge, a rich publican, who was a churchwarden in 1614. The high windows have on them subjects from the life of Christ, the five in the apsis being the oldest. We see on them the apparitions of Christ to the disciples at Emmaus, to Magdalen, to his mother, to St. Peter and St. John. In the Chapelle des Cathéchismes are windows on which is pictured the history of the Eucharist. One of these records the miracle which happened in 1291 in the Rue des Billettes, where the holy sacrament having been stabbed by a Jew, blood issued from it. Another of the windows displays the mystic " Wine Press." In the centre Christ is seen under the press, blood issuing from His body. Around are angels, apostles, and patriarchs, who collect the sacred liquid. The composition is by Pinaigrier, and the window, like that of the Apocalypse, was given to the church by the publican or wine merchant Le Juge, already referred to.[1]

The " Tomb " of St. Geneviève is, for pious Catholics, the great, the unique, treasure of the church of St. Étienne du Mont. According to the Abbé Perdreau, curé of the parish, and also to the official record of the *Moniteur*, of the 24th November, 1793, all the body of the holy shepherdess was not burned on the Place de Grève by the Revolutionists. Some bones had previously been distributed to different churches and monasteries, and

---

[1] This is stated by the Abbé Perdreau in his work on the church of St. Étienne du Mont, from which the above details are taken.

ST. ÉTIENNE DU MONT.

fragments of the relics, including a lock of the saint's hair, are now in three reliquaries at the foot of the statue of the Patroness of Paris, in St. Étienne du Mont. The whole is surrounded by ornamental ironwork, and is an object of the veneration of the faithful during the devotions every year in honour of St. Geneviève. The entire chapel, as well as the tomb, is elaborately ornamented, and the windows record the life of the saint. In front of the altar, in the chapel, is a monument, containing the heart of Monseigneur Sibour, who was murdered in St. Étienne du Mont. The flamboyant Gothic decoration of the tomb and its surroundings was begun by the Abbé de Voisins in 1802. It was carried to completion by the Abbé de Borie, curé of the church in 1853, and who was aided by the plans and suggestions of Père Martin, of the Company of Jesus. Before leaving this church a word must be said about the peculiar leaning of its choir and altar towards the right. This slant is peculiar to many Gothic churches, and by some is attributed to the desire of the early architects to symbolize the position of Christ at the moment of His death on the Cross, " And He bowed His head and gave up the ghost."[1]

[1] St. John xix.

St. Sulpice.

CHAPTER XI.

ST. SULPICE—ST. JULIEN LE PAUVRE— ST. SÉVERIN.

St. Sulpice and its district—The "Temple of Victory," the Banquet to Bonaparte—The "Clarionet" towers—The seminary of St. Sulpice—Ernest Renan's connection with the church and the college—The Sulpicians: Servandoni's façade—The work of Eugène Delacroix—The meridian line—The shells—St. Julien le Pauvre and its pictured screen—A terrible district—St. Séverin—The stained glass—The daughter of Herodias dancing—Historical operation on a criminal.

JEAN II.

THE churches of St. Sulpice, of St. Julien le Pauvre and of St. Séverin, although of different interest and dates, may be taken after the Panthéon and St. Étienne du Mont, as they are in the vicinity of these buildings. None of these churches are remarkable from the historic point of view, with the exception, perhaps, of St. Julien le Pauvre, which was once closely connected with the University of Paris. St. Sulpice was begun in 1646, the foundation-stone being laid by Anne of Austria, widow of Louis XIII., during the minority of her son who was to be known as the Grand Monarque.[1] The parish was noted as the most wealthy in Paris before the great Revolution. It is so still, to a certain extent. It stands in the midst of the academical quarter of Paris, near the schools of theology, law, medicine, and military and civil engineering.

Around it are grouped the shops or stores which may be said to supply the world with church furniture and ornaments of every kind from imitation Calvaries, big crucifixes, altars and confessionals to flower vases, paschal candles and ex-voto tapers. From these marts, too, are sent out daily, heaps of ecclesiastical vestments, breviaries, rosaries, prayer-books, scapulars, medals and religious pictures. In St. Sulpice take place many of the "ordinations" as priests, of the students from the contiguous theological college founded and controlled by the members of the Sulpician order. The festival of St. Fiacre, patron of gardeners, is also celebrated there with great pomp.

During the Convention the great, wealthy church of the "Rive Gauche," was temporarily transformed into a temple of victory. The Revolutionists held it, or rather the Theophilanthropists or Deists founded by La Réveillère-Lepeaux, one of the five members of the Directory, and from

[1] This church is also under the patronage of St. Peter.

HISTORIC CHURCHES OF PARIS.

whom it received its new title. On the 5th of November, 1799, a grand banquet was given in the church to General Bonaparte, fresh from his victories in Egypt. Only a few days after that event, on the eighteenth Brumaire, Bonaparte profiting by the weakness and the unpopularity of the Directory, at the head of which were La Réveillère-Lepaux, Letourneur, Barras, Rewbell and Carnot, caused his grenadiers to disperse the Council of the Five Hundred, destroyed the constitution of the year III., and made himself master of France.

The saint to whom the church is dedicated is little known and there are conflicting testimonies concerning him. There were two saints of the name, first Sulpicius Severus, the "Christian Sallust," who wrote some valuable works, including the life of St. Martin of Tours. This ecclesiastic, who was at first a lawyer, is not in the Roman Martyrology, but there is an "office" or service in his honour in the breviary of the Tours diocese. Alban Butler, in his "Lives of the Saints," calls him Saint Sulpicius Severus. The other Sulpicius, to whom the church now under consideration is dedicated, was Bishop of Bourges in the seventh century.

Victor Hugo compared the two enormous towers of St. Sulpice to "big clarionets." The poet is not, naturally, accepted by Catholics as an authority in matters of any kind appertaining to their Church. It is true that the Comte de Montalembert, the great champion of Catholicism whose mantle has nowadays descended on the Comte de Mun, regarded the romance "Notre Dame de Paris" as a splendid attack on the Vandals who desecrated the works, of the middle ages by their injudicious restorations. The author of the "Monks of the West" wrote, in fact, a letter to Victor Hugo on the subject, but, as M. Douhaire points out in an article on the Renaissance of Christian Art in the *Correspondant* of April, 1872, it is doubtful if Victor Hugo saw anything in the art of the middle ages except a new literary mine to be exploited. The same writer doubts if the poet had seized and penetrated the Mediæval spirit, but this is going too far. A man of Victor Hugo's poetic temperament could not have treated Gothic art in an artificial manner. But be all this as it may, the author of "Notre Dame de Paris" wrote what was true when he called the Panthéon a bad imitation of St. Peter's, and compared the towers of St. Sulpice to "big clarionets." The exterior of the church, which is neither Gothic nor mediæval, for it was commenced in 1646 and only finished, with the exception of the south tower, about 1777,[1] is very

[1] Another date is 1749, but it was in 1774 that the architect Chalgrin finished his alterations in the north tower.

ST. SULPICE.

fine, so far as imposing bulk is concerned. St. Sulpice looks an enormous building viewed from any part of Paris as well as from the fine square which extends in front of it. This is flanked on the right side, as one enters the church, by the monastic-looking college or seminary wherein the Sulpicians train young men for the priesthood, and where Ernest Renan studied before he took the step which led to his permanent separation from the religion of his forefathers. The Sulpician order was specially founded for the education of secular priests by Jean-Jacques Olier, usually called M. Olier, who was curé of St. Sulpice Church in the reign of Louis XIII. This ecclesiastic refused a bishopric in order to be able to continue his work. The first Napoleon greatly admired the Sulpician priests, but their method of education and rigid discipline have evoked the censure of Taine and other writers. Renan has fully explained his connection with the great seminary in his "Souvenirs de Jeunesse," and has left on record a description of his departure from the gloomy walls of the big building which forms one side of the Place St. Sulpice.[1] Before his final renunciation, the author of the "Vie de Jésus" had often assumed the surplice and taken part in the gorgeous ceremonies for which the church of St. Sulpice is famous. Little did the priests or the fellow-students among whom the young theologian then prayed, think that he was afterwards destined to assail the most precious traditions of Christianity in nearly as formidable a manner as Von Döllinger of Munich assailed its history. Renan and the Bavarian canon effected between them a terrible work. They may have been like those who, as Tennyson sings, seem to have "reached a purer air," but they were undoubtedly responsible for having confused with more than "shadow'd hint," many a life that led "melodious days."[2] By his great renunciation, Renan, in addition to his celebrity as a writer, gained the peculiar privilege of having a permanent place kept for him at the table of one of the members of the Rothschild family.[3]

Our business, lies, however, not with the seminary of St. Sulpice and its memories of Renan, but with the big church near which it stands. The façade of St. Sulpice is, according to Fergusson,[4] one of the grandest in Europe. It was the work of Servandoni, and consists of a large Doric and Ionic colonnade superimposed. The north tower, which

---

[1] The existing seminary was built in 1820. It has been compared to a barrack or hospital, as well as to a monastery.
[2] "In Memoriam," XXXIII.
[3] This is related in the diary or "journal" of Edmond de Goncourt.
[4] History of Modern Architecture, London, J. Murray.

is finished, is slightly higher than the similar construction on the cathedral of Notre Dame. The southern tower is unfinished, the work undertaken by Chalgrin having been brought to a full stop by the great Revolution. The interior of the church is also very stately and imposing with its eighteen side chapels. Of it, however, Fergusson remarks, that " it presents the defects inherent in Palladian churches where an Order of Architecture designed for external purposes is used on the scale, and with the simplicity which suits a large area exposed to the atmosphere, but which becomes offensively rude when applied to internal decoration in a building which not only pretends to, but demands elegance and richness of effect." He adds that the absence of a dome prevents one part of the building from overpowering the rest either by its height or its extent, and the interior consequently looks larger and is more harmonious than is usual in churches of this class. The unpictured windows give the church a Jansenist and almost Protestant aspect. Few of the mural paintings are worth more than a passing glance. The most notable are those in the first chapel of the right aisle, "Heliodorus expelled from the temple and beaten," "Jacob wrestling with the angel," and on the vaulting, "St. Michael," all by Eugène Delacroix, the great Romanticist of 1830, the "Shakespeare of painting," some of whose best work is in this very chapel of the angels, in St. Sulpice.[1] The other artists represented at St. Sulpice are Vanloo, Hein, Abel de Pujol, Lafon, Hesse, Drolling and others. The fresco of the Assumption, by Lemoine (1737), on the dome of the Virgin's chapel behind the high altar, is also noteworthy, as well as the statue of Mary, by Pajou. On the pavement of the transept is a meridian line traced in brass or copper, with the signs of the Zodiac. The direction due north is shown by a marble obelisk, and on the south is an opening in the transept window through which, on fine days, the sun strikes at noon, on the line, or the obelisk, according to the season. The meridian was traced between 1723 and 1748 by H. Sully and Lemonnier, to indicate the vernal equinox and Easter Sunday. Among the other principal features of this majestic church are the organ, built first by Cliquot and reconstructed by Cavaillé-Coll in 1861, and the holy water fonts, which are two big shells on rock-work designed

---

[1] Other works by Eugène Delacroix (1799—1863) are in the Chamber of Deputies, the Luxembourg and the Apollo Gallery of the Louvre. This painter had narrow escapes in his youth. Once his cradle was burned, on another occasion he swallowed some verdigris, twice he was nearly choked, and he fell into a dock at Marseilles, narrowly escaping a watery grave, from which he was saved by a sailor.

ST. JULIEN LE PAUVRE.

by Pigalle. The shells were given to Francis I., by his allies the Venetians. On the square outside the Church is a fountain on which are statues of Bossuet, Fénelon, Massillon and Fléchier, the great ecclesiastical writers and preachers of the eighteenth century. These ornamental basins, designed by Visconti, serve to accentuate the thoroughly ecclesiastical character of the whole neighbourhood wherein the few inevitable wine taverns and tobacco shops seem out of harmony with their clerical environment. Even the very hotels and lodging-houses of the district are called after famous ecclesiastics, and the majority of the shops with their profusion of altar-pieces and general church ornaments look like small, exterior chapels of the colossal edifice which towers over them and comparatively dwarfs them by its imposing size.

The old church of SAINT JULIEN LE PAUVRE is in the heart of the genuine historic Latin quarter, near the fountain of St. Michael and not far from Notre Dame. There are numerous St. Julians, but it is generally admitted, from the testimony of St. Gregory, of Tours, that the martyr was the first patron of the church and subsequently St. Julian of Mans. Around the edifice are the haunts of some of the most notorious rascals in Paris, but of late years this neighbourhood has been pierced with new streets which have done a good deal to alter the reputation of the district. Some of the old historic streets, like Dante's "Vico degli Strami," or the Rue du Fouarre, still exist, but have nothing academic in their aspect or environment nowadays.

The existing church of St. Julien le Pauvre dates from 1170 or thereabouts, and was attached to the old hospital or Hôtel Dieu. It was also closely connected with the University of Paris. The church is a blending of early French and Romanesque, which was the order of architecture prevailing before the Gothic replaced it throughout the more northern and western parts of France. The arches in the nave are round-headed, those in the choir being pointed. The church is small, but very interesting to the archæologist owing to the specimens which it still possesses of the fanciful work of the mediæval sculptors, notably on the capitals. There is a curious monument in the church to Maistre Henri Rousseau, an "Advocate in Parliament," who died in 1445, and a statue to Antoine de Montyon, founder of the Academical "Prix de Vertu," stands in the left aisle. The edifice is in a very dilapidated condition, without a tower or a porch. The entrance is through a back yard in the Rue St. Julien le Pauvre, off the Rue Galande, the main thoroughfare of a district which has much in common with the Seven Dials, of old, or the labyrinths of Whitechapel. The walls are crumbling, and the interior of the church is like that of a poor, out-of-the-way, roadside chapel-of-ease in the depths of the country. There is some brightness, however, communicated by the pictured screen drawn across the chancel, after the manner of Greek churches. St. Julian's has, in fact, been handed over to the Greek Catholics of Paris and is administered by an Archimandrite, Monsignor Ignatius Homsy, who is also director of a college for the training of young men intended to act as missionaries in the East.

Antiquity has also left its traces on the adjacent church of ST. SÉVERIN.

ST. SÉVERIN.

ST. SÉVERIN.

This handsome edifice, with its tower, spire and sculptured portal, was begun towards the end of the eleventh century, was reconstructed in the sixteenth, and enlarged in the eighteenth. The architecture is of the late Gothic order. Inside the church, the gloom is greatly relieved by the fine stained glass windows, some dating from the fifteenth and the sixteenth centuries, others being modern. On the right side of the nave is pictured the decapitation of St. John the Baptist. There is a realistic picture of the daughter of Herodias in the dancing dress wherein she appeared before the King. In her hand she has the "charger" containing the Baptist's head, around being the "lords, high captains, and chief estates of Galilee."[1] The scene is striking, but one is rather surprised to find so theatrical a figure as that of Salomé in the holy place. The artist has arranged her drapery in a manner calculated to arouse other thoughts than those of devotion in the minds of worshippers. The figure is more fitted for the interior of the opera house than for that of an edifice the very existence of which is a protest against the ensnaring pleasures of the world.

The church is dedicated to a recluse who died in a Paris garret and was buried in the oratory of St. Clement, which, in the sixth century, occupied the site of St. Séverin's. The death of the holy Solitary is pictured on one of the windows near the choir. Other interesting features in the edifice are the arches and vaulting, and the mural paintings by the two Flandrins, Hippolyte and Paul, by Heim, Hesse, Gérôme, Lenoir and others. One is surprised to see so much art lavished on a church in a poor neighbourhood, but it must be remembered that some of the best monuments and treasures of antiquity in Paris are to be found, not in the monotonous and ultra-fashionable Champs-Elysées, but in dilapidated, and sometimes disreputable districts. Fashion, as a rule, does not care for antiquity, so it gathers up its train and hastens away from its neighbourhood.

The first organ ever heard in Paris was that of St. Séverin. On the southern side of the church there is part of an old cloister, and in the garden of the presbytery, formerly a cemetery, the operation for stone was first performed in Paris. That was in the year 1374, the person operated upon being a thief who had been condemned to death. Having survived the operation, the man was pardoned.

[1] St. Mark vi. The Catholic version is "princes and tribunes, and chief men of Galilee."

Val-de-Grâce

CHAPTER XII.

THE SORBONNE—THE VAL-DE-GRÂCE—ST. LOUIS
DES INVALIDES—ST. FRANCIS XAVIER'S—THE
CHURCH OF ST. JOSEPH DES CARMES—ST. THO-
MAS D'AQUIN—ST. LOUIS EN L'ILE—ST. JACQUES
DU HAUT PAS—ST. MÉDARD'S—ST. NICOLAS DU
CHARDONNET.

Richelieu's tomb—Stealing the Cardinal's head—Opening of the tomb in 1895—Mignard's frescoes in the Val-de-Grâce—St. Louis des Invalides. The Hôtel des Invalides—The Sombreuil family—The cup of blood—Napoleon's tomb and funeral—The church of St. Francis Xavier—The church of St. Joseph des Carmes—The massacre of the priests—The spots of blood—The crypt Joséphine de Beauharnais in the prison of the Carmelites-St. Thomas d'Aquin—St. Médard's.

AFTER the lapse of several centuries the church of the Sorbonne is now nearly all that remains of the old scholastic buildings erected by the munificence of Cardinal Richelieu between 1635 and 1659. These constructions, which were intended for the Theological Faculty of the Paris University, were not finished at the time of the Cardinal's death. The expenses of the restoration were borne by Richelieu, who had a predilection for the famous institution, founded by Canon Robert de Sorbon, in the thirteenth century, for poor students, who, until then, had been obliged to beg, in order to obtain food and lodging. Later on the institution of poor scholars developed into the headquarters of scholastic theology, and Richelieu, among other notable men, studied there. Napoleon the First united the University and the Sorbonne, and in the new buildings erected since 1885, but not yet quite finished in parts, literature and science, as well as theology, are represented. The institution is also true to its old traditions, for lectures are given there gratuitously between December and July, and the merest man in the street is at liberty to attend them.

Richelieu's tomb is the main feature of interest in this church which has been called a "little St. Peter's." The Cardinal Minister of Louis XIII., who died in 1642, after an agitated and eventful life, during which he strengthened the French army, routed foreign foes and virtually ruled France, was interred near the place where he had studied in youth. Sismondi, in his history of the French people, condemns Richelieu as the founder of despotism in France. It was this powerful minister and ecclesiastic who, when told that the poor should be allowed to live, as well as other people, said that he did not see the necessity. At the approach of death, however, he is said to have asked God to condemn him, if he had any other motive at heart, in ruling with a rod of iron, save the welfare of his religion and his country. His tomb was the work of Girardon, from Lebrun's design. The Cardinal, in his ecclesiastical robes, is half raised from his recumbent attitude and looks heavenward. He is supported by Religion, and there is a weeping female figure at his feet. The monument is considered theatrical, but the composition is fine. The memorial extends nearly the whole length of the chapel in which it is placed.

During the great Revolution the tomb was opened under circumstances

THE TOMB OF RICHELIEU.

of a peculiar character. In December, 1793, the Revolutionists decreed that the monuments in the Sorbonne should be demolished, or, as the phrase is, "profaned." While the workmen engaged in opening the tombs were at breakfast one morning, a bonnet-maker, named Cheval, entered the Sorbonne church, and approaching the opened tomb of Richelieu, stole the Cardinal's head and a fragment of the coffin. The tradesman soon after gave up the ghastly relics to a priest, the Abbé Armez, who, in his turn, transferred the head to his brother, a country mayor. In the meantime, the body of Richelieu was flung to the winds by the Revolutionists. The

THE SORBONNE.

head was subsequently re-interred in or under the Sorbonne monument, the Armez family having given it to the government. There was a ceremony on the occasion of the re-interment of the head in 1866, when M. Duruy, Imperial Minister of Public Instruction, Archbishop Darboy, and the Dean of the Sorbonne were present. The funeral oration of Richelieu was preached by Monseigneur Perraud, Bishop of Autun, who was afterwards to be a member of the French Academy.

This is the usual version of the recovery of Cardinal Richelieu's head. The statements of the Armez family were accepted, but they have frequently been challenged. A writer in the *Temps* of Thursday, the 5th of September, 1895, referring to the opening of Richelieu's tomb in the presence of the architect of the Sorbonne, M. Nénot, and of M. Hanotaux, Minister for Foreign Affairs in the year mentioned, who is the historian of the Cardinal, and others, stated that the head and body of the great statesman were then seen in the coffin. The spectators of this gruesome scene were deeply moved, and at the same time surprised at the excellent state of preservation of the Cardinal's head and face, which were exactly as Philip de Champaigne had painted them in his portraits now in the British National Gallery. One of those who were privileged to witness the unsealing of the tomb with M. Hanotaux told the writer in the *Temps* that the head emerged from a lace or ruffled collar much browned, that the moustache and beard were perfect, and that the tuft of hair on the Cardinal's chin was cut square. · This was explained by M. Hanotaux on the following ground. In his last illness Richelieu was much inconvenienced by the drops of the syrups and tisans which he had to drink falling on his *barbiche*, or small peaked beard. He accordingly told his attendants to shorten the *barbiche*, so they cut it square with a scissors.

This story of "Richelieu Redivivus," as the narrator terms it, is worthy of all respect. It appears in a serious newspaper over the *nom de guerre* of "Candide," which is supposed to be the name by which M. Jules Claretie, academician and manager of the Comédie Française, veils his return to the columns of the same journal wherein of old appeared his weekly articles on "La Vie à Paris."[1] On the other hand, an equally estimable writer, M. Georges Montorgueil, controverted "Candide" in the columns of *L'Eclair*, so that the dispute about the real contents of Richelieu's tomb in the church of the Sorbonne still remains unsettled. There is still another account of the peregrinations of Richelieu's head, and according to which it was sawed

[1] M. Claretie now contributes regularly to the *Temps* in his own name.

HISTORIC CHURCHES OF PARIS.

in two by the person who stole it. Archæologists and scholars generally cannot fail to be disappointed owing to these contending and contradictory opinions and statements. As in the case of the Royal tombs at St. Denis, for instance, such vandalism has to be borne with, and regret must be expressed that there have been Frenchmen, Revolutionists, Royalists and Imperialists, so deficient in appreciation of the great past of their country as to deface or destroy monuments and tombs invested with deep historical interest.

There is little else to say of the small church of the Sorbonne. Its architecture, as has been remarked, is imitative of that of St. Peter's of Rome, with some of the improvements in the style introduced by the school of Andrea Palladio of Vicenza, the last great architect of the Renaissance. The pictures in the church are Timbal's "History of Theology," in which saints and doctors such as Bernard, Bonaventure and Thomas Aquinas are seen, and Hesse's "Presentation of Students to St. Louis by Robert de Sorbon." The spandrels of the dome were done by Philippe de Champaigne, the Belgian artist, who painted religious subjects for Marie de' Medici, Richelieu and Louis XIII. Timbal, who died in 1880, was of the school of Drolling and Signol.

Another notable church in the same neighbourhood, is that of the VAL-DE-GRÂCE, at the southern end of the Rue Saint Jacques, near the Boulevard de Port Royal. The abbey, now a great military hospital for the Paris garrison, was formerly a convent for Benedictine nuns. It was founded, together with the church, by Anne of Austria, in thanksgiving for the birth of her son, soon to be Louis Quatorze, at St. Germain-en-Laye in September, 1638. Seven years after, the child, already ruler of France, under the regency of his mother and the direction of Cardinal Mazarin, laid the foundation stone of the Val-de-Grâce. Mansard was the architect, and his plans were carried to completion by Lemercier, Lemuet, Leduc and Duval. The dome is imitated from that of St. Peter's, and the whole effect of the building is fine, although a good deal of fault has been found with it, chiefly on the ground that the aim of the designer was out of proportion with the means at his command, or the object for which he was building. His church was to be far smaller than the great Roman Basilica, but he insisted on using the plan of St. Peter's for a building of minor dimensions. At the time, however, Italian art and architecture were in fashion, and everything mediæval was regarded as barbarous and obsolete. In the interior

VAL-DE-GRÂCE.

of the church there is a baldachino like that over the high altar and the tomb of St. Peter at Rome. The ceiling is coffered, and on the dome is a faded fresco by Pierre Mignard, called the Roman, to distinguish him from the less celebrated Nicholas Mignard, of Avignon, his brother. Molière, in his poem, "La Gloire du dôme du Val-de-Grâce," lauds this painter to the skies:—

> "Toi qui dans cette coupe, à ton vast génie,
> Comme un ample théâtre heureusement fournie,
> Es venu deployer les précieux trésors,
> Que le Tibre t'a vu ramasser sur ses bords."

The comic dramatist cannot find anything better than an "amply-furnished theatre," by way of comparison with the church. In spite of Molière's extravagant praise which led him to call Raphael and Michael Angelo the Mignards of their century, the once popular painter of the Val-de-Grâce frescoes, of the "Ecce Homo," the portrait of Madame de Maintenon and of many other celebrities of his epoch, has now lapsed into oblivion. It was in this church that Bossuet made a great funeral oration over the coffin of Queen Henrietta, third daughter of Henri Quatre, and wife of Charles I. of England. The modern military character of the Val-de-Grâce is testified to the visitor before entering the church by the bronze statue of the famous Surgeon-General of the first Napoleon's "Grand Army," Baron Larrey, who died in 1842.

The most important church on the left bank of the River Seine is undoubtedly that of ST. LOUIS DES INVALIDES. It is a notable landmark of visitors owing to its connection with the tomb of Napoleon and the Hôtel des Invalides. It may, therefore, be appropriate to give a brief account of the whole cluster of buildings, which correspond to Chelsea Hospital. Many kings of France had thought of erecting a refuge for dilapidated old soldiers, but it was Louis XIV. who first took any practical measures for the protection and shelter in their old age of the men who had lost limbs, or passed the best of their lives in the service of the country. There are statements to the effect that Louis was much moved by the fact that many disbanded warriors not only begged, but robbed people on the highways. In any case the old pensioners were in a sad plight, and in 1670 a royal edict appeared ordering the foundation of the Hôtel des Invalides. It was finished after Bruand's designs in 1674, and the place was opened by Louis Quatorze himself, who arrived there in a carriage drawn by eight white horses, and followed by a large retinue, among the persons taking part in the royal procession being two old soldiers who had fought at Arques and at Ivry. The garden front of the hospital is garnished, if not defended, by some pieces of historic cannon forming what is called a "Triumphal Battery." These comprise Austrian, German, Dutch, Venetian and Russian guns, and near them is a statue of Prince Eugène de Beauharnais. In the internal part of the building are the principal curiosities of the place—the Artillery Museum and the dome over the ashes of Napoleon. Before dealing with the church, it may be worth mentioning incidentally, that the battery was drawn upon as well as the artillery museum in July, 1789, by the Revolutionists, who wanted guns to demolish the Bastille. Penvern, curé of St. Etienne du Mont, at the head of his parishioners, joined the rabble in clamouring for arms at the Hôtel des Invalides. Under the first Republic the place was called the "Temple of Humanity," and also the "Temple of Mars." The Lion of St. Mark, taken from Venice by Napoleon, once stood on the Esplanade in front of the great military refuge, but the Austrians recovered the monument in 1815.

The church of St. Louis, which, with the dome, forms the "Eglise des Invalides," is approached from the southern side of the imposing "Court of Honour." It is here that the old pensioners attend mass on Sundays, and as they pray, they see around them many memorials of battle. The pillars of the church are inscribed with the names, on tablets, of many notable French warriors, and overhead hang the flags captured in war, among them being a Union Jack. Some of the old trophies of victory in the church dated from the time of Francis I., but with the flags taken by Napoleon's Grand Army, and the others sent to the place by Louis XIV. and his successors, they were burned in 1814, before the entry of the allied forces into Paris. The pensioners had previously signified their intention of dying in defence of the Imperial standards and trophies, but the governor of the Invalides persuaded them to burn the tattered memorials of war in the Court of Honour. In the reign of Louis Philippe the flag collection was re-organized, and the Senate sent to the Invalides the trophies of the Grand Army which it possessed. The church has monuments to Marshal Moncey, the Duke of Conegliano, to Oudinot, Duke of Reggio, to Jourdan, Duke of Padua, and also to several governors of the Invalides. In the vaults are buried Turenne, removed from St. Denis, Jourdan, Moncey, Oudinot, Duroc and Bertrand, the faithful henchmen of the first Napoleon, Mortier, Grouchy, Bugeaud, Sebastiani, Exelmans, as well as later heroes

The Invalides—
Interior.

To face p. 150.

THE INVALIDES.

like St. Arnaud, of Crimean fame, and MacMahon. There are also in the place the hearts of Vauban, Kléber, General Négrier, and Mademoiselle de Sombreuil, daughter of the Governor of the Invalides, who, in August, 1792, was arrested for having taken part in the defence of the Tuileries against the people. There was a story to the effect that the Revolutionists made Mademoiselle de Sombreuil, who followed her father to prison, drink a cup of blood. This is, however, now disbelieved. Father and daughter were acquitted by Maillard and his associates, but they were afterwards re-arrested with the younger son of M. de Sombreuil. The Governor of the Invalides and his son were guillotined among the fifty-four persons who perished in the "fournée," or "batch" of the 17th of June, 1794. Among these were Montmorency-Laval, De Rohan-Rochefort, Madame de Saint Amaranthe with her son and daughter, as well as the faithful servitors of the doomed aristocrats, the actress Granmaison, and the little dressmaker Nicolle, who was barely sixteen years old. The elder son of De Sombreuil was shot as an emigrant by a military tribunal of the First Republic, and Mademoiselle de Sombreuil, whose heart is in the Invalides, languished in want, and, as Carlyle says, "hid her woes from history." The father, with the others who perished at the same time by the perfected guillotine of "improved velocity," was buried in the cemetery of Picpus, called the "Cimetière des Guillotinés." Through the pale-blue window over the altar of the church the dome or tomb of Napoleon is dimly seen.

This building is also approached from the Place Vauban, on which is, indeed, the public entrance. Here are chapels containing the tombs of Turenne and Vauban, whose remains are in the vaults, of Joseph Napoleon I. and Jerome Napoleon I.[1] Two of the chapels are empty. The tomb of Napoleon is circular and was designed by Visconti. The body of the Emperor was transferred hither from St. Helena in 1840, and Thackeray has left us a notable description of the whole affair in his "Miscellanies." The preliminaries of the transfer were arranged between Guizot, Louis Philippe's Minister, and Lord Palmerston. The English Government gave orders that the body should be disinterred when the French ships arrived at St. Helena, and that "every respect and attention should be paid to those who came to carry back to their country the body of the famous dead warrior and Sovereign." Then there was a debate in the French Chamber as to where the body should be buried when it reached home. Some

[1] These temporary monarchs were also known as Joseph Bonaparte, King of Naples and then of Spain, and Jerome Bonaparte, King of Westphalia.

suggested the Place Vendôme where stands the bronze column, an imitation of that of Trajan in Rome, and erected as a memorial of Napoleon's victories over the Russians and Austrians in 1805.[1] At last it was resolved that the remains of the conqueror who had filled the world with his fame should be placed under the gilded dome of the Invalides. The expedition to St. Helena was commanded by the Prince de Joinville. The disinterment was effected by the English, the French officers, with the exception of the Prince de Joinville, being present. The body was in a good state of preservation. "The features of the face, though changed, were perfectly recognized, and," as Doctor Guillard wrote in his account of the exhumation, "the hands left nothing to be desired (les mains ne laissaient rien à désirer: nulle part la plus légère altération)." The same authority states that Napoleon's toe-nails had burst through his boots, that his beard had grown after death, and that all his medals and decorations had become black, with the exception of the gold crown of the Cross of the Legion of Honour.

The body was transferred to the *Belle Poule* frigate, the English authorities of the island attending. These were General Middlemore and Colonel Trelawney, the latter commanding the artillerymen who escorted the funeral car. General Churchill, chief of the staff in India, was also present, having come expressly from Bombay. Thackeray mingles the gay with the grave in his description of the great funeral ceremony at the Invalides when Napoleon's body was placed under the great dome on "the banks of the Seine, among the people whom he so well loved," according to the inscription over his tomb. "Bertrand," says the English humorist, "put on the body the most glorious, victorious sword that has ever been forged since the apt descendants of the first murderer learned how to hammer steel, and the coffin was placed in the temple prepared for it. The six hundred singers and the fiddlers now commenced the playing and the singing of a piece of music: and a part of the crew of the *Belle Poule* skipped into the places that had been kept for them under us, and listened to the music,

[1] Thackeray, in the "Miscellanies," is rather misleading when he states that the Vendôme Column was "melted out of foreign cannon." The monument is of stone encrusted with bronze plates obtained from 1200 Russian and Austrian cannons. In 1814 the statue of Napoleon was taken down by the Royalists, but Louis Philippe had it replaced. The Emperor Napoleon III. had another figure of his uncle substituted for that made by order of the "Citizen King," and in May, 1871, the whole column was pulled down by the Communists. It has since been restored, and remains another of the many proofs of French fickleness in political matters.

THE INVALIDES.

chewing tobacco. While the actors and fiddlers were going on, most of the spirits-of-wine lamps went out."

Napoleon's sarcophagus, which rests on a mosaic ground representing a laurel wreath, is fourteen and a half feet high, and consists of one immense block of Finland granite. Over the entrance to the crypt are the words above referred to, "Je désire que mes cendres reposent sur les bords de la Seine, au milieu de ce peuple Français que j'ai tant aimé." The body is encased by no fewer than five coffins. The vast monument and the funeral

TOMB OF NAPOLEON, INVALIDES.

ceremonies cost 6,744,000 francs, or nearly £270,000. The dome rises 160 feet high over the crypt, and on its sections and compartments are paintings by Jouvenet and Delafosse, pupils of Le Brun, the accredited historical painter, or, it may be said, "decorator," employed by Louis XIV., in whose reign the Hôtel des Invalides was erected. The gilded dome of the tomb of Napoleon is, according to Fergusson in his "History of Architecture," one of the most elegant structures of its class, and resembles St. Paul's in plan more than any other domical church on the Continent.

Not far from the Invalides is the church of ST. FRANCIS XAVIER, dedicated to the memory of the great apostle of the Indies, who is also the glory of the Company of Jesus. This church was erected between 1861 and 1875, the old church of St. Francis Xavier having been handed over to the Foreign Missions. The architecture is pseudo-Renaissance, and the interior is ornamented by stained glass and mural paintings by Bouguereau, Bonassieux and others. There is a very large oratory in the apsis.

More interesting is another church in the same part of the city, namely that of ST. JOSEPH-DES-CARMES, in the Rue de Vaugirard, a large domical edifice approached from a court, slightly resembling a cloister. This is the old church of the monastery of the bare-footed Carmelites, called also "Discalced," or "Discalceated," and by the French "Déchaux," or "Déchaussés." The monastery was founded in 1611 by two Carmelites from Italy, to whom Nicholas Vivian, a God-respecting Controller-General of Accounts, gave the ground on which stood a hall where the Calvinists had preached their doctrines. This hall was used by the Carmelites as a chapel and was afterwards enlarged. Then, owing to the increase of the popularity of the friars, the church was erected, the foundation stone being laid by Mary de' Medici in 1613. The chief historical event with which this church is identified was the great Revolution. In the year 1792 the monastery was suppressed and the church was used as a prison in which royalists and priests were confined. Nearly all the ecclesiastics were murdered by the "Septembriseurs," who massacred thirty other non-jurant priests outside the gates of the Abbaye prison of St. Germain-des-Prés. During these September days Sans-Culottism ran riot through Paris, and about one thousand and eighty-nine people, including two hundred and two priests, were butchered in the various prisons. These are the figures given by Carlyle as quoted by him from "accurate Advocate Maton." The butcheries were perpetrated on the 2nd, 3rd, 4th and 5th of September, 1792. The stains of blood in or around the church of the Carmelites have been partially preserved. They are notably to be seen in a little oratory in the garden called the Chapel of the Martyrs. Strange to say, the Terrorists did not molest the friars of the convent, and only attacked the arrested priests. The murdered ecclesiastics are buried in the crypt of the church. After these

ST. JOSEPH-DES-CARMES.

terrible events, a public dancing place was organized in the gardens of the monastery, and was called the "Tilleuls" or "The Limes." There, on the ground reeking with the blood of the victims of Sans-Culottism hopped and frisked the gay nymphs of the Latin quarter and their admirers, and probably also, some of the very men and women who had rushed shrieking through the streets after the doomed royalists calling out for their heads.

In 1793 the monastery again became a prison. Among those temporarily confined there were General Hoche, Santerre the brewer, the Marquis de Soyecourt, and notably Josephine Tascher Beauharnais, afterwards to be the wife of the first Napoleon. Josephine was first thrown into Sainte Pélagie prison about the same time as Madame Du Barry, ex-mistress of Louis XV., who had returned from London only to be arrested as a suspect and to die by the guillotine.[1] Josephine was recognized as she was waiting about in the gardens of the Luxembourg Palace, also a prison, and wherein her first husband, Alexandre, Vicomte de Beauharnais, was confined. Like other persons of her rank, Madame de Beauharnais, dressed shabbily, was looking out for some fond signal from the Palace or prison windows. At the prison of the Carmelite convent—St. Joseph-des-Carmes—Josephine heard of her husband's death on the scaffold and swooned ; blood, it is said, streaming from her lips. While she was ill and anxious in prison, fully expecting that she was about to follow her husband to the guillotine, and that her children would become penniless orphans, a hope beamed on her and on her fellow prisoners. It is related that one morning as she sat at the window of her jail, she saw a poor woman out in the street behaving as if she were a lunatic. This shabbily dressed person, after having danced frantically in the middle of the road would look long at the prison windows, next take a stone from the ground, hold it up and finally roll it in her dress, or robe. Then she would immediately draw her hand across her throat. These antics were performed for the purpose of letting the prisoners in the Carmelite convent know that Robespierre, the "sea-green tyrant," had gone also to the guillotine. The *pierre*, or stone, rolled in the woman's *robe*, or dress, symbolized the tyrant's name, and the hand drawn across the throat

[1] Carlyle calls Dame Du Barry "unfortunate female," in the street sense of the term, and an "ex-harlot of a whilom majesty." Vatel, in his history of the favourite of Louis XV., labours to prove that she had not been a "fille publique" before her connection with the king, but only a "kept woman, in the widest sense of the word." In England, Madame Du Barry wrote love-letters to one of the members of the Somerset or Seymour family. They are given in the "Mémoirs sur le dix-huitième siècle" (1833-1867), edited by Barrière. See also, as well as Vatel, the work of the brothers Goncourt, "Les Maitresses de Louis XV."

signified his decapitation, which happened in Thermidor, year 2, or July, 1794.

After 1797, the cloister and church of the Carmelites were bought by the Marchioness de Soyecourt, daughter of the Marquis. In 1841 the Archbishop of Paris purchased the place and founded there a theological college, or "school of advanced ecclesiastical studies," and in 1849 part of this property was given to the Dominicans and their famous head in France, Père Lacordaire. Little else need be said of the church of St. Joseph-des-Carmes except that it was built in 1625, has the first dome, on the St. Peter's plan, which appeared in France, possesses good frescoes painted by the Belgian artist, Flamaël, in the cupola, and, near the entrance to the vestry, a marble monument containing the heart of Archbishop Affre, who was shot at the barricades in June, 1848. The chief curiosity of the church, however, is the crypt, with its tombs and ghastly mementoes of the savage days of September 1792.

Not a long distance from St. Joseph-les-Carmes is the small church and cloister of the ABBAYE AUX BOIS, near the big shop of the Bon Marché. This place is chiefly remarkable for Madame Récamier's connection with it, and must not be confounded with another—the older Abbaye aux Bois—by the wood of Verrières outside Paris. It was to the Abbaye aux Bois, formerly a Cistercian convent, that Madame Récamier, whose rival in beauty was Pamela, wife of Lord Edward Fitzgerald, retired in 1819, when "Son vieil époux," as M. Récamier has been ungraciously called, had suffered a second reverse of fortune. The *salon* of Madame Récamier at the Abbaye was moulded on that of the Marquise de Sablé in the Faubourg Saint-Jacques. The Marquise had also half-retired to a monastery, that of Port Royal, where she died in 1678. As Sainte-Beuve says in his "Causeries de Lundi," she had a window open on the convent and a door open on the world. This was exactly the case of Madame Récamier, who had around her, in the Abbaye, all the friends and admirers who remained faithful to her in her comparative adversity.

In the same district, but nearer to the river, are the fashionable churches of the Faubourg Saint-Germain, namely, ST. THOMAS D'AQUIN and ST. CLOTILDE. The building named after the Angelic Doctor of the Dominicans must be taken first, as it is an old church. St. Clotilde's, being modern, must take its place amongst those like it. Formerly the church of St. Thomas, now resorted to on Sundays by members of the stately families of

ST. THOMAS D'AQUIN.

the aristocratic Faubourg, was attached to the Novitiate of the Dominicans founded in 1631, under the patronage of Cardinal Richelieu. The monastery stood in the Rue des Vaches, "Cow Street," but the name of the locality was altered by the friars to that of their founder, St. Dominic, by which it is nowadays known. In 1638 the Dominicans began to build a larger church, that which now exists. The foundation stone was laid by the Archbishop of Albi and the Duchess de Luynes, Anne de Rohan Montbazon. In the days before the Revolution the church contained the tombs of Marshal de Navailles and of Francis Romain, a Dominican from whose plans was constructed the Pont Royal. Gabriel and Mansart are also mentioned as architects of this bridge. In 1795 St. Thomas D'Aquin became the Temple of Peace and was handed over to the Theophilanthropists. The name of Temple of Peace was wrongfully applied, for it was here that the sect of Theophilanthropists was first split up by internal dissensions. The church has been restored to the Catholics since 1803. The façade of the edifice has two good bas-reliefs of St. Dominic and St. Thomas Aquinas. In the interior are frescoes by Blondel, Lemoine's "Transfiguration" scenes on the ceiling, Ary Scheffer's "St. Thomas Aquinas calming a Storm," Guillemot's "Descent from the Cross," and Bertin's "Christ on the Mount of Olives."

Among the other old churches on the left bank of the river are ST. LOUIS-EN-L'ILE, that is to say, on the island of St. Louis. It may be classed, at least, as on the left bank, like Notre Dame and the Sainte Chapelle. It was commenced in 1679 and was finished in 1725. It has not much history, except that the poet Quinault was buried there in 1688. There are in it pictures by Mignard, Coypel, Perron, Perrin, Vouet and Hallé, with woodwork and stained glass lately restored and very interesting. The church is at the end of the long, narrow and thickly-populated street forming the nucleus or centre of the island, and called the Rue St. Louis. It is a queer, out-of-the-way part of Paris and looks provincial, although it is within a stone's throw of the Law Courts, and, it may be said of the Louvre Palace.

Of the other left-bank churches there is not much to say. SAINT JACQUES-DU-HAUT-PAS, in the Rue St. Jacques, near the Luxembourg, was begun in 1630 from Gittard's designs, the foundation stone having been laid by a royal prince. It contains some good pictures, one of which, "Faith

Hope, Charity and Religion," is attributed to the seventeenth-century master, Lesueur.

SAINT MÉDARD'S, dedicated to the French St. Swithin, is supposed to be one of the poorest of Paris churches. It was once a small chapel attached to the Abbey of St. Geneviève, but this was enlarged in the sixteenth century. This church was the scene of a great struggle between the Huguenots and

ST. MÉDARD.

the Catholics in 1561. According to one version, the Protestants, who had a meeting-house close by, were annoyed by the sounds of the Catholic bells, and broke into St. Médard's. The Catholics showed fight, and the conflict was only stopped by the royal archers. Another version is that the clergy of St. Médard incited their parishioners against the Protes-

ST. MÉDARD.

tants. The two places of worship were sacked, but St. Médard's was restored, whereas the "Temple of the Patriarch," as the Huguenot meeting-house was called, remained closed. The cemetery of St. Médard was a miracle-working locality in the eighteenth century, and the sect of "Convulsionists" had their headquarters there. Louis XV. ordered the graveyard to be closed, and somebody accordingly wrote on the walls of the place that "By order of the King" God had been ordered to perform no more miracles on the spot.

Another church in this district is that of ST. NICOLAS-DU-CHARDONNET, Rue St. Victor, which derives its name from the thistle or "chardons" once abounding in the locality, and not from the word "chardonneret," or goldfinch. In this church is a pyramid to the memory of Le Brun, the accredited painter of Louis XIV. The monument is crowned by a bust of the famous court artist. With this church the minor and less interesting religious edifices of the Latin quarter and of the left bank of the Seine must come to a close.

ST. EUSTACHE—ST. GERVAIS, ST. PROTAIS—ST
LEU, ST. GILLES—ST. MERRI—ST. NICOLAS-DES-
CHAMPS — ST. LAURENT — STE. ELIZABETH—
NOTRE DAME DES BLANCS MANTEAUX—ST.
PAUL, ST. LOUIS—STE. MARGUERITE—NOTRE
DAME DES VICTOIRES — NOTRE DAME DE
LORETTE—ST. ROCH—NOTRE DAME DE L'AS-
SOMPTION.

St. Eustache and its three patrons—Jacob the Hungarian—The Butchers—Scarron's wife—A terrified congregation—Mirabeau—Madame Momoro, Goddess of Reason—The women's club—The Communists and the Market-women—Molière's funeral—St. Gervais—Scarron's tomb—St. Leu—The bleeding statue—St. Merri's—St. Nicholas-in-the-Fields—Mademoiselle de Scudéri's tomb—Other churches—Rabelais and the man of the Iron Mask—The monuments to the Mignons—Cardinal Richelieu's first mass—The Dutch Dauphin—The English converts—Barras, Bonaparte and the Venus of the Capitol.

CHARLES VII.

ITS enormous size is the chief characteristic of St. Eustache. The church of the market-women, situated near the combined Billingsgate and Smithfield of Paris, is a colossal and lofty edifice. It comes next to the Cathedral in vastness, and is one of those churches which every one must see. The edifice occupies the site of a chapel once dedicated to St. Agnes. The chapel had taken the place of a Roman Temple to Cybele, and was attached to the parish of St. Germain L'Auxerrois. It was built with the money of one Jean Alais, manager or director of the mystery-players. The whole parish was originally under the patronage of St. Eustatius, a Roman captain of the time of Trajan, who became a Christian, of St. Agnes, whose memory Tennyson has enshrined in undying verse, and of St. Louis of France. It was while the latter was absent at the crusades that the old church of St. Eustache was invaded by the Pastoureaux or peasants, who, under the leadership of the ex-monk Jacob the Hungarian, gave much trouble in Paris in 1255, by fighting against the nobles and priests. In 1414 the church was the meeting-place of the butchers who, just before the domination of the English, vowed vengeance against the Armagnac party and, instigated by the Duke of Burgundy, were nearly masters of Paris. The existing church was begun in 1532 on the plans of Lemercier of Pontoise, and it was only in 1642 that it was all finished save the portal and one of the towers. It was in the church of St. Eustache that Françoise d'Aubigné, afterwards Madame de Maintenon, wife of Scarron and then of Louis XIV., used to say her prayers when she quitted Calvinism for Catholicism. The ecclesiastical chroniclers of the parish relate that for a long time before she met the cripple Scarron, Françoise d'Aubigné was befriended, pecuniarily, by a charitable lady who was one of the regular worshippers in the church. It is said that the young woman in her first fervour rose at midnight in order to attend matins at St. Eustache.

Louis XIV. made his first communion in St. Eustache, as he was then living not far away, in the Palais Royal, under the tutelage of his mother, the Regent Anne of Austria. In 1676 Fléchier, Bishop of Nimes, preached there before Louis XIV., the funeral oration of Henri de la Tour d'Auvergne, Vicomte de Turenne and Marshal of France, who was killed by a bullet at Salzbach, like Wolfe, in the moment of victory. A more famous sermon was heard at St. Eustache in 1704, when Massillon terrified the audience by his references to the day of judgment, so much so that they rose from their seats. In 1791 the Curé of the church had to hide from the Revolutionists, and with his vicars conducted the work of the parish by stealth. In the same year the body of Mirabeau was carried to St. Eustache by the Revolutionists, and a funeral oration was made by Cerutti, the ex-Jesuit from Piedmont, who subscribed to the opinions of 1789 and became a member of the Legislative Assembly. The ceremony was concluded by the discharge of firearms which, as Carlyle says, " brought down pieces of plaster." In the evening Mirabeau's body was carried to the Panthéon. In the May following, the barbers' assistants in Paris had a service in St. Eustache for Mirabeau. The church was next given over to the Women's Revolutionary Club or Society which was composed of abandoned and profligate adventuresses who alarmed the Committee of Public Safety by their conduct, attitude, discussions, and the bold extravagance of their petitions.

Then followed the Feast of the Goddess of Reason, which was carried out here as well as in the Cathedral of Notre Dame. Mercier has left a picture of the desecration of the church, which is quoted by Carlyle, who is inclined to look upon the statements of the Frenchman as extravagant. Enough happened, however, to give so lively a chronicler as the author of the " Tableau de Paris " full scope for his pen. The church was converted into a vast tavern and eating house. Sausages, poultry, vegetables, were brought in there from the adjacent markets. " Reason sat in azure mantle aloft, in a serene manner; Cannoneers, pipe in mouth, serving her as acolytes." Out of doors the drunken crowd danced around " a bonfire of chapel-balustrades, of priests' and canons' stalls." The Goddess of Reason at St. Eustache was Madame Momoro, wife of one of the Antiaristocrats. He was a bookseller by trade. Carlyle calls him a Bibliopolic and Bibliopolist who " knew something of Agrarian law." Momoro was guillotined with the Hébertists in March, 1794. His wife, according to the great Scotchman, " made one

ST. EUSTACHE.

of the best goddesses of Reason, though her teeth were a little defective." Abbé Torré, quoting from the book on St. Eustache by M. Goudreau, Curé of the parish in 1855, says that, during the feast of Reason, the interior of the choir of the church was turned into a mock-rural place with thatched huts or cabins and rocks, between which there were paths leading to mysterious grottoes. The viands and drinks were piled on tables around the choir, and everybody who entered had a right to eat and swill, and then to join in the orgies. In the "charnier" of the building, the women had their club founded by an actress named Lacombe, who wore a red bonnet or Phrygian cap while she was in the chair. The club was dissolved as ridiculous by Robespierre, just before he abolished the cult of Reason, and officiated as the high priest of the Supreme Being. Abbé Poupart was at last allowed to return to his cure in June 1795. St. Eustache having been opened in advance of other religious places. He had, however, to share the vast building with the Theophilanthropists and the town councillors who held their meetings there. In 1801 the Abbé Bossu obtained full possession of the church, restored it after the ravages of the Revolutionists, who as usual had done much damage, received pictures for the embellishment of the chapels and was substantially aided by the pious people of his extensive parish in preparing the edifice for divine worship. In 1844 the parish priest of St. Eustache was the Abbé Deguerry, during whose term of office a fire broke out in the church and destroyed the organ. The damage was soon repaired by the proceeds of a lottery. The Abbé Deguerry was removed to the Madeleine in 1848, and was shot by the Communists in 1871 with Archbishop Darboy. It was at this period, too, that the attention of the Communists was particularly directed to the great church of the " Dames de la Halle." The market-women had always been proud of St. Eustache, and once had a voice in the nomination of the Curés. The " nomination " was, of course, only a joke, but it did happen that Abbé Marlin, Curé in 1645, really owed his place to the intervention of the market ladies, who insisted that he should succeed his uncle.

On Holy Thursday, April, 1871, the Communists ordered the arrest of Abbé Simon, the Curé of St. Eustache. Six guards and a sergeant took him to the Prefecture of Police where he was locked up. His parishioners, old and new, immediately set to work in order to effect his release. The butchers of the parish of St. Eustache held a meeting of protest, the people of the parishes of St. Margaret and of Petit-Rouge, where M. Simon had been before, signed petitions, and the " Dames de la Halle " sent a delegation to the Prefecture of Police to ask for the release of their popular priest. The following conversation ensued between one of the women and the Communist chief:

" Citoyenne, what do you want ? "

" I want my Curé, M. Simon of St. Eustache. I am not here to ask a pardon from you, you understand. I want my Curé."

" Your Curé is like all the others."

" I have nothing to do with the others. I want my Curé. Tell me, I beg of you, why you arrested him ? "

" Because it has pleased us to do so."

Just then, somebody whispered into the ear of the Communist chief, and the market-woman overheard the terrible word " Mazas." This aroused her anger and she shouted out, " No, he shall not, must not go to Mazas. I am going to take him back with me, and if I don't you had better look out, for you will get a hot reception in the markets, I can assure you." This threat had some effect, and the "Dame de la Halle " was told that she would have her Curé safe and sound on Easter Saturday. M. Simon was in fact released. Accounts of his benevolence and charity, petitions for his release, were so numerous and emanated from such humble quarters that the Communists had to give in. Félix Pyat, Beslay, and the redoubtable Raoult Rigault, who was one of the first insurgents to be shot when the Versailles troops entered Paris, befriended the priest. M. Simon was released on Easter Sunday, much to his surprise. It was half-past three o'clock in the morning when his warder opened his cell door, and shouted out in stentorian tones, " No. 115, get up, make haste, take your traps and go down in the court-yard." " Where am I going to ? "asked the Curé in painful doubt. " I don't know," was the reply. " Perhaps you are going to be discharged, or perhaps you are going to be shot. Life, you know, is full of ups and downs. Anyhow, look alive and get down." M. Simon did as he was desired, and on reaching the courtyard was conducted by guards to the presence of a mock magistrate of the Commune who was in a room filled with tobacco smoke, around him being his friends or assistants. After having been questioned, the " Citizen Simon " was told that, owing to his good reputation in his district, he was at liberty to leave the prison, which he did, with a safe-permit from Raoult Rigault. The Curé at once went to his church, celebrated his Easter Sunday mass, offered the usual consecrated bread to his parishioners, according to an old custom in the Paris diocese, and made a short address to his congregation in which he thanked them for their solicitude on his

ST. EUSTACHE.

behalf. Thus M. Simon escaped the fate of the hostages of the Commune.

His troubles, however, were not all over. A few days after his return to his flock the church was invaded by a band of Communists who wanted to hold a meeting there. M. Simon managed to have his own way. He told the men quietly that the place was a house of prayer, and that they had no right to smoke, spit, harangue, argue and keep their hats on there. The insurgents accordingly retired, but the Curé had again some trouble with them as the Versailles army was advancing through Paris. The Communists ordered that the bells of St. Eustache should ring out as a tocsin of alarm, the city being in danger. The bell-ringer, in his haste, or fear, gave forth a jubilant peal, the "grande volée des fêtes," and a crowd soon burst into the church crying out for the Curé. M. Simon parleyed with the lunatics, but was dragged off to the police station, where, having explained the mistake of the bell-ringer, he was liberated amid the frantic acclamations of his parishioners.

According to the Abbé Coullié, vicar of the parish during the Commune, and subsequently Bishop of Orléans, the "Dames de la Halle" armed themselves with big knives on this occasion and were ready to fight the Communists if the Curé had not been discharged from custody. Joined by the butchers, the ladies of the market would no doubt have made blood flow copiously around St. Eustache on that occasion if their wishes had not been wisely taken into account by the insurgent chiefs. The "Dame de la Halle" who had distinguished herself in obtaining the liberation of the Curé from prison, died some years after the Commune, and there was a splendid funeral for her in the church of the markets. It may here be remarked that the names of the hostages who were shot by the Communists are inscribed on a wall in the south transept of St. Eustache.

The church of the Paris markets was built twenty-six years after St. Peter's of Rome, and is a mixture of late Gothic and Renaissance. According to Fergusson it is in reality a Gothic five-aisled church, and it is only in details that an experienced eye sees the influence of classical architecture. The arches are round and the pillars are of different orders. The frontage has a Doric great door, and a gallery above in the Corinthian style. The other doors, like the rest of the building, suffered a good deal in 1870-71, but the restorations have been effective and a good deal of the old Renaissance sculpture has been well reproduced or repatched. St. Eustache, although surrounded by lofty houses, appears a vast edifice, and its colossal size is

HISTORIC CHURCHES OF PARIS.

further realized when one stands inside, in the middle of the nave, and follows the lines of the tall pillars and arches until they lose themselves or merge into the lofty vaulting which is the highest of any church in Paris. A curious motive in the external decoration of St. Eustache is the stag's head and crucifix, which may be seen over one of the smaller rose-windows. The stag's head and crucifix—the arms of the parish—symbolize the legend of Placidus, the Roman soldier who became St. Eustace or Eustatius. Placidus was out hunting one day when a stag which he was about to kill revealed itself as Christ and a crucifix appeared between its horns. The statue of St. Eustache is seen in the central pier of the north door. The patron of the church is arrayed in the garb of a Roman officer.

This vast edifice is 348 feet long, 144 feet wide, and 108 feet in height. Its chapels are full of fine frescoes by Signol, Larivière, Vaugelet and others. The stained glass in the clerestory windows is by Cartaux, and there is a fine statue of the Virgin by Pigalle over the high altar. Other features are the boss which hangs from the centre of the transept with its large angelic figures supporting a cross; the ornamentation of the pillars, the exquisitely carved pulpit, the organ-case surmounted by figures of Saul and David, and also of St. Cecilia, the " banc d'œuvre," or space reserved for magnates of the parish, churchwardens, etc., with its woodwork representing carven scenes from the life of St. Agnes, and the tomb of Colbert, the Finance Minister of Louis XIV. This is a sarcophagus in black marble, the effigy of the statesman being in white. Several notable Frenchmen, such as Voiture and Benserade, the society poets, rivals and friends of Madame de Rambouillet, in the seventeenth century, Rameau the musician, were buried in St. Eustache or in the cemetery of St. Joseph near it. When Molière died in 1673, the Curé of St. Eustache refused Christian burial to the dramatist on the ground that he had not been reconciled to Mother Church. The king, however, was approached by the playwright's widow, and the Archbishop of Paris consequently allowed the body to be buried in St. Joseph's Cemetery, but on condition that it should not enter the church. Molière was accompanied to his last home by two hundred mourners bearing torches. Among these were two priests who said prayers over his grave and sprinkled it with holy water, so that he did not, after all, depart without benefit of clergy.

ST. GERVAIS AND ST. PROTAIS.

Before taking leave of this highly interesting church of the markets, it must be mentioned that it is the favourite place of worship of the musicians of Paris. Here are given oratorios and sacred concerts in Holy Week, and on St. Cecilia's Day, November 22nd. The music of the services is always fine, the organ being one of the best in Paris. The relics of St. Cecily, authenticated by Papal rescript dated November 28th, 1853, are in the chapel dedicated to the patroness of music. The same chapel contains the tomb of the musician Rameau, and on the altar-wood is painted the body of St. Cecily just as it was discovered in the catacombs by Pope Pascal I. in 822, and afterwards by Clement VIII., in 1599. Another chapel worth seeing is that of St. Louis, which is pictured with episodes from the life of that monarch. St. Eustache is full of relics, among them being bones of the patron, and of his wife and children, a fragment of the Holy Sepulchre, and bits of St. Vincent de Paul's body and clothes.

Next in importance to St. Eustache comes the Church of SAINT GERVAIS and SAINT PROTAIS, at the end of the Place de l'Hôtel-de-Ville, formerly known as the Place de Grève. The locality is one of the most historical in Paris. It was on the Place de Grève that Count Montgomery, of the Scottish Guard, was put to death by order of Catherine de' Medici, who made him responsible for the fatal accident which befell her husband, Henry II., during a tournament in the court of the neighbouring Palais des Tournelles, now the Place des Vosges. The church of St. Gervais and St. Protais was erected towards the end of the fifteenth century on the site of an older building. It was dedicated to the two martyrs Gervasius and Protarius who had suffered death in the persecution ordered by Nero. In 1616 the existing portal was erected, the foundation stone having been laid by Louis XIII.

Madame de Sevigné was married in this church, and in it were buried Scarron, the cripple and husband of Madame de Maintenon, the painter Philip of Champaigne, the poet and dramatist Crébillon, and Chancellor Le Tellier, whose mausoleum exists. In 1795 the church was known as the "Temple of Youth." The architecture is a combination of the Flamboyant and the Renaissance. The interior is Gothic, and the portal of 1616 is composed of the Doric, Ionic, and Corinthian orders. The frescoes are notable as well as the stained glass, two of the windows being old. One in the Lady Chapel is by Cousin, the other, in the chapel on the right-hand side of the choir, by R. Pinaigrier (sixteenth century). Notable, too, are the

HISTORIC CHURCHES OF PARIS.

altar ornaments, the carven stalls, the organ loft, and the pendentive or sculptured boss which hangs in the Lady Chapel. This chapel is a splendid specimen of Flamboyant Gothic, but it was disfigured about twenty years since with ornamentation out of harmony with the architecture. The five stained glass windows showing the history of the Virgin are the work of Pinaigrier, ably restored in 1846 by Gsell.

Almost midway between St. Eustache and St. Gervais is the church of ST. LEU-ST. GILLES, and below this is another old church, that of St. MERRI in the Rue St. Martin. The church of St. Leu-St. Gilles was raised on the site of an old chapel which was enlarged in 1320, and became a parish in 1617. The apsis of the church had to be reduced in proportions in order to preserve the alignment of the Boulevard de Sébastopol. One of the patrons of the church was a saintly French bishop, Lupus or Loup, the other was the gentle hermit St. Giles who sheltered a hind from the hunters. The exterior has a belfry with a spire which has openings. Among the pictures is one representing an incident said to have happened in June, 1418, when a Swiss soldier, having struck with his sword a street statue of the Virgin, it bled. The statue was then removed to St. Martin's-in-the-Fields, the Swiss was executed, and every year afterwards, until the Revolution, a dummy figure representing him was burned like a Guy Fawkes at the corner of the Rue-aux-Ours, where the effigy of the Virgin had stood. The event is described in an inscription in one of the chapels.

The Gothic church of ST. MERRI was begun in 1520 and finished in 1612. The patron was St. Medericus or Médéric, of Autun, who lived on the spot when in Paris. Odo, the Falconer, built a church in the ninth century on the site which was subsequently replaced by the existing edifice. In spite of the transformations which it has undergone, the church interests by its sculptured bosses, its stained glass with fragments of sixteenth-century work, and its arches. The three painted windows over the apsis give that part of the church and the chancel a bright cheerful appearance, and favourably impress the entering worshipper or visitor. The high altar is surmounted by a large marble crucifix by Dubois. There is also a curious crypt which fills the place once occupied by the tomb of the patron saint. Before the Revolution the church contained the tombs of the poet Chapelain and of the Marquis de Pomponne, one of the Ministers of the Grand

ST. MERRI.

Monarque. The church suffered a good deal at the hands of the Revolutionists, and the exterior ornamentation is all restored work.

St. Merri's church is towards the river end of the Rue St. Martin.

ST. MERRI.

Another old and interesting church is that of ST. NICOLAS-DES-CHAMPS, which is near the Conservatoire des Arts et Métiers, the Gaité Theatre and the main boulevard, and in the same street of St. Martin. This edifice, which is Gothic, with a fine Renaissance portal on the southern side, was originally a chapel for the use of the servants of the priory of St. Martin-des-Champs and people of the district. The priory is now the Conservatoire des Arts et Métiers, a trade museum and educational institution which contains the old abbey church of St. Martin and the refectory of the monks. The chapel of St. Nicholas, the patron of pawnbrokers as well as of boys, maidens, and merchants, was enlarged at different periods between 1399 and 1576. The lower part of the nave has pointed arches of the fifteenth century, with round pillars, but towards the altar the columns are Doric or Ionic. It is one of the longest churches in Paris, and its interior, although full of pictures by Vouet, Sébastien Bourdon, Landelle, Caminade and others, looks rather Calvinistic when compared to the internal part of its neighbour, St. Merri's church. One of its most interesting features is the varied and delicate workmanship on the woodwork of the organ, which is by Cliquot. The privilege of seeing this is granted to whoever cares to apply to M. le Curé.

In 1797 the Theophilanthropists took over the church of St. Nicolas-des-Champs and called it the Temple of Hymen. It contained the tomb of

ST. NICOLAS-DES-CHAMPS.

Gassendi, the philosopher and professor who taught Molière, Chapelle, Bernier and Cyrano de Bergerac, only to mention a few of his notable pupils. This monument has, however, disappeared like that erected over the last resting-place of Mademoiselle de Scudéri, who has been called the "Richardson of France," and was bitterly satirized by Molière and Boileau. Her memory has been, however, eloquently defended by an English authoress.[1]

[1] "French Women of Letters," by Julia Kavanagh. In Besant's "French Humourists,"

St. Laurent.

To face p. 173.

ST. LAURENT.

Proceeding in a northerly direction from St. Nicolas-des-Champs, another old church, that of ST. LAURENT, is to be found near the Eastern or Strassburg Railway Station. It dates from the fifteenth century, and is on the site of an older church which was attached to an abbey of the sixth century. This monastic place was swept away in one of the invasions of the Northmen, and its exact site is difficult to determine. The patron is the Holy Deacon of Rome who, in the third century, was roasted on a gridiron, and who, during the terrible process, told his tyrants to turn him over, as one of his sides was already done enough. The Communists, who seriously damaged the church in 1871, pretended that they had discovered in the crypt the dead bodies of women who had been murdered, and then buried pell-mell under the building. Fragments of the skeletons of the victims were exhibited during the Commune, but according to Messrs. Virmaitre and Buguet in their " Paris Croque-mort," a doctor who saw the exhibition described it as a " put-up job," designed for the purpose of throwing discredit on the priests and of drawing money from the pockets of the credulous. St. Laurent's church has a fine Gothic frontage and spire. The tympan over the portal is ornamented with a painting representing the life history of the patron saint. The bright colours of this fresco give the exterior of the edifice a rather Italian appearance in spite of the Gothic architecture. The interior of the church lacks decoration, except for the bosses and the stained glass in the choir windows. The inevitable Theophilanthropists had charge of the church in 1795, and called it the " Temple of Old Age."

In the more eastern part of Paris is the church dedicated to St. Elizabeth of Hungary. This is situated in the Rue du Temple, and the first stone was laid by Maria de' Medici, in 1628. ST. ELIZABETH's has little to recommend it save the baptismal font in white marble of the sixteenth century and the exquisite fourteenth-century wood carving.

Near the Rue du Temple also, is the old church of NOTRE-DAME-DES-BLANCS-MANTEAUX. It stands in the street of the same name, and close to the great pawn-office, or Mont de Piété. The title was derived from the " Servants of Holy Mary," who wore white mantles, and had a convent in the locality founded by St. Louis, King of France, in 1258. The name remained in spite of the suppression of the " Servants of Holy Mary," in 1274, and

the authoress of "Clelia" is compared to Richardson, whose vigour, however, she lacked, as is stated in Sir W. Besant's book.

their replacement by the " Hermits of St. William," or " Guillemites," who wore black and were merged with the Benedictines of Saint-Maur, in 1648. The first stone of the existing church was laid by Chancellor Le Tellier, in 1685. It was in the former church that the body of the Duc d'Orléans, assassinated by order of Jean-sans-Peur, Duke of Burgundy, was brought from the neighbouring Hôtel Barbette, in 1407. The place is also interesting as it was in the monastery of the " Blancs Manteaux," to use the popular name, that the Benedictines of St. Maur began their splendid historical records, which are nowadays carried on by the Académie des Inscriptions et Belles Lettres. When the monastery was closed by the early Revolutionists, the Benedictines were authorized by the Constituent Assembly to remove the books of which they had need for their historical work.

Also in the east end is the church of ST.-PAUL-ST.-LOUIS, Rue St. Antoine. It occupies the site of a chapel dedicated to the Apostle of the Gentiles by St. Eloi, and enlarged in the reign of Charles V. Being the church nearest to the Hôtel St. Paul and the Royal palace of the Tournelles, many princes were baptized there. Near this church and connected with it by a passage was a cemetery in which were buried Rabelais and the mysterious prisoner called the " man of the iron mask." In the old church were buried Marshal de Biron, Nicot and the two Mansards. There were also in it mausoleums, erected by Henri III. to his mignons, Maugiron, Saint Mégrin, Quélus and Caussade, who fell by the hands of the followers of the Duc de Guise. These monuments were destroyed by the people during the uprising against King Henri III., in 1589. A few years before these tragic events, Cardinal de Bourbon gave the property over to the Jesuits, who established a novitiate there and laid the foundations of the present church, in 1627. The novitiate now belongs to the Lycée Charlemagne. Under the church were buried many famous Jesuits like Tournemine, Bourdaloue and La Chaise. The hearts of Louis XIII. and of Louis XIV. were once placed in the choir, and before the Revolution were transferred to the Val-de-Grâce. Later on, the first Napoleon ordered the ornamental urns which had contained the royal viscera to be removed to Fontainebleau palace, and there placed in the private chapel of the captive pope. Georges Cadoudal, chief of the Chouans of La Vendée, defeated by General Hoche in 1796, was buried at St.-Paul-St.-Louis, but under the Restoration his body was removed to loyal Brittany. Another memory connected with this church is that of Cardinal Richelieu, who said his first mass here.

NOTRE-DAME-DES-VICTOIRES.

The edifice was planned by the Jesuit François Derrand, and is an example of the style of Maderno, Borromini and the others who with them introduced elaborate ornamentation. The general effect of this—the Jesuit style—is rich and picturesque, although it is objected to as rococo and meaningless. The interior of St.-Paul-St.-Louis is elegant, with its square pillars on each side of the nave, the triforium with round-headed arches, the cornice with railed gallery, and the paintings, one of which, "Christ in the Garden," is by Eugène Delacroix.

In the Rue St. Bernard, Faubourg St. Antoine, is the church of STE. MARGUERITE, formerly a chapel, built in 1625, and enlarged in 1736 and 1765. In its cemetery was buried in June, 1795, the body of the Dauphin, son of Louis XVI., who died in the Temple, although there are those who maintain that the young prince escaped from Paris and went to Holland, where he lived under the name of Nauendorff. This church contains some pictures and works of sculpture of fair merit, but otherwise it is completely devoid of interest.

Turning now to the west, the first important church requiring notice is NOTRE-DAME-DES-VICTOIRES, which is a permanent protest against the long-vanished power of the Huguenots. It stands in the busiest part of Paris, although the Place de Petits-Pères around it is quiet enough. The Bourse, however, is not far away, and the bustling Rue Montmartre is close by. It was formerly the abbey church of the Discalced or Bare-footed Augustinians, who were first invited to Paris by Margaret of Valois. These friars were called the "Little Fathers," on account of their poverty; others say to distinguish them from the Grands Augustins, or non-reformed Augustinians, while it is also alleged that Henri Quatre bestowed the name on them in allusion to their diminutive size. The "Little Fathers" began to build the church in 1628, and in the following year Louis XIII. directed that the edifice should be called Notre-Dame-des-Victoires in commemoration of the defeat of the Huguenots at La Rochelle. The king himself, attended by all his court and by the notables of Paris, laid the foundation stone, which was of black marble, and bore in letters of gold a pompous inscription declaring the "Most Christian King of France and Navarre," "invictus et ubique victor."

This church has not much history. After the Terror it was used as a Bourse by order of the Directory (Eighteenth Nivose, Year IV. of the

HISTORIC CHURCHES OF PARIS.

Republic, or 8th of January, 1796). In 1803 it was restored to the clergy, and is nowadays a place of pilgrimage and the church wherein young ecclesiastics who are called upon to serve in the army hear mass before their departure to their regiments.

The church was constructed in Ionic style, the portal being like those peculiar to churches of the Jesuits. The interior has only one nave, also Ionic, and surrounded by chapels. On the cupola is painted an Assumption. The transept chapels are ornamented by windows painted by Perrault, and the woodwork around the choir is of fine finish. Lulli, the musician, is buried in this church. Notre-Dame-des-Victoires contains many votive offerings from pious Catholics. Among these ex-voto gifts is one from three English converts. It is numbered 2631 and the inscription runs:

THANK · OFFERING
FROM · THREE · ENGLISH · CONVERTS.

A. R.	I. A.	I. G.
4. May.	1. June.	2. July.
	1864.	

Under this is an inscription recording gratitude to Our Lady of Victories "at whose feet so many prayers had been made for the conversion of England at the demand of the Hon. and Rev. George Spencer, recently converted, and known since under the name of Father Ignatius of St. Paul, of the Order of Passionists, died October 1st, 1864."

Before 1871, when the church was plundered by the Communists, the crowns on the heads of the Virgin and child were very valuable. They were shown on fête days. Some of the ornaments had been presented by the Marchioness of Wellesley, others by Pope Pius IX. Abbé V. Dumax, by the way, who wrote a small book on the church,[1] makes a curious mistake about the Marchioness of Wellesley, an American lady, Miss Caroll, whom he talks of as ascending the throne of Ireland, of which country her husband was Lord Lieutenant. The excellent Abbé was evidenty misled by the title "Viceroy." Miss Caroll first married Mr. Patterson, brother-in-law of Prince Jérome Bonaparte. The Abbé further states that when the Marchioness left the Court she set apart some of her jewels to form with them a crown for Our Lady of Victory. The memorandum of the gift is on parchment, and is preserved among the archives of the church.

[1] "Le Pèlerin à Notre Dame des Victoires. Paris, 1881." After the plundering of the church by the Communists, the parishioners and others subscribed for the purchase of new crowns for the Virgin and child. These were consecrated by the Papal Nuncio in 1876.

The High Altar—
Saint Roch.

ST. ROCH.

Northward of the Church of Victories is that of Our Lady of Loretto, "Beatæ Mariæ Virgini Lauretanæ," according to the inscription on the entablature over the portico with its four Corinthian columns. The church is very modern, but it replaced an old edifice dedicated to Notre-Dame-des-Porcherons, built in 1645. NOTRE DAME DE LORETTE calls for little treatment. It was built between 1823 and 1836 from the plans of Lebas, in the style of a Roman basilica. The interior is elaborately ornamented. Painting and gilding unite to give the church a gay, rather than a devotional appearance. It has been called the Church of the Demi-monde, or of the "Lorettes," for whom its marble, stucco and gold would seem to have been intended. The Demi-mondaines, however, when they do go to church, which often happens, are to be seen in the Madeleine, the Trinité, and St. Augustin, as well as Notre Dame de Lorette. This church is also used by the artists of various categories, who dwell in the streets leading to Montmartre on one side, or in those verging towards the Conservatoire of Music and the main boulevards on the other. The best frescoes are those in the nave and choir, which deal with episodes from the Virgin's life.

To the south of the district in which this edifice stands, is the Church of ST. ROCH, a rococo, Renaissance edifice which has been subjected to much criticism for its elaborate ornamentation. The whole neighbourhood around it is full of historic associations. The church itself dates from March, 1653, when Louis Quatorze and his mother, Anne of Austria, laid the foundation stone. Its history is rather uninteresting until the year of the Republic, 1795, when it was a "Temple of Genius" in the hands of the Theophilanthropists. In that year a young and obscure artillery officer was selected by Barras to help in putting down the opponents of the Convention, who were Royalists endeavouring to incite the electors of Paris against the Republic. Bonaparte, who had been recommended to Barras by Madame Tallien, the lovely and clever Térézia Cabarrus, known as the "Venus of the Capitol," the "Egeria of the Mountain," and by other classical appellations common in those days, had already gained a little prestige at Toulon. It was at the Church of St. Roch, however, that he first showed the Parisians that he was made of the iron stuff from which Nature fabricates great commanders and famous figures in history. He had only 5000 men against 20,000, but he did not hesitate to act with promptitude and decision in spite of the odds. The Royalists held the ground fronting the Church of St. Roch, then extending to the Tuileries gardens. They

HISTORIC CHURCHES OF PARIS.

were also strong on the other side of the river. Bonaparte directed Murat to bring up the guns from the artillery park of Sablons, placed them on the quays from the Pont Neuf to the Pont Royal and around the church of St. Roch. On the 5th October, 1795, the "Sectionnaires," as they were called, began to advance, when Bonaparte ordered them to receive the famous "whiff of grape-shot." The whole episode must be read in the penultimate chapter[1] of Carlyle's "French Revolution." There it is enshrined in immortal prose, which no French or English chronicler of the dramatic events of the end of the eighteenth century has equalled. There we are told that the "firing was with sharp and sharpest shot ; to all men it was plain that here was no sport : the rabbets and plinths of St. Roch Church show splintered by it to this hour," and that by the historic whiff which "blew to air some two hundred men, mainly about the Church of St. Roch," the event called French Revolution was whirled into space and became a thing of the past.

These brief extracts will serve to show what an important part St. Roch played in modern history. Its architectural features may be out of harmony with its historical associations, but it remains a highly interesting church. Some of the paintings by Schneiz : "Christ blessing the Children," "Christ driving out the Money-changers," by Thomas ; the "Daughter of Jairus," by Delorme ; the "Triumph of Mordecai," etc., are good. The marble monuments are likewise notable. Most of these were sent to the church, after the restoration of the monarchy, from the Museum of French Monuments. Among these are the mausoleums of Maupertius, of Cardinal Dubois, and of the painter Mignard. From Mignard's monument some ingenious person detached the figure of his daughter, Madame de Feuquières, and placed it as that of Mary Magdalen, at the foot of the Cross of the Calvary. This Calvary is behind the high altar and has three groups of statuary, lighted from above. It is much visited by the faithful, especially in Holy Week. Among the other monuments or memorials worth noting are those of the Abbé de l'Epée, founder of the Deaf and Dumb Asylum, the bust of Lenôtre, the great landscape gardener, who designed Versailles and other places, by the elder Coysevox, and on the left pillar of the principal door a medallion portrait of Pierre Corneille, the dramatist, who died in 1684 and was buried in the church. His Bi-Centenary was solemnized by a Requiem Mass at St. Roch in 1884. The venerable curé

---

[1] Carlyle's words are : "The thing we specifically call French Revolution is blown into space by it, and becomes a thing that was."

NOTRE-DAME-DE-L'ASSOMPTION.

invited to it the actors and actresses of the Comédie Française, the leading playhouse being in his parish, and its company being the only one which keeps up the classical drama of which Corneille is the chief exponent. The church was crowded on the occasion, not only by the players of the great Théâtre Français, but by ladies and gentlemen of the dramatic profession generally.

Not far off, down the Rue St. Honoré, is the Church of NOTRE DAME DE L'ASSOMPTION, with its heavy dome and environing cloister. It was built in the seventeenth century for the nuns called the " Filles de l'Assomption," or " Haudriettes," from Jean Haudry, their founder. The cupola was painted by Lafosse, with the scene of the Assumption of Mary into heaven.

The Madeleine.

CHAPTER XIV.

Modern Churches.

THE MADELEINE—ST. PHILIPPE DU ROULE—THE CHAPELLE EXPIATOIRE—ST. AUGUSTIN — ST. CLOTILDE—THE TRINITÉ—ST. VINCENT DE PAUL—THE BASILICA OF THE SACRÉ-CŒUR—THE CHAPEL OF THE CONVENT OF THE SACRÉ-CŒUR AND THE SMALLER CHURCHES.

The fashionable church—The Madeleine and the Commune—A Temple of Glory—The cemetery of the Madeleine—Louis XVI. and Marie Antoinette—Rossini's funeral—The Sacré-Cœur and the old Church of St. Pierre—A famous hill—The Hallelujah of the Germans—Ignatius Loyola—Henri Quatre and the Abbess—The Temple of Reason and the Montmartre Goddess—Montmartre in 1814, 1871 and 1895.

MARY MAGDALEN'S memory is enshrined in one of the finest of modern churches. For the MADELEINE is undoubtedly modern, as, although its foundations were laid in 1764, during the reign of the Fifteenth Louis, it was not finished and consecrated until 1842. Unlike other edifices of the kind, even including, to a certain extent, Notre Dame, it stands out alone, unhidden by surrounding buildings. All its noble proportions are visible, it raises itself proudly and prominently in one of the finest parts of Paris, and eclipses its environment by its stateliness and its size. Here come to pray all the fashionable devotees of Paris. It is as great a centre of the latest modes in dress and finery as the Grand Stand at Longchamp, or the annual Horse Show in the Champs Elysées. Do the dainty devotees pray? The answer is difficult to give. There are many, no doubt, who are touched by the semi-celestial music, the gorgeous processions of priests and acolytes, and the fascinating eloquence of the favourite and fashionable preachers. A large proportion of the well-dressed congregation are there, however, mainly for the purpose of meeting each other, of seeing and being seen, and of fulfilling the duty of attending mass. It is not good form in the real fashionable society of Paris to be an atheist or a cynic in religious matters. There was undoubted atheism among the frequenters of the Salons of the old régime, but the modern descendants of the Crusaders, the Leaguers and the *ancient noblesse* generally are, or appear to be, good Catholics. The Madeleine is also a church for fashionable marriages, and it lends itself admirably, exteriorly and inside, to lavish display on the occasion of weddings. Its curé, the Abbé Deguerry, was one of the victims of the Communists, and, in order to avenge his death, the Government troops are said to have driven a whole crowd of insurgents into the church, and to have slaughtered them there.

HISTORIC CHURCHES OF PARIS.

Contant d'Ivry was the first architect of the Madeleine, and intended to build a church like the Panthéon. His successor Couture adopted other designs, and was erecting a new construction when he was brought to a full stop by the outbreak of the Great Revolution. In 1806 Napoleon issued a decree, while he was at Posen, ordering the work to be continued, and the edifice to be prepared as a "Temple of Glory" for his soldiers. Vignon carried out the new designs, and the construction assumed the appearance of a Greek temple, with fluted Corinthian columns, a colonnade all round the body surmounted by a sculptured frieze. The façade was done by Lemaire, with its inscription "D.O.M. Sub Invocatione Sanctæ Magdalenæ," its pediment with bas-relief representing the Last Judgment, and its frieze and cornice. The composition lacks life, and, perhaps, the bronze doors sculptured with subjects from the Ten Commandments by Triqueti, form the most interesting features of the exterior.

Gilding is abundant in the interior of the splendid church, which is lighted from the top. The most important feature is the high altar, on which is a marble work by Marochetti representing Mary Magdalen being carried to Paradise by Angels. On the vaulted top of the choir is a fresco by Ziegler on which the history of Christianity is depicted. It is not a great work of art, but it answers its purpose well and includes figures of Constantine, Clovis, Barbarossa, Dante, Joan of Arc, the Wandering Jew, Napoleon, Pius VII., in fact, nearly every remarkable historical personage who has been connected with the Christian Church in a special manner.

There is not much to be said of the Church of St. PHILIPPE DU ROULE in the Faubourg St. Honoré, except that it stands on the site of an old leper's hospital, that it was built in the Greek style by Chalgrin between 1760 and 1784, and that it contains a "Descent from the Cross" painted by Chasseriau. Not far from this edifice is the small church of St. PIERRE-DE-CHAILLOT, which, like St. Philippe du Roule, is in the parochial district of the Madeleine.

The CHAPELLE EXPIATOIRE, in the Boulevard Haussmann, which has a connection with the Madeleine, was built by order of Louis XVIII., over the place where the remains of Louis XVI. and Marie Antoinette were supposed to have been for twenty-one years, before their removal to St. Denis. This place was formerly the cemetery of the Madeleine, and other victims of the Revolution were buried there. The

MODERN CHURCHES.

monument is in the form of a Greek cross with dome and portico. Under the chapel is a crypt marking the spot where the bodies of the murdered king and queen were supposed to have lain. Inside the chapel are two marble groups. On the right is Bosio's figure of Louis XVI., his will inscribed beneath. On the left are the queen and a figure supposed to be that of Madame Elizabeth, sister of Louis XVI., who was also guillotined.

S^T AUGUSTIN

The more modern churches of Paris call for little notice in these pages. ST. AUGUSTIN'S, on the Boulevard Malesherbes, is a much-criticized edifice which was erected between 1860 and 1868. It is a modern blending of Romanesque and Gothic. The nave has an arched roof on arcades of open ironwork, and over the altar is a gilt baldacchino.

HISTORIC CHURCHES OF PARIS.

Another modern and fashionable church is that of STE. CLOTILDE, on the left side of the Seine, and close to the War Office and the Chamber of Deputies. Its Gothic spires with crockets and openings appear above the thick cluster of houses marking the most aristocratic and the most tranquil part of the Faubourg St. Germain. The church was built between 1846 and 1859. The interior is interesting, although it lacks light, and the

excellent paintings cannot, therefore, be seen to advantage. The altar, the carven stalls of the choir, and the stained glass are notable features in this fashionable house of prayer.

The Church of the TRINITÉ was built on Ballu's plans between 1861 and 1867. It stands in the Rue St. Lazare, in front of it being a garden

The Trinité.

To face p. 187.

MODERN CHURCHES.

ornamented with fountains and statues of Faith, Hope, and Charity. Like St. Augustin's, the Trinité has fallen in for much censure owing to its elaborate decoration. Everything is florid, perhaps even theatrical. It was one of the churches built during the Second Empire, and shows the taste of that gilded and grandiose period.

The most important event in the history of the Trinité was the funeral service for Rossini in November, 1868. The new church, as it was then, was crowded with celebrities. The music was the finest ever heard out of St. Peter's. Nilsson was there, and the duet between Alboni and Patti, the "Quis est Homo," from Rossini's own "Stabat Mater," set strong men, as well as sentimental women, weeping until their eyes were red. Rossini's coffin was covered with Parma violets, his favourite flower, and with ivy. Then the remains were transferred to Père La Chaise, where they were disinterred a few years ago to be placed beside "Angelo's, Alfieri's bones" in the Santa Croce at Florence.

One more important church is that of ST. VINCENT DE PAUL, which is towards the north of Paris, and was built between 1824 and 1844 in the basilica style. The exterior is made specially imposing by the wide semi-circular steps leading to the doors. These form a sort of amphitheatre at the foot of the façade, with its portico of fluted Ionic columns supporting a heavy entablature on the pediment of which there is a relief representing that firm friend of the poor and the foundling, St. Vincent de Paul. The interior is especially interesting, owing to the stained glass, the statuary, and the paintings. In the nave is a fresco by Hippolyte Flandrin representing early Christians. The painter took suggestions from the mosaics of the Church of St. Apollinare Nuovo of Ravenna, which have inspired many other artists, and writers as well. The Chapel of the Virgin contains a fine group by Carrier-Belleuse and paintings by Bouguereau. The bronze Crucifixion by Rude, over the high altar, is a masterpiece.

Towering still farther to the north is the newest of modern churches in Paris—the Basilica of the SACRÉ-CŒUR. This edifice, still unfinished, is on the historic hill of Montmartre, now one of the poorest parts of Paris. Near it is the old church of ST. PIERRE DE MONTMARTRE. The two buildings, the new and the old, occupy the site of a rich abbey. Towards the end of the tenth century this hill was invaded by the forces of Otto the Second, who wanted to take some revenge for the entry of his cousin

HISTORIC CHURCHES OF PARIS.

Lothair's troops into Germany, and their excesses at Aix-la-Chapelle. Otto sent a proud message to the Duke of Paris to say that his men would sing on the Mount of the Martyrs a Hallelujah such as the city and its rulers had never heard before: "Parvenu sur les hauteurs de Montmartre, il fait chanter à ses soldats un Alleluia si bruyant, qu'il pouvait s'entendre de Notre-Dame de Paris." There is also a picture of it in Latin, by one of the old chroniclers, who tells us that the clergy gathered on the hill, and the German legions sang in so loud a voice their Alleluia to the Martyrs "ut attonitis auribus ipse Hugo et omnis Parisiorum plebs miraretur." All the events of this fighting period are inaccurately chronicled, but there are other historic memories connected with Montmartre which can be vouched for. In 1534, Ignatius Loyola, Francis Xavier and Peter Faber started singing from Notre Dame all the way up to Montmartre. This is more than the Salvationists have ever attempted to do in our days. Arrived on the hill, the three holy men made their vows there and practically laid the foundations of the great and powerful Company of Jesus. In 1590, Henry Quatre, while besieging Paris, made Montmartre his headquarters and visited the Nunnery or Abbey where the young and beautiful Marie de Beauvilliers was Abbess. The convent, which was called a royal abbey because the Abbesses were appointed by the king, was always full of noble ladies. In 1760, Marie Louise de Laval, Duchesse de Montmorency, was Mother Abbess. She was guillotined with all her nuns in 1793, the old convent was turned into a Temple of Reason, and a young Montmartre girl was elected Goddess. Soon afterwards the abbey was demolished, and the Church of St. Peter, originally founded by Louis VI. about 1135,[1] like the monastery itself, is all that remains of the antique edifices once crowning the hill. Montmartre also played an important part in 1814, when it held out against the Allies for a time. In 1871 it was the headquarters of the Communists who murdered Generals Lecomte and Clément-Thomas, and then, after some firing, retired to the Buttes-Chaumont and Père La Chaise. The Church of St. Pierre is frequently visited by archæologists, as it contains some columns and capitals supposed to have come from the older church and the abbey. The Calvary, or cemetery, hard by contains some tombs, and there is also the old graveyard of Montmartre.

The Church of the SACRÉ-CŒUR was built from Abadie's designs in the Romanesque-Byzantine style. Its history is elaborately set forth in the book written by Père Jonquière, a priest of the Order of Oblates of Mary

---

[1] The date is very dubious. 1147, given by Baedeker, is altogether wrong. .

MODERN CHURCHES.

Immaculate. It was decreed as a work of public utility by the National Assembly in July, 1873, and it has been raised by subscriptions amounting to nearly twenty-nine millions of francs. The strengthening of the foundations alone cost £140,000. Impressive services are periodically held in this church, and it is also a place of pilgrimage visited by pious Catholics from all parts of the world. The lower part of Montmartre is full of Communistic memories. It is likewise the abode of Parisian frivolity, the centre of dancing-halls, and night-houses, but over all these towers the holy citadel of prayer founded by the pious Cardinal Guibert in atonement for the excesses of Revolution and the sins of Paris.

Here must end the series of important historical churches destined for Catholic worship in Paris. There have been few religious edifices omitted from the list, for nearly all the churches have had a history. Buildings like St. Louis d'Antin, St. Pierre-du-Petit-Montrouge, St. Ambroise, St. Bernard, St. Eugène, near the Conservatoire of Music, Notre Dame des Champs, St. Ferdinand of the Ternes, and the handsome church for English-speaking Catholics in the Avenue Hoche, directed by the Passionists of the British province of their Order, must be unavoidably excluded. Their time for a place in a book of this kind has not yet arrived. Before concluding the series, however, it will be necessary to direct the attention of readers of the volume to the fourteenth-century chapel of the Château of Vincennes, with its splendid glass, and to the more modern chapel of the Chateau of Versailles. Noteworthy, too, is the chapel of the great Convent of the Sacré-Cœur in the Rue de Varennes, near the Hôtel des Invalides. This famous institution was founded by Madame Barat, who was of plebeian origin, and has since been succeeded by Mother Superiors of patrician birth. The present head of the Order is an Englishwoman of the noble house of Digby. Nearly all the titled ladies of France have been educated in this extensive establishment, which possesses a vast garden wherein once wandered and studied the daughters of Queen Isabella of Spain, the Duchesse de Rohan, the Duchesse de Brissac, and a host of others.

The Russian Church
(Winter.

CHAPTER XV

THE PROTESTANT CHURCH OF THE ORATORY—
THE RUSSIAN CHURCH—THE SYNAGOGUES.

French Protestants before the Reformers—" Little Geneva"—Calvin and Cop—Abbot Briçonnet and Marguerite de Navarre—Burning heretics—The Protestant tailor—The Huguenot hedge-schools—The first Synod—St. Bartholomew's Day—The League—The Edict of Nantes—George Washington and the French Protestants—The " White Terror"—The Bible Society—Jonathan the Jew—Early persecutions of the Children of Israel—Removal of Jewish disabilities.

PROTESTANTISM, according to some French writers, was heard of in France before the Reformers. Its cradle and nursing-place was the left bank of the Seine, among the schools where the daring Peter Abelard, the remarkable predecessor of Martin Luther, taught and preached. The "Gallic Liberties," which have also been regarded in the form of protests against the domination of Rome, dated, too, from the early days of the Paris University, and the uncompromising enemies of the Papacy go so far as to claim St. Louis

FRANÇOIS I.   himself as the first of the French Protesters or Protestants, because he is supposed to have signed a Concordat in 1268, and to have firmly resisted the intrusion of the Sovereign Pontiff in temporal affairs. Without going back, however, to the thirteenth century for proofs of nascent Protestantism in France, it will be sufficient to note for present purposes that in 1512 a professor named Lefèvre d'Etaples published a commentary on St. Paul, in which, five years before Luther, he explained the essential doctrines of the Reformation. The book was actually dedicated to the Abbot of St. Germain-des-Prés, Briçonnet, who thought highly of it, and endorsed its teachings. So, too, did many in the district of the monastery until that part of the Faubourg St. Germain became known as "Little Geneva." One of the pupils of the professor was burned for heresy in 1524, and he is supposed to be the first Huguenot who was put to death in France. Calvin was in Paris soon after this, and was directed by Cop, Rector of the University, to write an address for the opening of the schools. He did so, and his daring theories were condemned by the monks. He and Cop had narrow escapes. The latter succeeded in reaching Basle, while Calvin hid in Paris.

Briçonnet, the abbot above-mentioned, induced Margaret of Navarre, sister of Francis I., to hearken to the new doctrines, and she became unpopular thereby. In 1535, Francis I. attended the burnings of heretics on the Place Maubert, as well as outside St. Germain L'Auxerrois, or other localities. Henri II. did likewise, but was so frightened at seeing a

HISTORIC CHURCHES OF PARIS.

Protestant tailor burned alive, that he desisted from witnessing the executions. At that time the Protestants of Paris had neither pastors nor churches. They had, however, schools which were called *buissonnières*, that is to say "hedge-schools," as they were once called in Ireland, where they were common. One of the most notable Protestants at this epoch was the poet and translator of the Psalms into French verse, Clément Marot, who was once befriended by Francis I., but had to fly for his life in 1537.

In 1559 the Protestants first assembled in Synod in Paris, and re-united all the Reformed Churches of France into one. Then followed the terrible persecutions which culminated in the massacre on St. Bartholomew's Day. In spite of opposition and dangers which they incurred, the Protestants began to meet for prayer, secretly, in different parts of the environs of the city, and among their pastors was Bèze, who preached regularly. At last, after the horrors of St. Bartholomew's Day and the wars of the League, came the Edict of Nantes in 1598, and the two religions were recognized by the State. The Protestants, however, had to meet five leagues from Paris, but later on they were allowed to assemble at Ablon on the Seine, and then at Charenton, which is at the gates of the city. The death of Henri Quatre, who had been a Protestant, was a severe blow to the Huguenots. The "temple," as Protestant churches are called in France, was burned, as well as houses near it at Charenton. A new place of worship was erected in 1624, and among its congregation were Conrart, who is called the real founder of the French Academy, and Théophraste Renaudot, the creator of journalism in France. Among the noble Protestants were the Bouillons, the Turennes, the La Trémouilles and the De Rohans.

The Edict of Nantes was revoked in 1685, and the Protestants were again proscribed. Bossuet, in spite of his Gallicanism, which makes him so great a favourite with some Protestant writers, was one of the first to applaud the proscriptions, and he was followed by Madame de Sévigné, La Bruyère, La Fontaine, and thousands of others in Paris. The light of Protestantism was not quenched, however. Its followers were long sheltered by the representatives of England, Holland and Denmark. George Washington also made La Fayette promise, on leaving freed America, to do his best to obtain liberty for the descendants of the Huguenots. Matters, however, did not improve much until 1789, when liberty of conscience was proclaimed by the Convention. Then the Protestants, protected by La Fayette, were able to worship openly and without molestation. The First Napoleon afterwards

THE ORATORY.

recognized them, gave three of their preachers Crosses of the Legion of Honour, and allowed them three "temples."

The chief church accorded was the Oratory, still existing in the Rue de Rivoli, and against the apsis of which stands the monument to Admiral Coligny, with the open Bible at his feet. This church was built by the French Oratorians, or priests of the Oratory founded by Cardinal de Bérulle, in 1630, on the site where Gabrielle d'Estrées, the friend of Henri Quatre, had lived. It was to the Oratory that the utterly bad man, Philip of Orléans, Regent during the minority of Louis XV., used to go "on retreat," in order to prepare for his Easter Communion. The Order had many illustrious men like Massillon, Malebranche and Daunou, and from it also stepped forth the Jacobin Fouché, Duke of Otranto, Minister of Police under the First Napoleon and Louis XVIII., and whose remarkable personality, revived by Sardou in the play of "Madame Sans-Gêne," creates as much interest, almost, as that of his master. The Protestants of Paris were not troubled during the Restoration, although their brethren in the South of France suffered during what was called the "White Terror." The Bourbons, however, were less friendly towards the descendants of the Huguenots than Napoleon, who had invited three Protestant pastors to his coronation in Notre Dame, and had promised them that he would respect and support their religion. It is needless to dwell here on the disruptions which occurred among the followers of the Reformers in France after they had obtained freedom. They were supposed to have lost their orthodoxy, and the English Protestants, after the peace of Amiens, and especially after the downfall of Napoleon, undertook to bring them back to it. The language of the English Revivalists, however, often offended the ears of the French Protestants, who were patriots, and many of whom had taken part in the Revolution. It was to English example, however, that the French Protestants owed the foundation of a Bible Society which strengthened their hands.

The ORATORY, in the Louvre district, is still the great headquarters of the Reformed Church in Paris. It is a heavy and rather gloomy building in Corinthian style, and, as has been already pointed out, offers a striking contrast to the lighter and more elegant church of St. Germain L'Auxerrois, its near neighbour. Other Reformed Churches are the TEMPLE DU SAINT-ESPRIT in the Rue Roquépine; the EGLISE DE L'ETOILE, Avenue de la Grande Armée, both new buildings; the older "Temple de Sainte-Marie," Faubourg St. Antoine, formerly attached to a Convent of Nuns of the

HISTORIC CHURCHES OF PARIS.

Visitation, and built by Mansart in 1632 on the lines of the Roman Pantheon. It was sadly damaged by the Communists in 1871, and was restored by Varcollier. Another fairly old church is that of the Lutheran section of the Protestants of France, in the Rue des Billettes. It was formerly a Catholic place of worship, constructed from the plans of a Dominican monk and built over an old chapel, on the portal of which were the words, " Here God was boiled." This was in allusion to the miracle recorded in the Chronicles of St. Denis, which happened in 1290. A Jew, vaguely named Jonathan, was said to have stabbed a Host and then to have boiled it. A Gothic cloister of the old chapel still remains.

The Russian Church in Paris, which is in the Rue Daru, was built between 1859 and 1861 in a Byzantine-Muscovite style. Its form is that of a Greek cross with slightly irregular branches or arms, and a porch in front. In the centre is a tower with open bays and a gilded pyramid above. The spire is surmounted by a six-branched Russian cross. On the " iconostasis," or screen, in the interior, are paintings representing Christ, the Virgin, St. Michael, St. Stephen, St. Alexander Newsky, patron of the church, St. Nicolas, etc. These and the frescoes are by the Sorokines, Bronnikoff and Wassilieff.

The chief synagogue is in the Rue de la Victoire, not far from the bank of the Rothschilds. It is constructed in a style analogous to the Roman. The exterior comprises a porch of large dimensions, a principal nave and two aisles surmounted by galleries. In front of the choir is the Théba, or place for the officiating Rabbi, with marble balustrade. On either side of the choir are the stalls for the members of the Consistories of Paris and France. There are three other synagogues in Paris—those of the Rue Notre Dame de Nazareth, the Rue des Tournelles, with frontage on the old and picturesque Place des Vosges, and the Rue Buffault, where Jews of the Portuguese rite assemble for prayer on their Sabbath.

Since the Revolution, when the Constituent Assembly decreed liberty of conscience, the Israelites have been unmolested in Paris and France, although in these days a vigorous campaign has been conducted against them by the so-called Anti-Semites, of whom M. Edouard Drumont is the chief champion. The Napoleonic Concordat, which brought the churches under State control, established the legal right of the Jews to have synagogues, and gave them full civic rights. In previous ages those professing the Hebrew religion in Paris were energetically persecuted and frequently hunted out of their dwellings, their property being then

Israelite Temple.

THE SYNAGOGUES.

confiscated by their Christian tormentors. Episodes of this sort occurred under Philip Augustus, St. Louis, and Charles VI. During the reign of Henri Quatre, the Israelites, or some of them, returned to Paris. Louis XIII. banished them again in 1615, but with the dawn of new ideas in the eighteenth century came the era of their emancipation.

CHAPTER XVI.

INSCRIPTIONS AND EPITAPHS.

A ghastly memorial—The " Sorrows of Death"—Eccentric epitaphs—The Bouvines memorial—Strange epitaph of Jean de Creil—The glory of Louis XIII.—The tomb of Lulli—The Inscriptions in the Scotch College.

HENRY II.

EAN DE CHELLES, who has been alluded to in the chapters on Notre Dame de Paris, left one of the most remarkable of the inscriptions recorded on the stones of the cathedral. It perpetuates his name at the foot of the southern portal in Gothic capitals which are the finest specimens of their kind extant. The inscription, which is on one line, has already been quoted, and is terminated by the figure of a dragon. Some of the other antique inscriptions, like that recording the money gifts for stained glass offered by Pierre de Fayet, in 1303, were taken out of the church. That of Fayet is to be seen in the Louvre Museum.

One of the most curious memorials in the cathedral is the "pierre tombale" of Étienne Yver on the left wall, entering by the Virgin's door. This gruesome as well as curious memorial was formerly in the Chapel of St. Nicolas near the cloister. It dates from 1467, and was put in its present position in September, 1762.

At the bottom of the memorial are inscribed the following words, which are undecipherable owing to lack of light. One has, in fact, to use a lamp or a candle in order to read them, and hence they are necessarily overlooked by the average visitor :—

   Ante hanc ymaginem jacet Stephanus Yuer in jure canonico
licentiatus huius Parisiensis Rothomagensis ecclesiarum canonicus
Archidjaconus magnj caletj Dominj nostrj Regis in sua parlamentj
Curia Consiliarius Oriundus de perona Nouiomensis diocesis
habeat deus quam creauit animam ejus habet natura quod suum est
Expectans Resurrectionem et utriusque vitam aeternam.
                  Opporte enim
corruptibile hoc induere incorruptionem et mortale hoc induere immortali-
tatem. Obiit anno dominj millesimo CCCC°. LX°. VIJO. mensis februarij
die vero vicesima quarta Orate pro eo.

All this sets forth that "In front of this image lies Stephen Yver, licentiate in canon law, Canon of this church and of Rouen, Archdeacon of Grand Caux, Counsellor of the King in his court of Parliament, native of Péronne, diocese of Noyon. May his soul return to God who created it. May nature take what belongs to it, in awaiting the promised Resurrection, that both then may enjoy life eternal. For this body must become incorruptible and put on immortality, as being mortal. He died in the year of our Lord 1467, twenty-fourth of February. Pray for him."

The device on either side of this inscription is "la mercj Dieu," and on the sarcophagus are the words :—

> Preocupauerunt me dolores mortis torrentes iniquitatis conturbauerunt me. Nunc sum vermis et non homo induta est caro mea putridine et sordibus pulueris cutis mea aruit et contracta est. Deus, Deus, meus Respice in me et miserere mej quia tibi pecauj et malum coram te fecj.

The first line is from the 18th Psalm, "The sorrows of death compassed me, and the floods of ungodly men made me afraid." In the Catholic version of the Bible this is in the 17th Psalm, "The sorrows of death surrounded me ; and the torrents of iniquity troubled me." The second line is in the 21st Psalm, Catholic version, and in the 22nd in the Protestant Bible, "But I am a worm and no man." The third line is from Job, chapter vii., fifth verse, "My flesh is clothed with worms and clods of dust ; my skin is broken and become loathsome," but the Latin words of the inscription are more closely rendered in the Catholic Testament : "My flesh is clothed with rottenness and the filth of dust, my skin is withered and drawn together." The last line is the invocation for mercy, "Look upon me," etc., from the 85th Psalm of the Catholic version, and the "Miserere."

In the scroll held by the defunct are the words, "Non intres in judicium cum servo tuo, Domine, sed miserere mej. Nam imperfectum meum viderunt oculj tuj et in libro tuo omnes scribentur "—" Enter not into judgment with thy servant," and " Thy eyes did see my imperfect being, and in thy book all shall be written." These quotations are from the 142nd and 138th Psalms of the Catholic Bible. They are in the 143rd and the 139th in the other version.

On the book held by the Redeemer are the words :—

Miserebor	quem michi
cuj voluero	placuerit
et clemens	Exodj
ero in	XXXIIJ°.

INSCRIPTIONS AND EPITAPHS.

"I will have mercy on whom I will, and I will be merciful to whom it shall please me;" or, as in Protestant version, "I will be gracious to whom I will be gracious, and will show mercy on whom I will show mercy" (Exod. xxxiii).

On the summit of the memorial, above the head of Christ, are the words: "Clamabant alter ad alterum. Sanctus, Sanctus, Sanctus."

Yver's memorial, as has before been shown, represents the canon's body, on the lower part, being devoured by worms, and above, the priest is assisted out of his tomb by St. Stephen and St. John the Evangelist. The Redeemer, crowned with thorns, is over all. He has two swords in his mouth, and is represented as "God in Majesty." The work was executed in accordance with a fifteenth-century custom, and other specimens of the style are on the tombs of Louis XII., Francis I., and Henri II., at St. Denis. The conception is ghastly and realistic.

In the Sainte Chapelle the epitaphs are mostly those of canons buried beneath the church. One of the most curious is that of Guillaume Belier, canon in 1428. The stone is a sort of mosaic with a cross on it, and the canon's initials, as well as a kneeling figure of the defunct. Above is this inscription in Latin :—

>Qui teritis tritis similes eritis bene scitis
>quos pedibus premitis precibus releuare velitis,

which is of the "As I am now, so will you be" order of epitaph, common enough in the graveyards of Great Britain. "Help with your prayers those on whom you walk," is the concluding invocation. The remaining inscription is in French, and refers to the deceased canon, who died in 1428. He is an obscure man, unknown save for this eccentric epitaph, composed, perhaps, by himself or one of his colleagues.

Here is an example of one of the epitaphs at St. Denis :—

CY GIST LA ROYNE ISABEL DE BAUIERE ESPOUSE DU ROY CHARLES VI*. ET FILLE DE TRES PUISSANT PRINCE ESTIENNE DUC DE BAUIERE COTE PALATIN DU RHIN QUI REGNA AUEC SOND EPOUSE ET TRESPASSA L'AN M : CCCC ET XXXV LE DERNIER JOUR DE SEPTEMBRE. PRIES DIEU POUR ELLE.

This, as will be seen, is the epitaph of Isabeau of Bavaria, wife of Charles VI. Another interesting inscription is that on the memorial of the battle of Bouvines, formerly in the Church of St. Catherine of the Students'

HISTORIC CHURCHES OF PARIS.

Vale, in Paris. The valiant sergeants made a vow to found a church in honour of "Madame Sainte Katherine," if they gained the victory. They did so, for the Flemings were defeated, and King Philip Augustus was not only triumphant, but was able, through his victory, to consolidate the French monarchy, in spite of Otho of Germany, and John Lackland, the monarch of England. Charles V. founded a confraternity or guild of the "sergents d'armes," and had the following inscription engraved on the memorial of Bouvines :—

A LA PRIERE DES SERGENS D'ARMES
MONR. SAINT LOYS FONDA CESTE EGLISE ET Y MIST LA PREMIERE
PIERRE ET FU POUR LA JOIE DE LA VICTOIRE
QUI FU AV PONT DE BOUINES L'AN MIL. CC ET XIII.
LES SERGENS D'ARMES POUR LE TEMPS
GARDOIENT LE DIT PONT ET VOUERENT QUE SI DIEU LEUR DONNOIT
VITTOIRE ILS FONDEROIENT
UNE EGLISE EN L'HONNEUR DE MADAME SAINTE KATHARINE
ET AINSU FU IL.

Bouvines is between French Lille and Belgian Tournay, and the battle was fought in 1213, according to this inscription, but in some of the histories the date is 1214.

St. Germain L'Auxerrois is full of epitaphs, but they are mostly those of obscure persons or of donors to the church. In St. Germain-des-Prés are epitaphs to Boileau and Descartes. Of the latter, it is recorded on his tombstone that he "took the scales from the eyes of blind mortals, and guarding the respect due to altars, showed them the structure of the world."

There is a long epitaph on Racine's memorial in St. Etienne du Mont, and in it the social and professional gifts of the poet are extolled to the skies. Another inscription records the existence and death of "Blasius Pascal Claromontanus Stephani Pascal in suprema apud Avernos subsidiorum curia præsidiis filius"—"Blaise Pascal, son of Stephen, President of the Court of Clermont in Auvergne."

St. Nicolas-des-Champs, in the Rue St. Martin, is another church full of quaint tombstone or tablet inscriptions. There is one to a worthy named Jean de Creil, who was a counsellor of King Henri Quatre, and whose life-history is recorded amid a jumble of Christian and Pagan references and reminiscences. He was, for instance, born "under favour of Hercules," everything went so well with him that he "seemed to have discovered the

INSCRIPTIONS AND EPITAPHS.

secret of appeasing Nemesis," and, in fact, Jean would not have died at all but for "the anger of the Fates." There is added to this remarkable inscription an anagram establishing Jean de Creil's right to enter heaven. This inscription has been much injured, and is now on the floor of the Chapel of St. Vincent de Paul in this Church of St. Nicholas.

The Church of Notre Dame des Victoires is another of the sacred edifices of Paris where inscriptions abound. The foundation stone was inscribed with one of those pompous compositions common in the reigns of Louis XIII. and of his successor Louis XIV., and often imitated by the recorders of the victories of the First Napoleon. The full text was this:—

> Ludovicus XIII., Dei gratia, Francorum et Navarræ rex christianissimus, invictus et ubique victor, tot victoriarum coelitus partarum profligatæque hæreseos non immemor, in insigne pietatis monumentum FF. Augustineanis discalceatis, Conventiis Parisiensis, hoc Templum erexit, Deiparæque Virgini Mariæ, sub titulo de Victorias dicavit, Anno Domini MDCXXIX die IX monis Decembris, regno vero XX.
> Translation:—
> Louis XIII., by the grace of God, most Christian King of France and Navarre, everywhere and always victorious, in memory of all the victories with which Heaven favoured him, and mindful especially of the triumph gained over heresy, hath constructed this remarkable monument of pious gratitude for the bare-footed Augustinian Friars of the Paris monastery, and hath dedicated it to the Virgin Mary, Mother of God, under the title of Our Lady of Victories, the year of our Lord 1629, the 9th of December, and the 20th year of his reign.

Another stone was found in the church in 1863, inscribed with a record of the munificence of the founder, and the month of his death:—

> XIV° Maio Anniversarium
> Triumphantis Memoriæ Ludovici XIII.
> Regis Francorum et Navarræ
> Hujus Conventus Fundatoris Munificentissimi.

Another notable inscription which is still to be seen is that on the tomb of M. Des Genettes, curé of the parish for twenty-eight years, and who died in 1860. The epitaph was composed at Rome by Commendatore Rossi and Monsignor Lacroix, Apostolic Protonotary. The conclusion seems to foretell the events which happened in France in 1870-71.

> Ave anima fortis pietissima
> Huic fatiscenti ævo plurimos tibi similes
> Coelitus donandos præcibus impetra.

Translation:—
Hail strong and pious soul! May you obtain for us from heaven, in this century of unrest and ruin, many men like yourself!

HISTORIC CHURCHES OF PARIS.

The ex-votos, or votive tablets, to the Virgin abound in this church. They remind one of the similar offerings or memorials in the churches of Munich, Innspruck, Vienna, and other towns in Catholic Bavaria and Austria, wherein one reads so often on scrolls, wreaths or tablets the words " Maria hilf," and " Maria hat geholfen." Similar records of successful appeals for help to the Virgin are in St. Germain L'Auxerrois, but especially in Notre Dame des Victoires. In this latter church there is also a tablet recording the fact that the people of the parish of St. Laurence made a pilgrimage there in May, 1871, in order to ask the Virgin to " preserve their church from the impious and to obtain for them the return of their exiled priests." The prayers were heard, and a tablet was accordingly offered to Notre Dame des Victoires.

In 1855 the exiled Poles in Paris placed a fine tablet near the choir of Notre Dame des Victoires, in commemoration of the twenty-fifth year of their banishment and of the promulgation of the dogma of the Immaculate Conception. The conclusion of the inscription is peculiar :—

> Hi in Curribus et hi in equis ; nos autem
> In nomine Mariæ invocabimus.

Translation :—
Some trust in chariots, others in horses, but we confide in the name of Mary which we have invoked.

The other inscriptions in this church comprise a long one, in Latin, recording the foundation. There is another, to the same effect, in French, and both are in the Chapel of St. Augustin.

There is also the tomb of Lulli, the composer, which is largely inscribed in French and Latin. The Latin epitaph is interesting, and reproaches Death with being deaf and with having robbed the king and the people of Lulli's music.

> Perfida mors, inimica, audax, temeraria et excors,
> Crudelisque et cœca, probris te absolvimus istis ;
> Non de te querimur, tua sint hæ munia magna.
> Sed quando per te, populi Regisque voluptas,
> Non antè auditis rapuit qui cantibus orbem,
> LULLIUS eripitur ; querimur modo ; surda fuisti.

There must also be recorded the Greek inscription over the holy-water fonts, which reads both ways :—

> νιψον ανομηματα μη μοναν οψιν
> ABLUE PECCATA NON SOLAM FACIEM.

INSCRIPTIONS AND EPITAPHS.

The Greek text is taken from the Church of St. Sophia at Constantinople. It is graven in red characters on a ground of white marble, and the letters join together. Père Lefèbre, of the Company of Jesus, thus rendered it :—

Cest l'âme et non le corps qu'il faut purifier.

The Scotch College, near the Sorbonne and the Pitié hospital, now devoted to other purposes, has many inscriptions of a historical character. This establishment was founded in 1325 by Bishop Murray for Catholic students. It contains the tombs and epitaphs of James II., the Duchess of Tyrconnell, Patrick Menteith, a knight, Robert Barclay, priest, Marianus O'Cruoly, John Caryl, James Drummond, and a few others.

Fuller information on the subject of epitaphs in Paris churches, convents, and colleges, may be found in F. de Guilhermy's " Inscriptions," where they are treated in a detailed manner.

FINIS.

INDEX.

ABBAYE AUX BOIS, 156.
Abelard, Peter, 7, 9, 82 sq., 193.
Ablon, 194.
Affré, Archbishop, 27, 53, 56.
Agnadel (Vaila), 23.
Albert de Luynes, 104.
Albi, Archbishop of, 157.
Albigenses, 16.
Alboni, 186.
Alcuin, 33.
Alexander III., 38, 43, 113.
Amiens, Peace of, 195.
Anaqui, 19.
Angoulême, Count of, 62.
Angus, Earl of, 114.
Anjou, Duke of, 20.
Anne de Bretagne, 95.
Anne of Austria, 135, 148, 177.
Anselm, 82.
Antiaristocrats, 164.
Arago, 124.
Armagnacs, 21, 22, 163.
Armez, Abbé, 146.
Army, the Grand (trophies), 150.
Arnold of Brescia, 84.
Astrolabius, 84.
Attila, 57, 123.
Augustinians, 175.
Austerlitz, 27.
Autun Cathedral, 35.

BALDWIN II., 64.
Baltard, 115.
Balzac, 103.
Barat, Madame, 189.
Barbarossa, Frederick, 15.
Barclay, Robert, 207.
Barras, 136.
Bauchal, 31.
Bayard, 23.
Bedford, Duke of, 22.
Belier, Guillaume, 203.
Belle Poule (frigate), 152.

Benserade, 168.
Bérenger of Tours, 82.
Berneval, Alexandre de, 67.
Bernier, 172.
Berri, Duc de, 21, 92, 96, 105.
Berruger, Philip, 68.
Bertin, 117, 157.
Bertrand, 150.
Bérulle, 195.
Beslay, 166.
Bèze, Theodore de, 104, 194.
"biberon," 69.
Biron, Marshal de, 174.
Black Prince, 20.
Blanc, 124.
Blanche of Castile, 17, 68.
"Blancs Manteaux," 174.
Blondel, 157.
Boileau, 63, 65, 172.
—— (epitaph), 204.
Bonaparte, 136, 177.
Boniface VIII., 18.
Boniface, Pope, 69.
Booth, General, 111.
Bordeaux, Duc de, 27.
Borie, Abbé de, 131.
Borromini, 175.
Bosio, 185.
Bossu, Abbé, 165.
Bossuet, 129, 194.
—— (statue), 139.
Bougainville, 124.
Bouguereau, 187.
Bouillons, the, 194.
Bourbon, Cardinal de, 174.
Bourdaloue, 174.
Bourdon, 172.
Bourguignons and Armagnacs, 21, 22.
Bouvines, Battle of, 203.
Briçonnet, Abbot, 114, 193.
Bronnikoff, 126.
Bruand, 149.
Buci, Bishop Matiffas de, 54.
Buckle, H. T., 8.

INDEX.

Bugenud, 150.
Buguet, 173.
buissonnières, 194.
Burgundy, Duke of, 62, 163.
Butler, Alban, 136.

CABANEL, ALEXANDER, 124.
Cabarrus, Térézia, 177.
Cadoudal, Georges, 174.
Calvin, 104, 193.
Caminade, 172.
Candeille, Demoiselle, 26.
"Candide," 147.
Carlyle, 178.
Carmelites (Déchaux), 154.
Carnot, Lazare, 123, 125, 136.
Carnot, President, 11, 22, 28, 125.
Caroll, Miss, 176.
Carrier-Belleuse, 187.
Cartaux, 168.
Carvallo, 124.
Caryl, John, 207.
Casimir V., 114.
Castellans, 114.
Catherine de Bourbon, 114.
Catherine de Courtenay, 94.
Catherine de' Medici, 23, 103 sq., 169.
—— (tomb), 95.
Catulla, 78.
Caussade, 174.
Cavaillé-Coll, 56, 138.
Cerutti, 164.
Chalgrin, 138.
Champs Élysées, 113.
Chapel of the Martyrs, 154.
Chapelain, 170.
Chapelle, 172.
Chapelle des Catéchismes (St. Germain l'Auxerrois), 106.
Chapelle Expiatoire, 184.
Charenton, 194.
Charlemagne (statue), 96.
Charles d'Étampes, 97.
Charles the Bad, 102.
Charles the Bold (tomb), 89.
Charles IV., Emperor, 68.
Charles V., the Wise, 20, 61.
Charles VI., 89.
Charles X., 23.
Chartier, Jean, 82.
"Chasse" (Saint Chapelle), 73.
Chavannes, Puvis de, 124.
Cheval, 146.
Childebert I., 54, 112.
Childeric III., 79.
Chilperic I., 95.
Chouans, 174.
Choublier, M., 33.

Churchill, General, 152.
Claretie, M. Jules, 147.
Clément, Jacques, 103.
Clément, Thomas, 188.
Clement V., 19, 20.
Clement VIII., 169.
Cliquet, 56, 138.
Clootz, Baron Anacharsis, 26.
Clovis, 22, 125.
Cluny, 34, 35, 84.
Colbert (tomb), 168.
Coligny, 101, 102 sq.
Compassion Chapel (St. Germain l'Auxerrois), 107.
Concino Concini, 104.
Condé, Prince de, 94, 101 sq.
Conegliano, Duke of, 150.
Conrart, 194.
Conservatoire des Arts et Métiers, 171.
Constant d'Ivry, 184.
Convulsionists, 159.
Cop, 193.
Coquelin, 124.
Corday, Charlotte, 122.
Corneille, Pierre, 178.
Couillié, Abbé, 167.
Cour des Réservoir, 44.
Cousin, 169.
Couston, 117.
Couture, 184.
Coypel, 106, 157.
Coysevox, 106, 178.
Crébillon, 169.
Crown of Thorns, 64, etc., 72.
Cyrano de Bergerac, 172.

DAGOBERT I., 78, 95.
—— (tomb), 89.
Dagobert II., 79.
D'Aligre, Etienne, 107.
D'Amboise, Cardinal, 94.
"Dames de la Halle," 165.
D'Ancre, Marshal, 104.
Danegelt, 80.
D'Angers, David, 123.
Dante, 9.
Darboy, Monseigneur, 27, 53, 147, 165.
D'Aubigné, Françoise, 163.
Daunon, 195.
De Caumont, 31.
Dechaume, 44.
De Feuquières, Madame, 178.
Deguerry, Abbé, 165, 183.
Deists, 135.
Delacroix, Eugène, 138, 175.
Delafosse, 153.
De l'Epée, Abbé, 178.
Delorme, 178.

210

INDEX.

De Rohans, the, 194.
Derrand, François, 175.
Desaix, 27.
Descartes, 114, 115.
—— (epitaph), 204.
Des Genettes, M., 205.
D'Etaples, Lefèvre, 193.
De Verneilh, 31.
D'Harcourt, Claude Henry, 53.
D'Hulst, Monseigneur, 58.
Diana of France, 96.
Dominicans, 156, 157.
Dom Millet, 81.
Doublet, Jacques, 79.
Douglas, James, 114.
Douglas, William, 114.
Douhaire, M., 136.
Dourlat, 117.
Drolling, 138.
Drummond, James, 207.
Drumont, M. Edouard, 196.
Duban, 73.
Du Barry, Madame, 155.
Dubois, 170.
Dubois, Cardinal (mausoleum), 178.
Du Guesclin, 96.
Dumax, Abbé V., 176.
Dumouriez, 25.
Duns Scotus, John, 71.
Dupanloup, Monseigneur, 81.
Dupuis, 19.
Duroc, 150.
Duruy, M., 147.
Duval, 148.

EGINHARD, 79.
Eleanor of Guyenne, 81.
Elizabeth of France, 24.
Enguerrand le Prince, 130.
Escurial, the, 61.
Etienne de Garlande, 49.
Etienne Marcel, 20.
Eudes de Clement, 81.
Eudes de Châteauroux, 68.
Eugène de Beauharnais (statue), 150.
Exelmans, 150.

FABER, PETER, 188.
Façade (Notre Dame), 45 etc.
Félibien, 112.
Fénélon, 56.
—— (statue), 139.
Fieschi, 27.
Filon, M., 130.
Fitzgerald, Lord Edward, 156.
Flamaël, 156.
Flandrin, Hippolyte, 115, 116, 141, 187.
Fléchier, Bishop, 164.

Fléchier (statue), 139.
Fleurus, 25.
Fools, Feast of, 6, 15, 69.
Fosse, Edmond de la, 69.
Fouché, 195.
Franc-maçons, 34.
Francis II., 23.
François de Bourbon, 114.
Frédégonde, 95.
Froissart, 21.
Fronde, the, 90.
Fulda, 111.

GABRIEL, 157.
Gabrielle d'Estrées, 195.
Galigaï, Leonora, 104.
Gambetta, 124.
Garibaldi, Archbishop, 53.
Gassendi, 172.
Geoffrey, Duke of Brittany, 37.
Gerent, M., 71.
Gérôme, 141.
Gibbon, 8, 18.
Gittard, 157.
Gobel, Archbishop, 25, 26.
Goddess of Reason, 164.
Gondy, Jean-François de, 126.
Gothic architecture, 32.
Goudreau, M., 165.
Goujon, Jean, 166.
Granmaison, 151.
Gregory, XI., 20.
Gros, 124.
Grouchy, 150.
Gsell, 170.
Guébriant, Comte de, 53.
Guibert, Cardinal, 189.
Guillard, Doctor, 152.
Guillaume de Nangis, 82.
"Guillemites," 174.
Guillemot, 157.
Guise, Duc de, 24, 101.
Guizot, 151.

HALLÉ, 157.
Ham Fair, 6.
Hanotaux, M., 147.
"Haudriettes," 179.
Hébertists, 164.
Heim, 138, 141.
Heloïse, 82 sq.
Henri II., 63, 169.
—— (tomb), 95.
Henri III., 95, 174.
Henri IV., 10, 22, 23, 90, 91 188.
Henriet, 130.
Henrietta, Maria, 92.
Henry V. of England, 22.

INDEX

Henry VI. of England, 22.
Hesse, 138, 141, 148.
Hivert, 126.
Hoche, General, 155, 174.
Homsy, Monseigneur Ignatius, 140.
"Hudibras," 24.
Hugh Capet, 80.
Hugo, Victor, 52.
Huguenots, 10, 23, 90, 101 sq., 158, 175, 193 sq.
Hugues, Canon of St. Victor, 8.
Hyacinthe, Père, 58.

IMMACULATE CONCEPTION, 8, etc.
Ingelburgha of Denmark, 15.
Ingres, 116.
Innocent II., 84.
Isabella, Infanta of Spain, 23.
Isabella of Bavaria, 21, 68, 90, 203.
Isabella of Hainault, 15, 37.

JACOB THE HUNGARIAN, 163.
Jacques de Molay, 19.
Jansenism, 57.
Jean de Chelles, 201.
Jean de Creil, 204.
Jeanne d'Albret, Queen, 103.
Jeanne d'Evreux, Queen, 117.
Jean-sans-Peur, 174.
Jeaurat, 117.
Jehan de Chelles, 33, 50.
Jerome Napoleon I., 151, 176.
Jews, 196.
Joan of Acre, 89.
Jocelyn, Bishop of Soissons, 7.
Joinville, Sire de, 61, 63, 152.
Jonquière, Père, 188.
Joseph Napoleon I., 151.
Josephine Beauharnais, 155.
Jourdan, 150.
Jouvenet, 153.

KLÉBER, 151.

LA BROSSE, PIERRE, 68.
La Bruyère, 194.
La Chaise, 174.
La Fayette, 194.
Lacordaire, 58, 156.
Lacombe, 165.
Lacroix, Monsignor, 205.
Lacy, Lemaistre de, 129.
Lafosse, 179.
Lagrange, 124.
Lamartine, Madame de, 107.
Landelle, 172.
"Landit" Fair, 112.
Lanfranc, 82.
Lannes, Marshal, 122, 124.
Larivière, 168.
Larrey, Baron, 149.
Lassus, 27, 50, 73, 117.
Latil, 129.
La Trémouilles, the, 194.
La Vendée, 174.
Laurens, J. P., 124.
Lebouteiller, 55.
Le Brun, 153, 159.
Le Clerc, 117.
Lecomte, General, 188.
Leduc, 148.
Lefèbre, Père, 207.
Le Juge, 130.
Lemaistre, Antoine, 129.
Le Masurier, 117.
Lemercier, 148, 163.
Lemoine, 138, 157, 184.
Lemonnier, 138.
Lemuet, 148.
Lenepveu, 124.
Lenoir, Alexandre, 84, 92 sq., 141.
Lenôire, 75.
Le Réveillère-Lepeaux, 135, 136.
Lesclope, Thierry, 56.
Lescot, Pierre, 106.
Le Tellier, Chancellor, 169, 174.
L'Etoile, Église de, 195.
Letournier, 136.
Lévy, 124.
Lewis, Emperor, 80.
"Little Fathers," 175.
"Little Geneva," 193.
Lockroy, 124.
Lombard, Peter, 7.
Lorraine, Cardinals de, 103.
Lothair, 80, 188.
Louis VI. (le Gros), 81.
Louis IX., 17, 18, 61, 62, 66.
Louis XI., 69, 72.
—— (portrait), 96.
Louis XII. (tomb), 95.
Louis XIII., 10, 55, 175.
Louis XIV., 55, 69, 149, 164, 177.
Louis XV., 69.
Louis XVI., 124.
—— (statue), 96.
Louis XVIII., 22, 27, 92, 96, 124.
Louis de Sancerre, 96.
Louis d'Orléans, 96.
Lourdes, 11.
Loyola, Ignatius, 188.
Lulli, 206.
Lupus, Bishop, 170.
"Lutrin," 63, 65.

INDEX.

Luxembourg, Marshal de, 25.
Luynes, Duchesse de, 157.

MADILLON, 115.
MacMahon, 151.
Maderno, 175.
Maillard, 151.
Maillard, Demoiselle, 26.
Maillot, 124.
Maindron, 123.
Maintenon, Madame de, 82, 149, 163.
"Maïs," 57.
Malherbe, 106.
Malebranche, 195.
Malesherbes, 123.
"Man of the iron mask," 174.
Manichæans, 16.
Mansard, 148.
Mansards, the, 174.
Marat, 122.
Marceau, General, 125.
Marcel, Etienne, 101, 102.
Marengo, 27.
Margaret of Navarre, 193.
Margaret of Provence, 62.
Marguerite de Valois, 23, 156.
Maria de' Medici, 10, 90, 104, 154.
Marie Antoinette, 92, 96.
Marie de Beauvilliers, 188.
Marie de Clèves, 114.
Marie de Luxembourg, 68.
Marochetti, 104, 184.
Marot, Clément, 194.
Martel, Charles, 79.
Martin, Père, 131, 165.
Mary of Brabant, 68.
Mary Stuart, 23.
Massillon, 195.
—— (statue), 139.
Maton, Advocate, 154.
Matthieu de Vendôme, 81.
Mauclerc, Père, 62.
Maugiron, 174.
Maupertius (mausoleum), 178.
Maurevel, 102.
Mausart, 157, 196.
Mayenne, Duke of, 24.
Mazarin, Cardinal, 148.
"Mazas," 166.
Meissonier, 124.
Menteith, Patrick, 207.
Mercier, 164.
"Messe Rouge," 64, 69.
Middlemore, General, 152.
Mignard, 157.
—— (mausoleum), 178.
Mignard, Nicholas, 149.
Mignard, Pierre, 149.

Mirabeau, 121, 123.
—— (funeral), 164.
Molière, 149, 172.
—— (funeral, etc.), 168.
Momoro, Madame, 164.
Moncey, Marshal, 150.
Mons-en-Puelle, Battle of, 19.
Montaign, Jean de, 51.
Montalembert, Comte de, 113, 136.
Montereau, Pierre de, 63, 66, 67, 70.
Montfauçon, 115.
Montgomery, Count, 169.
Montmorency, Constable de, 104.
Montmorency, Duchesse de, 188.
Montmorency-Laval, 151.
Montorgueil, M. Georges, 147.
Montreuil, Eudes de, 62, 63.
Montson, Jean de, 10.
Montyon, Antoine de, 139.
Morand, Canon, 68.
Morard, Abbot, 113.
Morlot, Cardinal, 54.
Mortier, 150.
Mun, Comte de, 136.
Murat, 178.
Murray, Bishop, 207.

NANTERRE, 124.
Nantes, Edict of, 194.
Xanthilde, 89.
Napoleon I., 27, 124 sqq., 104.
—— (sarcophagus), 153.
—— (tomb, etc.), 151 sqq.
Nauendorff, 175.
Négrier, General, 151.
Nénot, M. 147.
Nestorius, 8.
Nicolle, 151.
Nicot, 174.
Nilsson, 186.
Nonilles, Cardinal de, 53, 55, 56.
Northmen, 80, 111.
Notre Dame des Champs, 189.
Notre Dame, Chapels, 53, etc.
—— Relics, 57.
Novena, the, 127.

O'CRUOLY, MARIANUS, 207.
Odo of Chateauroux, 68.
Odon de Deuil, 82.
Olier, M. 137.
Oratory, the, 194.
"Oriflamme," 81.
Orléans, Duc d', 21, 174.
Otto II., 187 sq.
Oudinot, 150.

INDEX.

Palissy, Bernard, 112.
Palmerston, Lord, 151.
Pame'a, 156.
Paré, Ambroise, 103.
Pascal, 129, 130.
—— (epitaph), 204.
Pascal I., 169.
Pasteur, Louis, 28.
Patin, Guy, 106.
Patterson, Mr., 176.
Patti, 186.
Paulicians, 16.
Penvern, Curé, 150.
Pepin, 113.
Pepin the Short, 79.
Perdreau, Abbé, 130.
Perraud, Monseigneur, 112, 147.
Perrin, 157.
Perron, 157.
Peter of Capua, 70.
Philip Augustus, 15, 204.
Philip II., 61.
Philip III. (le Hardi), 68.
Philip the Fair, 18, 19, 47.
Philip of Orléans (Regent), 193.
Philip of Valois, 37.
Philippe de Champagne, 148, 169.
Pierre de Fayet, 201.
Pigalle, 138, 168.
Pinaigrier, 129, 130, 169, 170.
Pitié Hospital, 207.
Pius VII., 27.
Pius IX., 8, 176.
Placidus, 168.
Poirier, Dom, 92.
Poles, 206.
Pompadour, Madame de, 121.
Pomponne, Marquis de, 170.
Portals (Notre Dame), 46, etc.
Porte de la Sainte-Vierge, 46.
Porte Rouge (Notre Dame), 43, 49.
Poupart, Abbé, 165.
Prudentius of Troyes, 80, 111.
Pujol, Abel de, 138.
Pyat, Félix, 166.

Quélus, 174.
Querini, Nicholas, 65.
Quesnel, 56.
Queynon, M. 38.
Quichard, 107.
Quicherat, 31.
Quietists, 56.
Quinault, 157.
Quinet, 121.

Rabelais, 174.

Racine, 129, 130.
Rambouillet, Madame de, 168.
Rameau, 168, 169.
Ravignan, Père, 58.
Ravy, Jean, 55.
Raymond VI., 17.
Raymond VII. of Toulouse, 16, 17.
Reason, Goddess of, 26.
—— Temple of, 27.
Récamier, Madame, 156.
Reggio, Duke of, 150.
Regnier, 106.
Renan, Ernest, 137.
Renaudet, Theophraste, 194.
Renée de France, 103.
Retz, Cardinal de, 24.
Rewbell, 136.
Richard II. of England, 68.
Richard Philippe, 103.
Richard Plantagenet, 15.
Richelieu, Cardinal, 157, 174.
—— (tomb, etc.), 145.
Rigault, Raoul, 166.
Rigord, 82.
Robert, King of France, 9, 113.
Robespierre, 27, 155, 165.
Rollin, 120.
Romain, Francis, 157.
Rondelet, 121.
Roscelin of Compiègne, 82.
Rossi, Commendatore, 205.
Rossini (funeral), 186.
Rothschild, 137.
Rousseau, 122, 123, 124.
Rousseau, Maistre Henri, 132.
Russian Church, 196.

Sacré-Cœur, Convent, 189.
St. Agnes, 163.
Saint Amaranthe, Madame de, 151.
St. Anne's Portal (N.D.), 48.
St. Antony, 112.
St. Arnaud, 151.
St. Bartholomew, 23.
St. Bartholomew's Day, 102, 194.
St. Benoit, 113.
St. Bernard of Clairvaux, 8, 9, 84, 189.
St. Cecilia, 168, 169.
St. Charles Borromeo, 129.
St. Denis, 54, 55, 69, 77 sq.
St. Dionysius (St. Denis), 78.
St. Eleutherius, 78.
St. Elizabeth of Hungary, 173.
St. Eloi, 79, 94, 174.
St. Epiphanius, 8.
Saint-Esprit, Temple de, 195.
St. Euchère, 79.
St. Eugène, 189.

214

INDEX.

St. Ferdinand of the Ternes, 189.
St. Fiacre, 135.
St. Francis of Assisi, 106.
St. Francis Xavier, 117.
St. Germain, 54.
St. Germain l'Auxerrois, 23.
St. Gregory of Tours, 139.
St. Julian of Mans, 139.
St. Louis, 61, 69.
St. Louis d'Antin, 189.
St. Lucien lez Beauvais, 94.
St. Marcel, 48.
St. Marcel Portal (Notre Dame), 43.
St. Martin, 79.
St. Mary of Egypt, 106.
St. Médard, 158.
St. Medericus, 170.
Saint Mégrin, 174
St. Nicholas, 171.
St. Nicolas, Chapel of, 201.
St. Nicolas-du-Chardonnet, 159.
St. Ouen, Borough of, 77.
St. Ouen (Rouen), 67.
St. Pierre-du-Petit-Montrouge, 189.
Saint Pol, Count of, 62.
St. Remi, 22.
St. Rusticus, 78.
St. Stephen (body), 127.
St. Stephen's and St. Mary's, 5.
St. Symphorien of Autun (monastery), 112.
St. Victor, 7.
St. Vincent, 112.
Sainte-Beuve, 156.
Ste. Geneviève, 7, 57, 121 sqq.
—— (tomb), 130.
Ste. Marguerite, 175.
Sainte-Marie, Temple de, 195.
Salle des Pas Perdus, 63.
San Guste, 61.
Sans-Gêne, Madame, 195.
Sanson, 106.
Santerre, 155.
Sarden, 195.
"Satyre Ménippée," 24.
Scarron, 163, 169.
Scellières, Abbey of, 122.
Scheffer, Ary, 157.
Schneiz, 178.
Sciarra Colonna, 19.
Scudéri, Mademoiselle de, 172.
Sebastiani, 150.
Sébastien, 172.
"Septembriseurs," 154.
Servandoni, 137.
Sevigné, Madame de, 169, 194.
Sibour, Monseigneur, 53, 131.
Sigebert, 89.
Signol, 168.
Simon, Abbé, 165.
Soissons, Council of, 84.

Sombreuil, Mademoiselle de, 157.
Sorbon, Canon Robert de, 145 sq.
Sorokines, 196.
Soufflot, 3, 121 sqq.
Soyecourt, Marchioness de, 156.
Spencer, Hon. and Rev. George, 176.
Steinheil, M., 71.
Stephen III., Pope, 79.
Steuben, 117.
Suger, Abbot, 80 sqq., 90, 94, etc.
Sully, H., 138.
Sully, Maurice de, 7, 49, 104.
Su picius Severus, 136.
Sylvester II., 18.
Sylvestre, Israel, 106.
Synagogues, 196.

TALLIEN, MADAME, 177.
Templars, 19, 20.
Temple of Genius, 177.
Temple of Glory, 184.
Temple of Hymen, 172.
Temple of Old Age, 173.
Temple of Peace, 157.
Temple of Reason, 188.
Temple of the Patriarch, 159.
Temple of Youth, 169.
Tennyson, 163.
Tessé, Marshal de, 103.
Thackeray, 152.
Théba, the, 196.
Theophilanthropists, 135, 157, 172, 173.
Theophilus, 49, 71.
Thomas, 178.
Timbal, 148.
"Tilleuls," the, 155.
Torré, Abbé, 165.
Tournelles, the, 63.
Tournemine, 174.
Trelawney, Colonel, 152.
Triqueti, 184.
Turenne, Marshal, 90, 150, 164.
Turennes, the, 194.
Tyrconnell, Duchess of, 207.

"UNIGENITUS," Bull, 56.

VALENTINE DE MILAN.
Vanloo, 138.
Varcollier, 196.
Vauban, 151.
Vaugelet, 168.
Verdier, 117.
Vézelay Church, 35.
Victor Hugo, 3, 24, 25, 121, 136.
—— (tomb), 124.
Vignon, 184.

INDEX.

Villani, 19.
Vincennes, Chapel of the Chateau, 189.
Viole, Madame de, 129.
Viollet-le-Duc, 4, 27, 31, 36, 43, 45, 47, 63, 73.
Virmaître, M., 173.
Visconti, 151.
Visitation, Nuns of the, 195.
Vitry, Baron de, 104.
Vöge, Herr, 36.
Voisins, Abbé de, 131.
Voiture, 168.
Voltaire, 11, 122, 123.
Von Döllinger, 137.
Votive tablets, 206.
Vouet, 157, 172.

WALDENSES, 16.
Washington, George, 194.

Wassilieff, 196.
Wellesley, Marchioness of, 176.
Wickliff, 20.
William of Champeaux, 7, 83.
William of Nogaret, 19.
Winslow, Jean Benigne, 129.

XAVIER, FRANCIS, 188.

YVER, ETIENNE, 52, 201.

ZACHARY, POPE, 79.
Ziegler, 184.
Zola, 52.

www.ingramcontent.com/pod-product-compliance
Lightning Source LLC
Chambersburg PA
CBHW021406230426
43666CB00006B/656